STEPHAN SCHIFFMAN'S

SALES ESSENTIALS

BUSINESS

AVON, MASSACHUSETTS

This book incorporates material from the following books, all published
by Adams Media and all Copyright © by Stephan Schiffman:
Cold Calling Techniques (That Really Work!)
Upselling Techniques (That Really Work!)
Closing Techniques (That Really Work!)
E-Mail Selling Techniques (That Really Work!)
The 250 Sales Questions to Close the Deal

Published by
Adams Media, an F+W Publications Company
57 Littlefield Street, Avon, MA 02322 U.S.A.
www.adamsmedia.com

ISBN 10: 1-59869-228-3
ISBN 13: 978-1-59869-228-0

Printed in Canada

J I H G F E D C B A

Library of Congress Cataloging-in-Publication Data
is available from publisher.

Contents

Contents

Contents

ACKNOWLEDGMENTS

It's hard to know where to start with a list of acknowledgments for a project whose genesis lies twenty years in the past. This book is a compilation of concepts and principles developed over a long series of years, and I would be remiss if I neglected to mention the following people, each of whom made important contributions to the material between these two covers. My profound gratitude goes out to:

Brandon Toropov
Stephanie Kip Rostan
Jim Levine
Daniel Greenberg
Gary Krebs
Shoshanna Grossman
Danielle Chiotti
Steve Bookbinder
Scott Forman
David Rivera
Alan Koval
Ben Alpert
Steve Mueller
David Toropov
Eric Blume
Chris Ciaschini
Carol Burr
Sheldon Gilbert
Bob Adams

Read This First

A NUMBER OF years ago, I decided to take some golf lessons from a pro. (At that point, I should mention, I'd been golfing for quite a while, without ever having taken a lesson.)

During my first lesson, the pro showed me the proper grip for the club. It felt a little awkward, and I told him so. But my teacher assured me that the reason the new grip felt awkward was simple: I had been holding the club incorrectly for many years. Once I got used to the right way of doing things, he assured me, the right way of holding the club would feel just as "natural" as the way I had been holding it. And with that, he demonstrated not only the right grip, but also the right swing and follow-through. It was beautiful.

Well, what he had said sounded logical enough, and it was certainly hard to argue with when he showed off that swing. If only I could get my swing to look as fluid, as graceful, and as powerful as my instructor's!

And yet I had a similar feeling of awkwardness when the golf pro showed me how to stand, where to put my feet, and how to swing. It all felt very uncomfortable. But during my lesson, I swung, as instructed, from that awkward position, and I hit the ball many, many times while the golf pro watched me and offered suggestions.

At the end of the lesson, the pro told me to keep practicing exactly as he'd instructed me. If I did, he promised, the new ways of holding the club, standing, and swinging would soon become second nature.

Well, once I got back on my own, I tried to hold the club, and stand, and swing, as the instructor had told me to. But it still felt strange. I found that when I moved my grip to a "more comfortable" position, it just felt better. And when I stood the way I was used to standing, it just felt better. And when I swung the way I was used to swinging, it just felt better.

So I dropped the lessons and went back to playing golf "my way."

I hit that ball with all my might. I hit it "my way." I hit it so I was "comfortable."

And my average score was 150. (By the way, if you're not a golfer, let me just offer a little bit of background information: the higher the score, the worse the golfer. And 150 is an extremely high—that is, bad—score.)

I couldn't understand why nobody wanted to play with me, or why I wasn't getting any better. In fact, I wasted a whole year wondering why my scores were so high.

After a year, I went back to the golf pro. This time, I followed his directions, stuck it out, and practiced the right grip, swing, and follow-through over and over and over again, until they became second nature to me. As the golf pro had promised, the correct way of doing things eventually—and the key word here is "eventually"—became "comfortable." And my score dropped!

The thing is, I had to *drill* the right way of swinging until it *became* comfortable.

Why do I tell you a story about golf in a book about selling? Because we all have our "comfortable" ways of doing things: swinging a golf club—following through on the swing—and connecting with people to make sales.

If we take the time to do what's right—what really works—over and over again, until it becomes second nature, it really will feel comfortable. And it really will deliver the results.

If what you're interested in improving is your golf swing, you should talk to a golf pro. If what you're interested in improving is your sales ability, you should read this book.

I say that because we've presented the techniques within these two covers to hundreds of thousands of salespeople in virtually every industry, all over the world, and to just about every kind of sales force. If the aim is to get a face-to-face meeting with someone you haven't talked to before, so you can discuss your product or service and how it might fit into that person's operations, and then eventually close the deal, this book shows you how to "hold the club," how to "swing," and how to "follow through."

Even if what I suggest that you do in the following pages feels a little awkward at first, I promise you—it works. The only reason it feels awkward now is that you're not used to it yet! Once you practice it enough, it won't feel awkward at all.

Years ago, when I first came up with some of the principles in this book, I bought a book that was written by someone who had sold a whole lot of book proposals to publishers. It outlined a system for selling your book idea to a publisher. It broke the system down into simple steps. I followed the steps, even though some of them felt a little awkward at first. The system worked!

Here's why I mention that. You are holding in your hands a system written by someone who has set a whole lot of sales appointments and closed a whole lot of business. This book breaks the system down into simple steps. If you follow the steps—the system will work!

Once you begin the book, do yourself a favor. Make a commitment to drill the many techniques you'll find here repeatedly until they become second nature. Don't waste a year—or more!—of your precious time doing the "same old thing" just because it feels more comfortable than trying something new! Do what works . . . and stick with it. And you will certainly see dramatic improvements in your sales ability and your overall income level.

■ ■ ■

Before we get started in earnest, I need you to write something down.

Yes, I really mean it. I want you to go get a piece of paper, or your sales notebook, or your call sheet, or whatever you use to write in your sales work. I want you to pull out the pen or pencil you always use. And I want you to copy the following sentence down verbatim before you do anything else in this book.

You cannot force a prospect to do anything.

Believe me when I tell you that that sentiment is worth framing and hanging where you can see it every morning as you settle into your seat, ponder the day ahead, and enjoy your Starbucks and your low-fat breakfast bar.

When we try to force prospects into committing to actions they're not ready to take, we lose. The exchange becomes polarized. The prospect starts to worry about all the things that need to get done as soon as this uncomfortable meeting is over. We start to sweat. We start to worry. We start to push.

And—paradoxically enough—we *don't win sales that ought to come our way.*

Now, even though you can't force your prospect to do anything, you certainly can find areas of agreement with your prospect! You certainly can highlight potential solutions for your prospect! You certainly can show things to your prospect that he or she may not have noticed before! You can always act on areas of mutual opportunity with your prospect! And you can keep this person on your radar screen, and take a minute or two to reach out once a week or so via e-mail . . . until you win a place on the *prospect's* radar screen! And you certainly can find *other* prospects to talk to.

At the end of the day, your objective is to find a prospect who will tell *you* what to do, or, at the very least, to work out a course of action on which you both are in complete agreement that moves the sales cycle forward. If your aim is to intimidate, to overrun, to conquer, to pressure your prospect into fitting into your preconceived notion of how the two of you will work together, you should resign yourself right now to the fact that you are not going to achieve your full potential as a salesperson. In other words, you are not going to close sales you should close.

Believe it or not, everything that follows in this book depends on the sentence you just wrote down on that sheet of paper. Read it again right now! Read it every day!

I would love to hear your reactions and results once you have implemented the strategies in this book. Please e-mail me at *contactus@dei-sales.com,* or call 1-800-224-2140.

Good luck!

Stephan Schiffman
New York City

Part One

Foundation Concepts

1 The Number One Reason Businesses Fail

A FAMOUS PROFESSOR at Harvard Business School once asked his students to name the number one reason that businesses do not succeed. He got all kinds of answers, ranging from bad management and bad programs to bad products, poor concepts, and lack of capital. After reading their answers he stood before his class and told them that the number one reason businesses fail is . . . "lack of sales."

That's it. It's lack of real sales—the work you and I do on the front lines. And if I can't get in the door to see people, I'm not going to sell.

In most selling environments, nothing can happen unless you're able to get that first appointment. No matter how well you sell, if you can't get in the door, if you cannot get an appointment to see somebody, you're not going to sell.

To become a successful salesperson, you have to develop a solid base of prospects. This base will only remain solid if you continue to prospect successfully—and the cold call plays a large part in successful prospecting. Cold calling is the best and most economical way for you to develop prospects on an ongoing basis. This book is devoted to helping you get in front of your prospects in the most efficient, profitable way—and to overcome your number one competitor.

Your Biggest Competitor

Who is your number one competitor? Interestingly enough, you can name every company in your business—and you'll be wrong. No matter what company you mention, I'll tell you you're wrong. You could tell me that you are your own competitor. You'd be wrong again. You could say to me that your energy level is your competition. Wrong.

Your number one competitor today is the status quo. The status quo is what people are doing right now. If you understand that, you're going to be successful. It's rare that we're really up against a competitor—we're usually up against the incumbent, the status quo. Remember, most of your potential customers are happy with what they've got—otherwise, they would be calling you!

Once when I was doing a training session I stated that your number one competitor is the status quo. A sales rep raised his hand and said, "Steve, I've never heard of that company. Who's Status Quo?" Don't get sidetracked. Remember: you're up against what the prospect is already doing.

Where Sales Come From

Now, I'm going to discuss something that upsets many salespeople. The fact of the matter is you're going to get one-third of all your sales no matter what you do. *Let me repeat that: You'll get one-third of all your sales no matter what you do.* In the United States nearly 1,000 copiers are sold every single hour of every single day. It's estimated that nearly 2,000 cellular numbers are installed in the United States every hour. What do numbers like that tell you about sales? They should tell you that there are people who need your product . . . just like you need to go to the supermarket to buy milk. That's a consumer-driven sale.

In fact, you and I have seen people who shouldn't be allowed to walk the streets without a leash who still make sales. The reason people like that are able to make a living is that their sales are based on needs for those consumer-driven products. Eventually something breaks; eventually you're going to need a new car; eventually you're going to need more lettuce; eventually you're going to buy a new television. Successful salespeople understand that they'll get one-third of their sales no matter what, simply because they knock on enough doors. But is that enough?

The Sales You'll Never Get

Then there's one-third of your sales that you're not going to get. For whatever reason, no matter what you do, you're just not going to get the last one-third of your sales. Sometimes it's because the other guy, the other salesperson, gets it. Sometimes there are internal changes at the target company that you can't control. Either way, you're not getting the business.

The Sales That Are up for Grabs

The last one-third is up for grabs. That's what we're going to discuss here. We'll show you how to develop your competitive edge, get more appointments, and get more of that last one-third, which is where the good salespeople separate themselves from the mediocre salespeople.

The interesting thing is that plenty of salespeople make their living by simply accepting the first one-third. That's really more of an order-taking situation.

In fact, there's a guy in Times Square who sells a little wallet-like card case. He simply stands there and says, "Wanna buy, wanna buy, wanna buy, wanna buy, wanna buy, wanna buy, wanna buy, wanna buy?" You get the idea. That's all he does!

That tells you something about the entire sales process. If you see enough people, you will eventually make a sale. In fact, as we mentioned earlier, you're going to make a certain number of sales no matter what you do. If you knock on enough doors, it doesn't make any difference what you do, eventually you're going to get a sale.

Suppose I went to the busiest street corner nearest my office (it happens to be Times Square), and I simply put out my hand. Do you think anybody would put money in my hand? Of course, eventually someone's going to do that. That's my first third. Now if I held out a cup, do you think I might make more money? Of course. If I add a cup and a bell, bing-bing-bing-bing, would more people give me money? Of course. Add a cup, a bell, bing-bing-bing-bing, and a sign, "Please help me." Would more people give me money then? Absolutely.

The point, again, is that you'll eventually make a sale if you see enough people. But this story illustrates that it's equally important to make the most of the opportunity. It's not enough to just see people or talk to people on the phone. You have to use the right tools.

The other day I was walking in Manhattan near our office and I noticed a bank with a table right outside displaying a sign that read, "SIGN UP FOR PC BANKING." Three bank employees simply approached every single person who walked past them. I went up to one of them and asked, "How did you do?" They said, "It was incredible today." In the last two hours they had signed up 200 people for their PC banking program—people who had simply walked past the building.

One of the great telecommunications giants in the country today started many years ago by setting up tables outside of major office buildings with a sign that simply said, "SAVE MONEY ON LONG DISTANCE." And people would sign up. You and I could make sales that way. Simply going after the first third, and doing nothing else, however, is not the way to build a successful sales career. I doubt even that telecom giant could survive today if all they had were a couple of tables and a few homemade signs!

Timing Is Everything

When we begin to look closely at the prospecting process, we can see why the concept of time is so important. I know that it takes me about eight weeks from the time I first sit down and talk to a prospective client to the time I make a sale. So let's play this out and see how it works. If I sat down with you on January 1, I'd know that, if we decide to do business together, I'm going to see a sale not in February, but in March—say, on March 1. January 1 to March 1. If my sales cycle is eighteen weeks, it's going to take me that much longer. The sale will be closer to May.

If, on January 1st, I'm busy because it's a holiday and I don't call anybody, and on January 2 I don't call anybody because I'm doing something else, I've pushed out the date when I can expect to see a sale. Say I don't prospect on January 3, 4, 5, 6, 7, 8, 9, or 10. Now instead of March 1, it's going to be March 2, 3, 4, 5, 6, etc. I think you get the point.

Think about it like this: When you get paid for a sale, when did you really earn that money? Depending on your sales cycle, it could have been as long as three months or even a year ago. If you didn't do some kind of prospecting a year ago, the odds are that you would not see any income now. If you look at it this way, what you suddenly realize is that the appointments that you generate today are what create the prospects you meet, which ultimately give you your sale at the end of your sales cycle.

Now that you've read about how important time is, you're probably jumping out of your chair saying to yourself "I've got to get started!" Please remember to finish the whole book before you try to implement the program.

Reducing the Sales Cycle

A couple of weeks ago I went on a sales call. It was a good sales call. How do I know it was good? Because while I was there, I set up an appointment to come back. By setting the next appointment on my first appointment, rather than waiting until later, I accelerated my sales cycle by three to five weeks.

Let me explain. Typically, on an appointment, a salesperson will tend to say to the prospect, "I'll call you in a week." Now we've added at least a week to the sales cycle. Then what happens? We might not get the person on the phone that next week. Now we have to wait. Finally, we get the person on the phone, setting an appointment for perhaps two to three weeks later. By setting the next appointment during the first one, we can save all this wasted time. We really can reduce the sales cycle by three to five weeks!

Gerbil Selling

Let me share another story. Recently a sales call of mine went very well. Since the presentation had gone so well, I asked for the sale:

Steve: It makes sense to me. What do you think?
Prospect: We can't do it now.
Steve: Why not?
Prospect: I gotta talk to my boss.
Steve: (Because time is so important) Okay. Let's go see him now.
Prospect: Well, we can't do that. I need a week.
Steve: I'll come back in a week.
Prospect: Nope, no good. I'll call you.
Steve: No, I'll call you.
Prospect: I'll call you.
Steve: I'll call you.
Prospect: Steve, trust me. I will get back to you. Honestly, I'll get back to you.
Steve: Okay.

There was nothing else I could do. One week went by, then two. I didn't hear from him. Three, four, five, six, seven, eight, nine, ten, eleven, twelve, thirteen, fourteen, fifteen, . . . It's now, I don't know, maybe ninety-eight weeks later and I still haven't heard from him. What do you think my chances are of making the sale? Virtually zero. The point is that time is of the essence.

The longer the sale goes out of the normal cycle, the less likely it is to happen.

Does this next example sound like a normal sales cycle? A woman in Rockville, Maryland, once told me she went on thirty-seven appointments to the same contact at one company. The same person, thirty-seven times, and she still hadn't made the sale! Would you do that? Of course not! What could the two of you possibly talk about on the thirty-seventh visit that hadn't already been covered on the first thirty-six? Isn't that a waste of time?

Years ago I went on a sales call, and the person I was dealing with knew that I usually only go back three times. I typically either close on my third call or conclude that the sale isn't going to happen right now. On the third call my contact at this company said: "I know you usually only come back three times. Would you come back one more time? It's going to be worth a half-million dollars to you." I said I'd come back.

When I went on that fourth meeting, the prospect said to me again: "This is really great. Would you come back one more time?" I came back one more time. At the end of the next meeting, he said to me: "This is really great. Would you come back one more time?" I came back one more time. And, of course, when the same thing happened at the end of that meeting I got suspicious. So I asked: "What am I coming back for?" He replied, "Well, I want you to meet Mr. Big. He's going to give you a million-dollar deal, not five hundred thousand." One million dollars!

Of course, I came back again. He asked again: "Would you come back one more time? I want you to meet some more people." I went back again.

In fact, I went back eleven different times for this company. What do you think happened the eleventh time? At the end of the eleventh meeting, they said to me: "Steve, we're not going to buy." What did they do to me? What they did was convince me, against my usual practice, to run around in circles and waste a lot of time.

I call that gerbil salesmanship. At home, my kids have two gerbils. One runs around continuously in the miniature Ferris wheel in the little cage. He's a very busy gerbil. In fact, he's absolutely exhausted at the end of the day. Gerbil salespeople run around in circles all day but get nowhere.

The Open Door

At my company we have an open door policy. Anyone who wants an appointment with me can get one. In fact, I try not to screen phone calls. I think it's important to meet each and every salesperson who wants to talk to me. I'm eager to meet them and understand what they have to sell. To me it's foolish for executives not to see salespeople from time to time. Why not keep up-to-date with what's going on in their fields? Granted, not everyone thinks that way. (Wouldn't our jobs be easier if everyone did?)

Whether your prospects have an open door policy or not—your goal has to be to get the appointment. To learn why that goal is so important, read on.

By the Numbers

WHEN I STARTED my company, years ago, I did not know how to get appointments. I sat in the office waiting for the phone to ring because I was convinced that people would call me. I hired a secretary and an associate to help me field the calls. We sat there saying to ourselves, "We have an ideal situation."

We knew exactly what it was we were going to sell. We knew that people needed it (there's the word "need" again) and we thought that all we had to do was send out enough announcements about our business, and people would start calling us.

How naïve was that? I would be glad to send you some of the 10,000 brochures and 10,000 pens with my name and telephone number on it that I still have. Circulating them didn't get people to call us!

I learned very quickly that if I was not able to get appointments, I was not going to be successful. The key to successful selling has to be getting appointments, but most salespeople don't realize that. Sixty-five percent of success, I've learned, is finding people and telling them what you do.

The A = P = S Formula

There's a formula that's more important to successful salespeople than any other: A = P = S. In other words, *Appointments* give you *Prospects* give you *Sales*. If you have no new appointments today, what's your chance of getting a new prospect? It's nonexistent. If you have no new prospects, what's your chance of making a sale? That, too, is nonexistent.

The real question is, how many appointments do you need to generate one real prospect? (A prospect is someone who consciously agrees to move through the sales process with you. We'll look at this definition more closely in Chapter 3.) Your appointment base is always going to be larger than your prospect base, which is going to be larger than your sales base. It's like a pyramid, with your appointments forming the base, your prospects forming the middle, and your final sales at the top.

For example, suppose that you don't make any new appointments today. You're not going to generate a new prospect. That means that, approximately eight weeks from now, you'll see no new sales. Now, you can argue with me and say, "People will call me." But that's not what we're talking about. We've already established that's going to happen; those are consumer-driven sales. We're talking now about how to get at that last third of all possible sales.

A = P = S. Or, if you prefer, zero A = zero P = zero S. no appointments, no prospects, no sales.

Know Your Numbers

How many appointments do you need to get your prospects? How many dials on the phone does it take to get those appointments? If you don't know those numbers, how can you know whether your sales approach is working? In my case, I know I need one appointment a day, or five new appointments a week. In order to do that, I have to call fifteen people each day. Fifteen times five gives me seventy-five. Over five days, I dial seventy-five people, I generate five new appointments, which ultimately gives me my one sale every single week. And that's the objective. That ties into the question I asked you before. If you don't know the numbers you need to reach your goal, you're probably not going to get there.

How many cold calls do you make each day? Do you know? If so, why do you make that number of calls? Are they true cold calls, or are they calls you've been repeating by calling the same people over and over again?

Every single day that I'm not in front of a group, I still pick up the phone fifteen times; that is, I still make fifteen calls. That's fifteen new people I haven't spoken to before.

Even on busy days I still try to find a way to make those fifteen calls. On those days when I cannot reach anybody during normal business hours, I call fifteen new people starting at 7:00 A.M. I know the odds are that I will not reach people that early. But I also know that I will have fifteen messages out there, and at least one of those people will call me back.

Typically, though, I call fifteen people a day, and I actually speak to seven of those people. For every seven people I speak to, I set up one new appointment. As a rule, I do that five days a week, so at the end of the week, I have five new appointments. That's five people that I have not met with before.

Now here's a trick question. If I make five new appointments this week, as I always do, how many total appointments will I have next week?

Do you know the number? It's eight. Why is it eight? Because I know for every five new appointments, I'm going back to three more for follow-through appointments.

If you say to me that you have five appointments for this week, but you have no follow-through appointments, then the odds are you did not have five appointments last week. My total number of appointments (eight) is every important. My closing ratio happens to be that for every eight appointments, I make one sale. This means that I will bring in something in the neighborhood of fifty new accounts a year.

Why is that important? Well, suppose I didn't make those fifteen calls a day. What would happen? I'd be out of business! The fifteen calls that I make every day give me the fifty new accounts a year. In other words, the fifteen calls drive the fifty sales. Cold calling is a numbers game (or, to be more precise, a ratios game). And this particular game drives your sales.

Now, I'll go back to my initial question. How many calls do you make each day?

Is it giving you the number of appointments that you require in order to be successful? I know that I must get one new appointment a day, and that I have to make fifteen calls, and speak to seven people, to set up that one new appointment. I do that five days a week. Those are my numbers. How many appointments do you require to be successful? If you must make five new appointments a week, are you getting them? If you require ten new appointments a week, are you getting them? More important, how did you settle on the numbers you're working with?

Here's a simple question. Do you know the mileage of your car? Most people can tell me automatically that their car has X amount of miles on it. They know how many miles per gallon they get in that car. Yet if I ask the same person, "Do you know how many appointments you went on last week?" they often don't know. Which figure matters more to your yearly income?

You need to know your numbers and understand your ratios. I'm going to show you how increasing your sales can be as simple as getting one or two more appointments a week. You are not going to get twenty more appointments a day. That's unrealistic. But if you get one more appointment a day, consistently, your sales are going to increase.

A lot of salespeople don't know where their numbers came from. What they do just evolved; it just kind of happened. That's not the way to take control of your career. Only use numbers that give you the actual number of sales and/or appointments you must generate each and every day, week, month, and year.

Numbers from the Real World

Let me give you a series of numbers that I think are important:

293 > 149 > 49 > 83 > 10

Now these are actual sales numbers. Let me tell you what they represent. In this particular case, this salesperson picked up the phone 293 times during a ten-week period. During that time, he spoke to 149 people and actually set up 49 first appointments. The 83 represents the total number of sales visits. Of course, that's higher than the number of first appointments because it includes repeat or follow-through visits. Ten represents the number of sales. When you analyze these numbers, what you start to understand is that the salesperson made one sale and went on an average of 8.3 appointments each week for ten weeks.

This person actually set up about five appointments every week for ten weeks and made about thirty dials a week, or six dials a day every day, for ten weeks. Not exactly a major blowout in terms of numbers, but successful nonetheless. Why?

Because this person understood his numbers. His goal was a new sale a week; he monitored his numbers and hit the goal.

I have somebody working for me who made $68,000 his first year with me; he picked up the phone 2,448 times. Now that may seem like a lot to you, but when you really think about it, it's only ten calls a day (assuming a 250-day working year). In other words, if I promised you that if you picked up the phone ten times a day you would definitely make $68,000, would you do it? Of course you would. The fact is, every single time you pick up the phone you're getting closer to a yes. If you understand that concept, you'll be successful in sales.

Avoiding Peaks and Valleys

Another reason prospecting and getting appointments is so important has to do with the peaks and valleys, the ups and downs that so many salespeople experience. What most of them don't realize is that there's no need to have peaks and valleys!

Let's look at why these peaks and valleys occur. Think about the ratios we just discussed. Think about the number of *no's* that you get in relation to each sale. You'll realize that, when you make a sale, you actually lose prospects!

Let's say, for argument's sake, that you're working on twenty prospects. These are twenty people whom you've met, and you're going back to meet them. They're working with you. Let's say your closing ratio is one out of five. When you make a sale within that group of twenty, what actually happens is that you've made one sale and four people have said no. That's one sale out of five prospects, which means you now have only fifteen prospects (even though nineteen still seem to be active). Now, if you make another sale from these fifteen prospects, you'll only have ten prospects left. If you make another sale, you'll have five prospects left. Soon you'll have nothing left.

Salespeople often repeat the process I just described. And in doing that they create peaks and valleys. They don't replenish prospects soon enough. They have highs and lows because they work their way through their prospects. They make their four or five sales out of the twenty prospects that they had, without replenishing that base of prospects.

In order to avoid these peaks and valleys, we have to replenish or re-establish that base constantly. How long does that take? Depending on your sales cycle it could be eight, ten, or twelve weeks, ninety days, or it could be a year. Whatever time frame your process demands, when you get a big sale (or even a little one), you have to check for peaks and valleys and replenish your prospect base.

Salespeople talk about the "big sale" all the time. They say, "Steve, I had the greatest month I ever had last month." I ask, "What did you do the month before?" "Well, it wasn't so good." "What are you doing the month after?" "It doesn't look so good." To really understand how well their sales are going, they need to average their sales over that three-month period. When they do, their sales numbers are probably going to look suspiciously like the one-third that they would have gotten anyway—unless they've continuously worked on developing new prospects.

CHAPTER

3   Prospecting and the Sales Cycle

THE NEED FOR "perpetual" sales prospecting becomes even more obvious if you consider how far your sales efforts take place in advance of your sales revenues. For example, if it takes sixty days to generate a sale, thirty days to implement the program, thirty days to use the service, thirty days to bill, and thirty days to get paid, that means six months pass between the start of the process and when you actually see the first dollar. You may think you're making sales today, but the sale you made today came from the work you did yesterday. Again:

Appointments = Prospects = Sales

Recently I was working with a software company that had had a tremendous year. I talked to the president of the company about what had happened that year. The conversation went like this:

Steve: What happened last year?
Company President: Well, from January to June we had a tremendous year. We had fifteen people call us and we got fifteen major accounts. It was just a great year.
Steve: And what happened after that?

Company President: Well, people stopped calling!
Steve: So what did you do?
Company President: Well, we, uh . . . *(Silence.)*
Steve: So what did you do?
Company President: Well, you know, we, uh, we started thinking
about what to do.

Because their sales cycle takes nearly a year, their sales have now plummeted, and they are in real danger of going under. And the fact is, that downturn didn't have to happen.

Keep on Prospecting!

Even if you have a successful week, a successful month, or a successful year, that doesn't mean you should ever stop prospecting. One of the biggest mistakes that we make is we convince ourselves that we don't have to prospect on a regular basis. We get happy and complacent with our existing business and we think we don't have to seek new business.

Prospect constantly, every single day.

I learned the importance of prospecting some years ago when my business got very busy. We got an assignment in August that sidetracked everyone in the organization. We stopped prospecting for about two months. It was incredible the amount of work that we had to do on that assignment, and every trainer and every staff person was involved. You know the rest of the story, don't you? You guessed it: in October our sales plummeted. It was December before it started to build up again, but, of course, December is a light month, and it wasn't until January that we saw the light at the end of the tunnel. That was a harrowing few months; I've promised myself that we'll never go through that again.

A number of years ago my number one salesperson, someone who's been with me for years, got very sick. I was extremely worried about her, as we all were.

Although she passed the crisis safely, she had to stay in the hospital for a number of weeks. When I was sure the worst was over, I became concerned about her appointments—because there weren't any! So there I was in the hospital saying, "Sit up, sit up." She said, "Well, I can't—I've got this thing in my nose and . . ." I said, "You're fine. You can talk on the phone. Make the calls; you have to make calls now."

Maybe that sounds harsh. Why did I do that? Because I knew that her sales would drop in eight weeks if she didn't make those calls. It's a terrible story, but it's true. Without her calls, her business was going to suffer a crisis, too, and I knew she didn't need that.

The key, then, is to keep prospecting on a regular basis. Making the sale is important, but it's not as important as managing your prospects. And the key to that is to replenish your base of prospects with new appointments. It's worth repeating. If you don't have enough appointments, you're not going to get enough prospects. If you don't get enough prospects, you're not going to get enough sales, and you're not going to be in business. A = P = S!

If you keep this concept in mind, and act on it, you should be able to avoid the peaks and valleys.

The Value of a "No"

Earlier in this chapter I asked you, "How many appointments do you need each week?" Then I asked, "How many calls do you need to make each day to get that number of appointments?" If you don't know these numbers, you're not going to be successful.

It can be frustrating—but you're going to get plenty of "no" answers when you make these calls. Ready for a surprise! You really shouldn't be too concerned about the number of "no" answers you're getting. Because if you're not hearing "no," you're not making sales. This addresses a basic criticism—that my cold calling approach doesn't work 100 percent of the time. It doesn't! It's not designed to work 100 percent of the time. It's designed to give you a competitive edge. Everything I'm sharing with you is designed to help you improve your numbers over where you are today. That's what this entire book is all about.

So realize that there is a ratio of "no" answers to "yes" answers. A typical ratio would look like this: You're going to make twenty calls, speak to five people, and set up one appointment. Or you're going to see twenty people, and set up one appointment. Or you're going to see twenty people, make five presentations, and make one sale. What's important to understand about that twenty, five, and one ratio is that in the process of doing that, you're going to hear "no" nineteen times. In other words, for every appointment or sale you get, you have to collect nineteen "no" answers.

My company does a lot of work with life insurance companies and HMOs around the United States. In fact, we train life insurance agents around the world. When we work with a brand-new life insurance agent, somebody who's just been hired, we will give that person a chart with 250 boxes on it.

Every single time that person talks to someone about life insurance and hears, "No, I don't want to buy," or "No, I'm not interested," the sales person puts an X in the box. When the chart is full, that is, when 250 people have said no, we give the person $1,000. Why can we do that? Well, if you stop to figure it out, you'll realize that in the process of getting 250 "no" answers, that salesperson will probably generate $10,000 in sales. In other words, we can afford to pay out $4 for every "no," because we know we're going to make it back.

It's important to understand that every time someone says no, you're getting closer to a yes.

Did You Hit Your "No" Quota Last Week?

Did you get enough "no" answers last week? Did you hear "no" enough times to generate a sale? If you don't know the answer, my guess is you don't know your ratios yet. If you're not getting enough "no" answers, you're not getting out there enough.

I meet with many different sales forces throughout the United States. Sometimes sales managers say to me, "Steve, we had a great week last week. Nobody turned us down!" I know they were either on vacation or they weren't selling at all. Learn to count the "no" answers!

There's a great insurance brokerage firm I know of, where the owner of the company literally walks around and says, "How many 'no' answers did you get?" And if a salesperson ever says, "Man, I had a rough day, everyone was turning me down," the owner says, "That's great! We're going to make a sale."

Interestingly enough, if you understand this concept, and know the ratios, you can predict how long it will take you to reach a certain level of sales. You can make a chart that shows that it's going to take you, let's say, three months to generate the "no" answers you need to reach the level you've identified.

We had a new representative in Chicago a while back who was not doing well his first few months on the job. As a manager, I knew that he had to get a certain number of "no" responses in order to be successful. One day, he called me and told me that he was discouraged because he hadn't yet closed a sale, and he was thinking of leaving the company. I asked what his calling numbers were; then I said, "Based upon what you're telling me, right now you need two more 'no' answers." He asked what I meant. I said, "If you make enough calls to get two more "no" answers, you're going to have enough, and you're going to make a sale." And that is exactly what happened—he stuck with it and closed his first sale on his 101st day with our company.

Five Ways to Double Your Income

Let me give you some more examples of numbers and ratios so you can have a feeling of what to expect. One sales force I worked with in New York picked up the phone 606 times, spoke to 315 people, and set up 152 appointments.

Here's another example. This person was selling advertising in the Chicago area: 736 dials, spoke to 358 people, and set up 138 appointments.

Here's another from a company in Los Angeles: made 203 dials, spoke to 99 people, and set up 66 brand-new appointments.

Here's another from a company in Florida: made 589 dials, spoke to 213 people, and set up 102 appointments.

These numbers are from across the country, so don't say, "Well, this program won't work here in (fill in the blank)," because it will! Let me explain why these numbers are so important. There are five ways in which you and I can double our income, based on what we do with these numbers.

1. Double the Number of Calls

The first way to double your income is to simply double the number of calls you make. In all the seminars that I conduct, and I do about 150 to 200 seminars a year, I ask people if they can double the number of calls they make. Every once in a while I get somebody who says, "Yes, I think I could double the number of calls." "Well, if that's the case," I immediately say, "then the seminar is over! There's no need for you to continue." If in fact you can double the number of calls you make every day, then just do it. You don't need me to tell you what to do. Double your number, and you'll get more sales.

For most people, unfortunately, that's probably not a realistic option.

2. Get Through More Often

A second way to double your income is simply to get through to more people. For example, on a typical day, I call fifteen people and speak to seven of them. Now, getting through to fourteen people might be tough. But if I got through to eight people a day, would it change anything? Well, one more person a day means over 200 more people a year. That's a big number. Think about how a similar change would affect your numbers.

3. Get More Appointments

A third way to double your income is simply to get more appointments. In other words, instead of speaking to seven people and getting one appointment every day, I could get two appointments, or even 1.2 appointments. As long as I increase that ratio over time, I'm going to be more successful. If I got one more appointment a day, the amount of additional income I could generate would be incredible! But even a smaller increase could make a dramatic difference. Later in this book, I'll show you how to get more appointments from the people you're speaking to on the phone.

4. Close More Sales

A fourth way to increase my income is to get more sales from my appointments. My closing ratio is one out of eight. For every eight appointments, I'm going to make a sale. What if I could improve that ratio? What if I could go to six to one or even four to one? Again, a dramatic improvement. Of course, I'd have to see the same number of people while I was improving that ratio.

5. Generate More Dollars Per Sale

Finally, I could go down to my last number, my fifty new accounts, and simply raise the stakes. If I could just get twice as many dollars out of each sale, I could (theoretically at least) double my income.

That idea isn't quite as outlandish as it may sound. A woman from a major oil company called my office at 10:00 on a Friday night to buy ten copies of an earlier edition of this book. I said to myself, "Here's a woman calling me at 10:00 on a Friday night. She probably doesn't have a life." Of course, it wasn't long before I thought, "Here I am at 10:00 on Friday night answering the phone. I must not have a life either!" In any event, I asked her, "Why are you calling this late on a Friday night?" She said, "Steve, I'm calling you because we have ten distributors down here in the Virginia area and we want them to make more appointments. We thought your book would help." I said, "You know something, I've got a great idea. Why don't we get together in person?" I turned an $80 book sale into a $250,000 program simply by asking the question. "What is it you're trying to accomplish?"

The point is that if I can increase the average dollar amount per sale, I'm going to be more successful, and sometimes there are opportunities to do just that.

So there they are—five ways I can increase my income: double the number of calls, do a better job of getting through, do a better job of getting the appointment in the first place, do a better job of closing, and finally, make higher-dollar sales.

Just One More Call a Day

If you watch sports, you know the difference between winning and losing is often one stroke, one run, or even one fraction of a second. You don't have to win by a mile. You just have to win. To be number one, to be the best, or even to just make a dramatically better living doesn't require that you get 1,000 more points. Just one more point is often the margin of victory. You don't need 1,000 more appointments a day. You may just need one.

Years ago I did a program for a pharmaceutical company. Their top representative was a young man who had beat out 650 other reps for the top spot in the organization. The senior managers had asked me as part of my speech to ask this particular salesperson what he did that made him so special. He was not briefed on this ahead of time, and he didn't know the question was coming. I'll never forget this, because he was a big guy—about six foot four—and I walked over and asked him to stand. Then I looked up at him and said, "Jim, just out of curiosity, how did you become number one?" He said, "I made one more call at the end of the day." And I said, "What do you mean?" I was just flabbergasted. I thought he would give me a whole elaborate story about what he did. What he said was very simple. He said he decided he wanted to be number one in the country. He normally made all of his prospecting calls in the morning. Every single day, just when he was ready to leave the office, no matter what time it was, whether it was 5:00, 6:00, 7:00, or 8:00, he sat down at his desk with his coat on and he called and spoke to one more person.

That's success. That's what it takes. You don't need to get a thousand more people on the phone. You may just need to get one more person on the phone every day.

Let's look at this more closely. Take a look at the set of numbers that I gave you before: 149 conversations with new people, 49 first appointments, 83 total appointments, and 10 sales. If that salesperson had merely spoken to one more person a day, gotten one more appointment a day, made one more sale a day or a week, or had increased any one of those numbers by one, he would have increased his income substantially.

If you want to be successful in sales, you have to understand that a seemingly minor change can have a major impact on your career!

The 60,000-Mile Man

Here's another real-life example. Once I was in Dallas, Texas, doing a program. I was about a quarter of the way into the discussion when a man by the name of Ed stood up and said, "Steve, I'm leaving," and walked out the door. Now, I hadn't had this happen in a very long time. During the break I went up to him and I said, "Ed, why did you walk out?" He said, "Look, Steve, I'm sixty-two years old. I've been selling for eight years for his company. Every single year I get in my car, drive from Dallas to Oklahoma, down through Arkansas and back to Dallas again. I drive 60,000 miles a year every single year. I don't need you or anybody else to tell me how to sell." I said, "Ed, let me take a wild guess at this. My guess is you're making about the same amount of money every single year." He said, "How did you know?"

I said, "Ed, you're driving 60,000 miles a year and you've been doing it every year for eight years. You have the same amount of appointments every year. You're seeing the same number of people every year. You're doing exactly the same thing every day. If you don't change something, you're not going to change the income." He kind of shrugged and walked away. (I eventually found out how much money he was making every year. It wasn't a lot.)

Are you a 60,000-mile salesperson? Are you doing the same things over and over again—and getting the same unsatisfactory result? If so, start thinking about what you're going to change.

Salespeople not only have to know what their ratios are, they must know how to work their ratios. You're going to make sales no matter what you do, but if you don't keep analyzing and keep making adjustments, you're not going to improve over time.

The way I've changed is by growing my company by bringing in new people, by adding more offices, by writing more books. I realized I needed to change something to keep myself sharp. You and I both need to change something if we're going to be successful, or else we'll plateau!

Winning the Numbers Game

I talk to many salespeople who actually do know how many people they saw over the past week, but then I say, "What are you going to do differently now?" And they don't know.

If you don't know what you're going to do differently, then you're in trouble. Remember—the best salespeople know how to work their numbers.

4   Where to Look for Leads

WHAT EXACTLY IS A PROSPECT? What's the difference between a prospect and a lead?

Many salespeople have difficulty defining the word "prospect." Let's take a careful look at the beginning of the sales process—to see where leads and prospects come from. Let's say, for example, that I identify a company I want to do business with. Typically, I find it, maybe do a little research on it, and put it in my database. At this point, what do I have? Do I have a prospect? If I really thought about it, I could call it a candidate. I could call it a lead. I could call it a suspect. I could call it any number of things. To me, those are simply opportunities. They're not prospects. There is, however, no question that there is a better chance of making a sale once you've identified a target company than before you've identified it!

Now, suppose I get to the next step—and get an appointment. Two weeks from today I'm going to sit down with a person for the first time to explain my product and try to learn a little bit about what he does and how he does it. Now do I have a prospect?

Well, there is a realistic chance that the person will cancel, postpone, or change that initial date. It won't happen all the time, but it will probably happen often enough for us to factor it in. Therefore, even setting the first appointment does not really mean we're dealing with a prospect. It still is simply an opportunity, a candidate, or a lead.

A prospect is someone who's progressing with you through the steps of the sales process. I'll discuss these steps in more detail later on in this book, but for right now, you should know that those four steps are: the *Opening*, the *Information Stage*, the *Presentation Stage*, and the *Closing Stage*.

As a practical matter, a prospect is someone who is in steps one, two, or three—someone who is allowing you to open up, get information, and make the proper presentation prior to closing the sale. Another way of thinking about a prospect is that this is somebody who is going to "play ball" with you.

So there are three types of potential customers in the world of sales:

1. **A customer, an account, or a client**—someone with whom you have closed a sale;
2. **A lead, suspect, candidate, opportunity**—someone you want to talk with;
3. **A prospect**—someone you are working with and who's already past the opening step.

Another way to think about it is to use the $A = P = S$ model you've already seen.

Appointments = Prospects = Sales. A prospect, then, is someone who's past the appointment stage, but has not yet formalized the sale.

Generating Leads

How do you get to those steps? How do you find your candidates? Let's spend a little bit of time exploring lead generation.

There are a number of ways in which we can generate leads. The most important tool you have for lead generation is probably word of mouth—that every single person you know probably knows an average of 250 people. Therefore, it's important that you understand the value of telling people what you do. The problem is that most of us fail to let people know what we do when we meet them.

I was at a dinner party the other night; someone came up to me and asked me what I did. I answered him: "Well, I'm the president of D.E.I. Management Group, a sales training firm here in New York City. I'm doing a lot of work with (I named a major company) in the areas of cold calling and prospect management."

My wife thinks I am obnoxious because I'm always using words like these to tell people what I do. I prefer to think of it as being consistent. The reason I'm consistent is that I'm concerned that you—or someone you know—might want to know about my services. Therefore, I want to be consistent in my message to all the people I talk to. If possible, I want to give you a mini-commercial for my business.

When asked what they do, most salespeople reply, "I'm in sales." Of course, that says nothing. You must develop a clear, consistent message that you can use to promote your business.

Everyone who's ever sold anything has thought, at one point or another, about selling to FRAs: friends, relatives, and acquaintances. That is a big mistake. It's not productive. It's not effective. It doesn't really work. What's more, it often creates enemies.

Try this instead: use your friends, relatives, and acquaintances as a way to generate leads. For example, when was the last time you told your life insurance agent what you do for a living? In order for that life insurance agent to be successful, he or she has to sell to at least 1,200 people. Did you know that? How many of those 1,200 people do you think could use your product or services?

Did you know that your accountant probably does about 300 tax returns a year? Does he or she ever call on you for your services? Do you know why? Because you've probably never told your accountant what you do beyond filling in your occupation as "sales" on your tax form. You've probably never told your accountant what kind of sales you do. Your accountant almost certainly has clients who could benefit from what you have to offer. Have you ever thought about using your accountant to reach them?

When was the last time you told your physician or your dentist what you do? You never know who's going to be in the dentist's chair or who'll be visiting the doctor's office. Your barber or hair-dresser, for that matter, is another source of people you can meet.

Too many salespeople don't take advantage of these opportunities. We overestimate how many people know who we are and underestimate how many people our acquaintances know. A barber or hairdresser might have as many as twenty customers a day, and yet few salespeople think about using them to generate leads. I give copies of my books to my barber! Every time I write a new book, I give several copies to my physician! (He tells me the books never stay in his office. They are constantly being taken out by salespeople.)

I got a lead at a major computer company through my life insurance agent. He called me shortly after I had sent him a dozen books, and said, "I gave your book to one of my clients, and he happens to work for such-and-such a company. Why don't you give him a call?" Reaching out to such people is a simple but extremely effective way to generate leads.

Civic Organizations

Another way to generate leads is by becoming involved in civic organizations: Rotary, Lions, Kiwanis, Chamber of Commerce, and so on. They're all important. I know most people don't want to bother. But even your church or synagogue gives you a platform to meet people. Why not use every resource available to get more leads? I've learned over the years that every time I give a speech, one out of ten people in the audience will come up to me afterward and prequalify themselves. That is, the person will say to me, "You know, you could help my company. You could help me. Here's how. This is what I'm looking for. This is what I want to do." Talk about an effective way to generate leads!

Conferences

On average, you'll get one lead from every 10 people you meet at a conference. A couple of months ago, I went to a conference sponsored by a major entrepreneurial magazine, with 750 business owners in attendance. I walked away with 83 business cards—none of which I actually asked for. People walked up and gave me the cards!

The T Call

A T call is what happens when you're on an appointment and, after that appointment you go to the right, to the left, and behind you—and come back to the office with three more contacts.

A sales associate once told me that after she got done prospecting at an appointment, she always "did the right thing." What she meant was, whenever she walked out of the appointment, she walked out of the contact's office, turned to the right and saw somebody else. Then she went to the right again and saw somebody else. Of course, I wondered what happened to all the people on the left, but I never asked her. The point is she was using her intuition to gather new contacts, and that helped her build her sales. (Whatever works!)

Newspapers

Newspapers are another good source of leads. You probably already knew that, but consider that most people look at the obvious sections: the business section, and maybe the front page. You should really be looking at the obituaries (not so you can call the person who died, but so you can identify the company he or she worked for), the classifieds, the display ads, and the wedding sections—in addition to the more obvious sections. All of these parts of the papers can give you good information about companies.

I worked with a major computer company about two years ago. We took a copy of the Sunday *Los Angeles Times*, went through the paper, and came up with 198 potential customers that company had never thought about calling before.

Newspapers are an incredible source of leads—especially old newspapers. (New ones can actually be trickier, since lots of people call newsmakers the day a story breaks.) Hold on to those newspapers and wait about six to eight weeks; then call, using the techniques you'll learn about later in this book.

Existing Business

Another way to generate leads is through existing business. You have a one-in-two chance of getting more business from an existing account. You even have a one-in-four chance of getting business from an inactive account. At the same time, every single business you work with will inevitably suffer from a downturn. They'll change—or their business will change. (Think about IBM. IBM once was famous for its typewriters. Have you seen a Selectric lately?) Learn to rethink your existing accounts—while you find new ones.

The Usual Suspects

And don't forget the standard approaches for new leads: directories, Yellow Pages, White Pages, and lists from list brokers. You should also think about joining clubs where people trade leads and create alliances with other companies.

Some people, because of the nature of their job (e.g., payroll, security, real estate), will know about new companies that are planning to come into your territory. These people can be a tremendous resource for you. Create alliances with them!

Now that you know how to identify the people you'll be calling—what should you say? That's the subject of the next section of this book.

Part Two

Calling Techniques That Really Work

Cold Call Mechanics

THERE ARE FIVE BASIC ELEMENTS to the initial cold call:

1. Get the person's attention
2. Identify yourself and your company
3. Give the reason for your call
4. Make a qualifying/questioning statement
5. Set the appointment

I'm going to cover these in order. As we work our way through this outline, take notes so that you can develop your own cold calling script.

"But I Don't Want to Use a Script!"

Have you recently seen a movie or a television show that you really enjoyed? Sure you have. Did the actors in that drama or that comedy sound like they were reading from a script? No. It doesn't sound like a script because the actor has internalized what has to be said. That's what you must do. You have to internalize what you're going to say so it sounds natural. For example, I've been teaching the *Cold Calling Techniques* program for years. I've learned it, I've memorized it, I've internalized it. I can, therefore, take that program and change it and adjust it as the circumstances require. It always sounds natural.

Do you remember the first time you drove a car by yourself? You were probably so nervous about driving that you actually forgot how to start the car. Or maybe you went through stop signs or you got lost. Now, though, as you drive you don't even think about the various elements of the process.

The objective here is not to "handcuff" you with a script. The objective is to help you develop a script that will help you say what you need to say, while freeing you to pay attention to the prospect's response—which is what's really important.

What is the response? What is the person saying? Are we creating an atmosphere that will make it easy to make positive responses? Or are people responding negatively because we've asked the wrong questions, or asked the right questions in the wrong way? Using a script makes it easier for you to listen for crucial information, since you know exactly what you're going to say.

Here then are the five elements.

1. Get the Person's Attention

I begin a cold call by making a statement that will get attention and open up the conversation.

Let's assume I'm calling you. Depending upon what I say, you're going to respond. No matter what I say, you're going to respond somehow. And the better I get at my opening, the more likely I am to get a good response from you!

People Respond in Kind

When you try to get the person's attention, remember that people respond in kind. Salespeople tend to forget this, so they try an opening such as, "If I could save you eight zillion dollars, would you be interested?" How do you feel when someone asks you a question like that?

Gimmicky openings don't work because they produce a gimmicky response. Ask a stupid question, and you'll get a stupid answer. If you ask a reasonable question or make a reasonable statement, on the other hand, you're going to get a reasonable answer. People respond in kind.

I got a call recently from a stockbroker. He said, "Mr. Schiffman, are you interested in investing in stocks?" I said, "No," because I wasn't. He hung up. End of call. I responded to the question in kind. Now, had he asked me, "Are you presently with a broker?" I would have said, "Yes," because I was with a broker, even though at that point I wasn't interested in reinvesting. But he would have had a conversation, and perhaps the beginning of a new relationship.

Here's another kind of call: "Good morning, Mr. Schiffman, Jack Smith calling from ABC Life Insurance Company. Do you have life insurance?" I say, "Yes." I always say yes because I'm responding in kind to that question. I have no reason to say "No." I say, "Yes." He says, "Well, would you be interested in changing?" I say, "No, I'm not." Awkward silence. End of conversation. The person hangs up. I am simply responding in kind to the questions! Now, had he said to me, "Gee, I'm just curious, why did you buy the life insurance you did?" then I would have said to him, "Well, I've been with my life insurance agent for the last seventeen years. He's a good friend." The salesperson could have used that information to move the sales call along. (Later, I'll show you how to get all the information you need to get to turn a call like this around.) But I never hear that question.

Another call I got recently went like this: "Good morning, Mr. Schiffman, this is XYZ Stock Brokerage House. We'd like to come over to your office and review your 401K plan for your company." I said, "Well, I'm really happy with what we've got." He said, "Okay," and hung up. That happens all the time! Ninety percent of all salespeople make that kind of telephone call. Later on, I'm going to show you how to move beyond that kind of initial obstacle in the conversation. For now, just remember that people really do respond in kind.

I notice that a lot of the stockbrokers who call me try to keep me on the phone by saying, "Well, Mr. Schiffman, if I send you information, would it be okay if I call you back?" You don't need permission to call somebody back. That's foolishness. Just call the person back. If people don't want to take the call, they're not going to take the call. In fact, what most people who sell on the phone don't realize is that the first call is incidental. It doesn't really matter. It's the second call that will matter, and it's a waste of time to try to win a promise that the contact will be interested in taking that call.

Don't talk fast or lie or mislead people to get appointments. Some people call and say they've found somebody's wallet, or that a raffle has been won, or they're calling from a doctor's office. Or they say, "Oh, I'm sorry I called this number by mistake." All these gimmicks are terrible. They don't work. They can get you in big trouble. Stay away from them.

I remember doing a program years ago for a company where the salespeople were taught to ask for the wrong name when making the cold call. If they were calling Bill Smith, they would say, "Can I speak to John Smith?"

Inevitably, the secretary or assistant would say, "There's no one here by that name. There's a Bill Smith." They say, "No, I want John Smith."

"There's a Bill Smith."

"Oh, then it must be his brother. Can I speak to him, please?"

So, Bill Smith gets on the phone because he can't figure out who would be calling him with the wrong first name. It doesn't make sense, especially if the name's a little bit odd. So he takes the call and immediately the salesperson says, "Oh, hi John," using the wrong name. Bill says, "No, this is Bill." "Oh, I'm sorry; you know something, I was looking at the wrong name. Anyway, let me tell you why I was calling." And then they get into their little script to see if Bill is interested in whatever they're selling. Such an approach is so irritating (and so ineffective) that you shouldn't even think about using it. Believe me, there are far, far more effective strategies for getting appointments!

The Best Way to Get a Person's Attention

Most salespeople think they have to say something unique or provocative to grab a prospect's attention. Such as, "If I could show you a way in which you could. . . ." Actually, that approach builds mistrust and makes your job harder. The easiest, simplest way of opening up and getting the prospect's attention is by saying his or her name. Call up and say, "Good morning, Mr. Jones."

It's that simple. It's so simple it's almost scary.

Think about it. When you were growing up, your parents called you by your name. You responded to that. If you hear your name yelled out in the middle of a crowded room, you respond. So the first way we get someone's attention is by saying, "Good morning, Mr. Jones."

When you analyze a call, you realize that the key points to focus on are response and turnaround. How well can you handle a response? How well can you turn that response around? Given this basic premise, we have to develop an opening that's going to lead to a response we want. "Good morning, Mr. Jones," or "Good morning, Bob," does that.

The opening of your call is going to lead to a response. You can anticipate that response. You are then going to produce an appropriate turnaround, which should get the appointment. The key to the call is actually not the opening, although most salespeople spend an inordinate amount of time worrying about what they're going to say in their opening piece. The reality is no matter what you say in the opening, people are going to respond to you, and you can prepare for those responses.

Most people will respond positively to a positive-sounding call. Usually, if you speak politely and intelligently to people, they'll speak politely and intelligently to you. There will be a response in kind.

Even a hangup is a response. If you're getting hung up on an awful lot, then the odds are you're probably being too aggressive. Ask yourself: what's turning people off? (Fortunately, if you follow the script we're developing and deliver it confidently and professionally, you won't run into many hangups.)

2. Identify Yourself and Your Company

If I called you up and simply said, "Good morning, Mr. Jones, this is Steve Schiffman from D.E.I. Franchise Systems, Inc." you probably would not know who I was—or what D.E.I. Franchise Systems, Inc. was—and you probably wouldn't give me the kind of response I wanted. Therefore, I have to go further. I have to build a brief introduction, or commercial, into the call. For example, I could say, "Good morning, Mr. Jones, this is Steve Schiffman from D.E.I. here in New York City. We're a major sales training company that's worked with over 500,000 salespeople."

3. Give the Reason for Your Call

Now, the third step, the reason for the call, becomes important. Let's go back to the concept of the man in Times Square who holds his hand out. When he holds his hand out, he does eventually get a response. But when he holds his hand out and adds a cup, and adds a bell, and uses a sign, and walks after people, what he's really doing is increasing the chances that he'll get a better response.

When calling for an appointment, I suggest you say the following: "The reason I'm calling you today specifically is to set an appointment."

Now, if that were all I said, if that were my entire program, what do you think would happen? I would get appointments. Not sure? Well, think about it. If you called a million people, and you said that a million times, would one person give you an appointment? If all you said was "The reason I'm calling you today specifically is to set an appointment," would one person give you an appointment? Absolutely; probably a lot more than one! On the other hand, if you don't give the person any idea whatsoever of what you're calling for, what's going to happen? Not much! You have to send a message. You have to let the other person know what you want.

We have a relatively new assistant in our office. She was in Rome, Italy, a number of years ago when she was a student. She was a junior in high and school and had been away from home for a while; one day, because she was very hot and tired, she happened to sit down on some church steps. She was wearing a baseball cap, and she took the cap off and put it down in front of her. Lo and behold, people started dropping money in the hat! She was in shock. She couldn't believe it actually happened. Her mother later asked her, "What on earth did you look like, if people started to do that?" But that's not the point. The point is that by putting her hat down, she conveyed that she was interested in receiving money. Even though she didn't mean to send that message, that's the message she sent. She got a response. People dropped lira into her hat. But notice: she had to put the hat out in order for that to happen.

If you don't say, "The reason I'm calling is to set an appointment," then no one can say "yes" to the idea of getting together for an appointment. Remember the cup, the bell, and the sign. If I simply say, "The reason I'm calling today is to set an appointment," someone will see me. In fact, my experience is that something like one person out of twelve will see you simply because that person is not sure what you're calling about and will agree to meet with you because you asked. Now do you see why it begins to make sense just to ask for an appointment in a straightforward way?

I can enhance that third element of the script. Instead of simply saying, "The reason I'm calling is to set an appointment," I can turn it into something more compelling by saying, for instance, "The reason I'm calling you today specifically is to set an appointment so I can stop by and tell you about our new sales training programs and how they can increase the productivity of your sales force."

Notice that what I've just said paints a picture for Mr. Jones. I've really given him a reason for my call. I've talked about increasing productivity. I've actually given him some reasons we should get together. The call is now very directed. I'm not calling to introduce myself. I'm not calling to send a business card. I'm not calling to ask permission to call again. I'm not calling to ask Mr. Jones any questions. And I'm certainly not calling to close the sale! I'm calling to set an appointment. That's it. This point is very important to any salesperson who hopes to be more effective at cold calling. You're calling to set the appointment . . . not to do anything else.

4. Make a Questioning or Qualifying Statement

Now, I'm going to add a questioning statement that's going to allow the prospect an opportunity to respond to me in kind—favorably. The question that I'm going to ask has to be based on my reason for calling Mr. Jones.

My qualifying or questioning statement has to follow easily and logically from that statement. It has to be a reasonable and nonmanipulative extension of what's gone before.

So what am I going to say? I could say, "Mr. Jones, are you interested in having qualified salespeople?" The problem is, that kind of question can produce a negative response. Because there are actually people who will say "no" in response to that question: "No, I'm not interested in increasing my sales." (Anyone who's ever tried to sell using such a question knows this is a fairly common kind of response.)

A better way to start out is, "Mr. Jones, I'm sure that you, like a lot of the other companies that I work with . . . " and here I insert some real names. I might mention a computer company, an HMO, or a life insurance company. It could sound like this: "I'm sure that you, like ABC Company, are interested in having a more effective sales staff." We now have a name inserted as a reference. Mr. Jones is much more likely to say, "Yes, I'm interested."

5. Set the Appointment

Suppose Mr. Jones does say that. Now I'm ready to set the appointment. Here's how:

> *Steve:* That's great, Mr. Jones, then we should get together. How about Tuesday at 3:00?

That's it. You are simply going to say something like: "That's great, Mr. Jones, then we should get together. How's Tuesday at 3:00?" The request must be this direct, this brief, and this specific. Don't change it.

Most salespeople don't want to take this approach. They want to say, "Well, that's great! Then we should get together. What's better for you—this week or next week?" or "What's better for you—Monday or Tuesday?" or "What's better for you—morning or afternoon?" or "What's better for you—2:00 P.M. or 3:00 P.M.?"

What I've just shown you is very different. I've said, "How about getting together Tuesday at 3:00?" Now the discussion focuses on when we're going to get together, not whether we're going to get together. Now I have a better chance of getting the appointment.

The biggest mistake most salespeople make is that they fail to ask directly and specifically for the appointment. If you wish to benefit from this program, you must pose the request for an appointment exactly as I have outlined it here. When I say, "Let's get together Tuesday at 3:00," I'm being specific, and I'm going to get a response in kind—that is, a specific answer about the appointment on Tuesday at 3:00—because people respond in kind.

All Together Now

So here's what one script might sound like:

> *Steve:* Good morning, Mr. Jones, this is Steve Schiffman from D.E.I. here in New York City. We're a major sales training company that's worked with more than 500,000 salespeople. The reason I'm calling you today specifically is so I can stop by and tell you about our new sales training program and how it can increase the productivity of your sales force. I'm sure that you, like ABC, are interested in having a more effective sales staff—*(Positive response.)* That's great, Mr. Jones. I think we should get together. How's Tuesday at 3:00?

How Not to Set an Appointment

A good friend I'll call Louie makes one of the classic ineffective cold calls. Louie calls and says:

> *Louie:* Good morning, Mr. Jones, this is Louie Blank from the Blank Company here in Boston. The reason I'm calling you is to see if you might be interested in learning a bit more about our company.

Inevitably people say:

> *Prospect:* Sure, would you send me a brochure?" or "Sure, send me some literature." Or, "Do you have anything you can mail me?" Or, "Thank you for calling. Send me something."

Louie then gets into a whole conversation about what he'll send you. He never asks for the appointment until it's too late. People are simply responding in kind to his question: "Would you like to learn more about us?"

You must emphasize that you're calling to set an appointment. You can't state any other goal for the call. If you do, you're in trouble. Here is an example of what I mean. I got a call from a stockbroker that went something like this:

Stockbroker: The reason I'm calling you today is to introduce myself and my company.

Steve: Hey, nice to meet you. *(He didn't know what to say to that. But that's why he's calling me, right?)*

Stockbroker: Well, we're XYZ Company.

Steve: That's fine.

Stockbroker: Anyway, would you be interested in getting some material about us?

Steve: Absolutely.

Stockbroker: By the way, I'm just curious, what kind of stocks do you have?

The problem is that, at this point, he's lost momentum. And let's face it, people don't want to reveal the type of stocks they have to a complete stranger! When a salesperson (in this case, a man) calls me up, he should ask for an appointment. That's what he wants. He's calling for my business. That usually means he wants to meet me. Why not say that?

When Do You Call?

One of the most common questions I encounter is, "When should I call?" I call between 7:35 and 8:30 A.M. I have my first appointment scheduled somewhere between 7:45 and 8:30 A.M. By 9:00 A.M. I'm usually done with my cold calls.

You should find the best time for you, but just as important, you should avoid calling when everybody else is calling!

I remember doing a training program for a production company in New York City. One discussion went like this:

Steve: What time do you call?

Salesperson: I call at 11:00 A.M.

Steve: Why do you do that?

Salesperson: Well, I get in about 10:00 so that's the best time for me to call—11:00.

Steve: Do you get through?

Salesperson: Well, no, they're always in meetings, I leave messages.

Steve: Why don't you call at 8:00?
Salesperson: I never thought to do that.
Steve: Why don't you do that?
Salesperson: I'd have to get in early.
Steve: Okay. Get in early.

You have to find the best time for your situation. I've had sales-people call me as late as 10:00 P.M. on a Friday, and I've called people as late as 7:00 P.M. on a Friday. I've even made calls on Saturday. If you haven't thought about that, you might be interested to learn that, in many industries (like mine), Saturday happens to be a pretty good day to call and reach heads of companies.

Getting Past the Gatekeeper

Perhaps you're running into the same problem I once did—getting past the gatekeeper. Consider the following story.

A number of years ago, when I first published a book on cold calling, I got a call from my editor, who told me that a major company in Chicago had bought 400 copies of my book. He suggested I call them. I thought to myself, "This is definitely a lead." If that's not a lead, what is a lead? I called the contact at this major Chicago corporation. I got him on the phone and he told me the organization was using my material. He said my program was a fantastic program. I asked for an appointment: "I've got an idea. Let's you and I get together so we can talk about it. Let me show you some of the things I do." He told me he was the wrong person to meet with and that there was someone in New York City to talk with who set up training.

I called that person in New York City the next day. The secretary answered the phone. The conversation went like this:

Secretary: What are you calling in reference to?
Steve: Well, I was speaking to Mr. John Jones in Chicago and he
    suggested I give Mr. Peters a call.
Secretary: Well, what is it the nature of the call?
Steve: It's about sales training.
Secretary: I'm sorry, we're not interested.

Steve: Wait a minute. I know you're using 400 copies of my book. I know that your managers are training with my program. Can I speak to your boss?

Secretary: No, we're not interested.

And around and around we went. I'm not insulting secretaries now; I'm just telling you the kind of problem you're likely to run into with gatekeepers.

What do you think I did? What would you do? Salespeople I tell this story to say that they would have called back the person in Chicago, or mailed a letter complaining about the secretary, or even called the president of the company.

The only approach I can recommend is what I actually did. I called at 6:30 P.M. I got through directly to the person I was trying to reach in the first place. And I got the appointment. I realized that I was not going to get through the gatekeeper, but I also realized that there was no real need to "get through" that barrier.

What I did instead was simply call late at night. You might call early in the morning. The point is, there was no reason for me to keep talking to the gatekeeper. In fact, you're going to get through 50 percent of the time no matter what you do, so why get hung up with gatekeepers?

Don't Make Repeat Calls

Not long ago, a participant in a program I did in Chicago said to me, "Every single time I call this company, the receptionist gives me a hard time."

What's wrong with her statement?

I'll tell you what's wrong with it. The phrase "every single time" told me that she was calling this company too many times!

I asked her how many other people she could call. She responded, "Well, gosh, there's a zillion."

I told her to call those people instead! "Don't call that company. If somebody gives you a hard time, say, 'Thank you very much, have a good day,' and hang up. Then call someone else." Don't take abuse on the phone. There are always other people to call.

A "Bad" Day to Call?

A number of years ago one of our trainers was conducting a program on the Friday afternoon before Labor Day weekend, which is perhaps your biggest nightmare in terms of selling times.

The program was drawing to a close late in the afternoon. The trainer finished and said, "Thank you very much for coming. Have a wonderful Labor Day." All the representatives got ready to walk out the door, ready to go home. After all, it was 4:00 on the Friday before Labor Day weekend. The senior vice president stood up and asked where everyone was going. The representatives replied, "It's Labor Day. We're going to go to the beach."

The VP replied, "Well, look, you have an extra hour. Why don't you get on the phone?"

So now they're facing every salesperson's worst nightmare—it's Friday, 4:00, on Labor Day weekend—and they're supposed to set up appointments. (It's also every sales trainer's worst nightmare—it's not the way most of us would like to test how effective our training is.) The trainer called me and asked what he should do. I told him to let them make the calls.

An hour later they finished with these numbers: 244, 112, 44. Translation: They dialed 244 people in that hour. They spoke to 112 people and they set up an incredible 44 brand-new appointments!

The program you're learning, the script you're developing right now, works. If that story doesn't prove it, nothing does!

Using a Cell Phone

Cell phones have their uses, but I draw the line when it comes to using them to make cold calls. Logic alone should dictate that cold calling on a cell doesn't work. Too much can go wrong.

Does the expression "dropped call" ring a bell? Despite advances in the technology and an increased number of cell sites, you're going to lose some calls. You will also lose parts of the conversation to ambient noise. It's extremely difficult to have a coherent conversation with someone (or even leave an intelligent voice mail) with the sound of flight announcements or street traffic in the background. It's difficult—heck it's impossible—to concentrate on both driving and pitching.

My experience is that you have to concentrate whenever you're on the phone with a client—but even more so on a cold call. Not only do you need to be aware of the text of the conversation, you need to be aware of the subtext. If the prospect tells you she's not interested, you have to figure out a way to change her mind. And you can't do that if you sound as though you're calling from a tunnel. I'm sure you've been at the other end of a cell call where the caller used a headset or Blue Tooth technology? It sounds horrible.

And there are some psychological considerations as well. You can almost always tell when someone is using a cell phone. When it comes to cold calling, it bespeaks a lack of interest, almost as though you're trying to fit me in on the run rather than making the call from your office. It cheapens it; it seems like a lack of respect.

CHAPTER 6

Six Specific Telephone Tips for Better Prospecting Numbers

HERE ARE SIX SPECIFIC TIPS that are going to help you be more effective on telephone. You should be doing these six things in order to implement the program successfully. It's crucial that you do all six, even though each one on its own will help you become more successful in making appointments.

1. Use a Mirror

This is a great $1.99 investment. Go out to a drugstore or specialty store and buy a small hand mirror. Take the mirror and put it where you can see it and look at yourself while you're making calls. You're going to smile while you make calls. Why? When you smile, those "smile" muscles affect your larynx. The result is, you sound better. In fact, you're going to sound better than your competition—the person who's not using the mirror. This gives you an edge.

One of my favorite stories is the one about the sales representative I worked with who sold a tree-pruning service. When I called his customers, they always said, "He made the tree sing." In other words, people could envision the benefits of what he was selling, simply by listening to him. He used his voice very effectively.

Sometimes your voice becomes squeaky because your back neck muscles are pulling on your vocal cords. This makes for a squeaky sound. The smiling relieves this pulling. That's why the mirror is so important—it makes you smile!

2. Use a Timer

Know how much time it takes you to make a good call. This is important because you don't want your calls to be any longer than they need to be. If it typically takes you two or three minutes to set the appointment, don't go further than those two to three minutes.

Here's another important rule: Block out your calling time.

I told you earlier in this book that I make fifteen cold calls, speak to seven people, and usually set up one new appointment every day. It takes me approximately forty minutes each and every day to do that. Accordingly, each and every day I'm not training I schedule forty minutes for cold calling.

Years ago I was in Indianapolis doing a program for a major oil company. There was a man in the back of the room who had said nothing for two whole days. I tried to get him to participate. He took notes, he was observant, he listened, but he never once volunteered to participate in the program.

Finally, at the end of the cold calling training, he raised his hand, stood, and asked, "How long does it take you to make those calls?" I said, "Well, it takes me about forty minutes a day to make my fifteen calls." He asked, "How do you do that?" I answered, "I block out the time. In other words, I make an appointment every single day with myself to make those calls."

He said to me, "Steve, the appointment you make with yourself, that forty-minute appointment you make with yourself each and every day, is really what gives you your entire year's worth of business."

This was the most insightful thing that anyone had said to me in years. The forty-minute prospecting appointment that I make and keep with myself does in fact guarantee me my income. His observation had been worth the wait!

3. Practice!

Once you finish this section on cold calling, it's going to take you a minimum of three hours of practicing the principles you learn here for you to be successful.

When I first started my business I was not a good cold caller. I simply could not get appointments. (In fact, the reason I learned how to make appointments was that I needed to make the appointments.) Once I realized that there were certain things that I had to say and that I had to learn how to say them, I practiced. My wife, Anne, and I sat at the kitchen table going back and forth with role plays until I learned the responses and developed the right phone approach.

It was the best time investment I ever made.

So do what I did. Practice. It will take you three hours or so, but if you practice properly, those three hours will be the most productive hours of your entire sales career.

When I say this to salespeople, they often say, "Well, I don't need to practice. I make cold calls every day." That's not really practicing. Practicing means drilling. Get someone to help you: your spouse, your friend, whoever. Make that person work with you until you get your cold calling responses down perfectly.

It just doesn't make sense to practice on a prospect! You're thinking about too many things; your mind is focused on connecting with that person, not on learning the fundamentals.

4. Keep a Record of Your Calls

In other words, learn to manage your numbers. Successful salespeople don't merely know their numbers; they know how to use their numbers, how to analyze the ratios and set appropriate goals based on them. Get in the habit of tracking three things: the number of dials, the number of completed calls, and the number of appointments you get.

A number of years ago a salesperson told me that it took him 400 dials to set up an appointment. I asked him, "Well, how many people did you actually connect with?" He didn't know that number. Therefore, there's really no way to determine whether his number was good or bad. Okay, it wasn't great. But consider this: for all we know, he could have spoken to 400 people to get only one appointment—which is, admittedly, terrible. On the other hand, suppose he only spoke to two out of the 400 people he dialed—and still got one appointment. Then, from a certain point of view, he's doing great! The question then becomes—what's keeping him from getting through 398 of 400 times?

What are your numbers? How do they fit into your revenue goals? What do you expect the numbers to be? What's your desired end result?

Usually when I'm doing a program I ask salespeople how many cold calls they've made in a year. They often don't know their numbers. Worse than that, they don't know the number of sales they need to complete at the end of the year.

Therefore, even if they knew their numbers, they wouldn't have known whether or not that number was sufficient to deliver on the goal!

Determine for yourself what numbers you need. Find out how many appointments you must make each and every day in order to make the total number of sales you need at the end of the year.

5. Tape-Record Your Calls

In many places it's legal for you to tape-record your calls and then listen to them if you do so for your own use. (You should, however, check whether your state's laws require you to notify the person you're talking to.) I recommend that, for a solid week, you listen to 100 percent of your calls. Pay attention to both sides of the conversations. How does what you say sound? What responses do you get? Listen to 75 percent of your calls the second week, 50 percent the third week, and 10 percent thereafter, and I guarantee you will get a one-third increase in first appointments.

I have received many letters over the years from people who've told me how much listening to their own calls has helped them improve their results. The reason this works is obvious—you get to listen to the mistakes you're making. Once you hear and truly acknowledge a mistake, you're probably never going to make that mistake again.

6. Stand Up

Stand up when you make your calls! For many years, I worked at a standup desk. My chair was a stool, the telephone was raised. I was one-third more productive than I had been when I was sitting down.

Most of us sit down and start to make our cold calls at the end of the day. There we are dialing away, tired, exhausted, bent over our desks and (let's face it) not sounding very good. When you stand up and make cold calls, you're going to sound more animated (especially if you make your calls while you still have some energy). You're going to feel better about yourself. You're going to sound better, and, once again, it's going to give you the edge that you need to be more successful.

Implement!

All of these techniques are tried and true. They've been proven to be effective time after time. But these ideas, like all of the things you're learning about in this book, will not help you if you don't implement them. (And by the way, the same ideas will help those whose job it is to close sales on the phone, rather than set appointments.)

Having said that, let me be very clear on one point. I think it's a fallacy for people who write sales books to claim their system (or any system) is going to work all the time. My approach isn't going to work on every call, but I can promise you this: If you follow this program, it will get you one out of ten more appointments.

If this program will increase your appointments by 10 percent, is it worth trying? Of course it is. Look at it this way: If you simply speak to one more person on the phone a day, it's worth it. That's over two hundred more contacts a year. If you get just one more appointment every single week, that's fifty more appointments than you've got right now. And if you implement the program as it's laid out here, that's what you can do.

Turning Around Common Responses

OF COURSE, NOT EVERYONE SAYS "YES" when you ask for an appointment. It's important to remember, though, that when someone says, "No, I don't want to see you," it's because that person is responding to you in kind. He or she is responding to the question you posed. Don't think of this as an "objection." Think of it as what it is—a response to what you've just said.

The Four Most Common Responses

You're soon going to realize that virtually every initial "no" response falls into one of these four categories:

1. "No thanks, I'm happy with what I have."
2. "I'm not interested."
3. "I'm too busy."
4. "Send me some literature."

The trick is to learn how to anticipate and handle these responses properly.

"No Thanks, I'm Happy with What I Have"

Earlier I told you that your number one competitor is the status quo. For the most part, people really are happy with what they already have. The vast majority of the people you'll speak to will be happy, relatively "set." Otherwise, they would have called you. And guess what? They're not calling you!

You don't operate a business that's like a pizza parlor. People don't walk in and talk to you because they want to order something from you. You're reversing the process. You're out on the street, as it were, dragging people in for pizza!

And initially, yes, that person says he or she is happy with what's happening now. In fact, at the moment you call that person, he or she is already doing something. In other words, you're interrupting that person when you call.

When a Prospect Gives You Lemons, Make Lemonade

I deal with a lot of banks. In fact, my company works with just about every major financial institution in the United States today. A number of years ago I called a bank at 7:00 A.M. and talked to a senior manager—the type who probably shows up at 4:00 A.M. The conversation went like this:

Steve: Mr. Jones, this is Steve Schiffman from D.E.I. Franchise Systems, Inc. We're a major sales training company here in New York City, and we've worked with . . .

Mr. Jones: Steve, let me stop you right there. *(It's almost as if he held up his hand.)* We're already doing sales training. In fact, today's the first day of the program.

At this point, he held up the telephone so I could hear the noise of the people getting ready for the meeting. There I am at 7:00 A.M., listening to the sound of someone else starting a sales training session. Noise. How do you think I felt?

Mr. Jones: Can you hear? Phil's coming in right now!

I didn't know who Phil was. (I didn't even care who Phil was.) I listened to the noise, as I'd been instructed. Suddenly, it dawned on me. I shouldn't feel bad. I should feel great! This person has just told me he's a potential customer—he does sales training. So without missing a beat, I said:

> *Steve:* You know something, Mr. Jones, that's great that you're using sales training. A lot of the other banks *(and I named several banks that we had worked with)* have said the same thing before they had a chance to see how our program, especially the cold calling program, would complement what they were doing in-house. You know something, we should get together. How about next Tuesday at 3:00? *(By the way, every word I'd said to Mr. Jones was absolutely true.)*
>
> *Mr. Jones: (After a pause.)* Okay.

I got the appointment.

Think for a moment about how I did that. What I said was, in essence, "Other people told me exactly the same thing you did. They had the same reaction you did before they had a chance to see how what we do complements (fits into, matches, supports) what they're already doing. We should get together. How about next Tuesday at 3:00?"

In other words, I reinforced what Mr. Jones was already doing. I simply said that we could complement what he does, that we fit into that plan, that we could match that plan. I told him that he should look at our programs because of what he's already doing. I didn't tell him how to feel about the situation, or pretend I knew how he felt. I simply told him how I felt ("That's great!") and then told him the facts.

Don't say, "I sure can understand that," which is the way most people have been taught to turn around responses. It sounds stupid. It's completely unbelievable. What is there for you to understand at this point in the conversation? Remember: If you speak intelligently with a prospect, the prospect will speak intelligently back to you. People respond in kind. So don't say things like "I know how you feel" or "I can understand that" at this early point in the relationship.

Much of the training salespeople get in cold calling encourages empathy. The problem is, you don't have the vaguest idea how the prospect feels—and it's condescending to say you do. Let's say you're talking to a guy who's fifty-five years old, and you're just starting in sales. Can you honestly call him and tell him you understand how he feels? No!

Once you understand that your objective is to get in the door, not to emphathize, you'll start to see how the sales process really works.

Tell the Truth!

Think again about what I did in the call I just told you about. The bank manager was happy with his current service and I still managed to get in the door. Why? Because instead of playing word games, I told him the truth: I'd heard similar reactions from other companies in his industry before they saw how what we offered complemented what they were already doing.

If that's true for you, too (and I'm betting it is), then you have a strategy for dealing with the "I'm happy" response.

"I'm Not Interested"

Let's take a look at the next most common response. Let's say I call someone up and he says to me, "Steve, look, we're really not interested." Has that ever happened to you? Sure. Now here's the big question: Have you ever sold to someone who initially wasn't interested? Your answer has to be yes, because that's what sales is. Sales is selling to somebody who wasn't interested prior to your call. Again, if they were "interested," they would have called you.

So here's what I say:

> *Steve:* Well, Mr. Jones, a lot of people had the same reaction you did when I first called—before they had a chance to see how what we do will benefit them.

Isn't that the truth? Well, then say that. While you're at it, why not tell the person the names of the relevant companies you've worked with? If you have appropriate referrals, you should certainly use them, and this is the perfect time. Tell your contact that the XYZ Company, the ABC Company, and the National Widget Company all had the same reaction he did before they had a chance to see how what you do could benefit them. It's the truth.

"I'm Too Busy"

The third most frequent response is "I'm too busy." In other words, you call somebody and they say, "Steve, I'm too busy. I can't talk now." Typically, salespeople react to that by asking, "Well, what's a better time to call?"

In my seminars, I have plenty of discussions like this:

Salesperson: Steve, I have to leave the program to make a call, because Mr. Jones said to call him at 11:00.

Steve: Really? Tell you what, we'll take a break and we'll just sit here and wait for you.

Salesperson: Oh, no, I'll be on the phone.

Steve: Trust me. We'll take a break, you'll be back in a minute or two.

Of course, that's exactly what happens. Think about it. Nine times out of ten, Mr. Jones has no reason to sit there and wait until the stroke of 11:00 for a salesperson to call him.

For Mr. Jones, specifying 11:00 was a way to get rid of you. That's all it was.

But how do you deal with the prospect who says, "I'm too busy?" There is an effective strategy you can use.

Let's say I call Mr. Jones, and he says that he's too busy to talk. Instead of asking, "What's a better time to call?" I say: "Mr. Jones, the only reason I was calling was to set an appointment. Would next Tuesday at 3:00 be okay?"

Look at what I just did. I took that first response, "Look, I'm too busy to talk," and responded with, "Oh—well the only reason

I was calling was to set up an appointment." After all, you don't really want to have a conversation now!

You want to get the appointment. The truth is, the other person doesn't want to have a conversation now, either.

Now the prospect generally will not agree to this suggestion. Instead, the prospect will probably raise another of the standard responses we're discussing.

For example:

> *Mr. Jones:* Well, I'll tell you the truth. I'm really happy with what I've got.

Now I can go back to the response I've prepared for that kind of statement:

> *Steve:* Oh, that's great! A lot of people tell me the same thing before they have a chance to see how what we do complements what they're doing.

Understand: The person hasn't yet said he won't see you. Now you've got another response, and you can deal with that.

Note: Don't try to turn around more than three answers at this point. Instead, you can simply say: "Okay, I'll call you back later." (And mean it!)

"Send Me Some Literature"

This next response is probably the most difficult to handle. This is the person who says to you, "Look, do me a favor. Mail me something." That response is difficult because the premise behind mailing something is that the prospect will look at it, will think about it, will respond to it intelligently, and then when you call, you'll have an intelligent conversation about it. That's a real problem! Too often, salespeople translate "send literature" this way:

> "Well, Mr. Salesperson, I might be interested in what you have to sell. Why don't you send me something. Let me look at it,

really study it; then call me. We'll have an intelligent conversation and I, who by that point will have read it all, will let you tell me more about what you offer."

The problem is that 90 percent of all salespeople we surveyed said that their mail somehow never gets through to the person they mailed it to. Obviously that's not correct. Think about it. Your credit card bills, your telephone bill, and your bank statement all get to you. And yet sales material never gets through?

It got through. Your prospects just don't remember it. They don't care about it. They didn't read it. The secretary threw it out. It doesn't really matter what happened to your material, does it? The point is that this approach doesn't move the sales process forward. It doesn't get you closer to an appointment.

Here's how to turn that response around. When the prospect says to you, "Look, why don't you mail me something?" Just say, "Can't we just get together? How about next Tuesday at 3:00?"

It's as simple as that! "Can't we just get together? How about next Tuesday at 3:00?" Don't get any fancier than that. If you don't get the appointment, nine times out of ten, the person will say, "Well, I'll tell you the truth. I'm pretty happy with what we're doing." And you know how to respond to that!

Don't Forget to Listen!

Listen to what the other person says. Suppose you hear: "Look, I'm really happy with what I'm doing because I'm using the ABC Widget Company to come in here and work on this."

Now you can say, "We really should get together because of what you're doing. My experience is that we can definitely complement ABC."

The First Response Isn't Worth Fighting Over

Typically, when you listen carefully, you'll find that the first response isn't really the obstacle it sounds like.

A number of years ago, I called a major bank. This is how the conversation went when I asked a decision maker at the bank for an appointment.

The person said, "Well, I'll tell you the truth. We're really happy with what we've got and everything's okay.

I responded to that by suggesting that what we did could complement what he was already doing.

He said, "Oh, well, the real problem is that we have no budget."

I said, "Well, that's okay, let's get together anyway."

And we got together!

This was the first major sale that I ever made—$75,000. I was so excited on the drive home that I got a speeding ticket! I learned a very important lesson from that call. What I learned was that the first response had very little validity. Once I handled the first response properly, the second response emerged.

In other words, responses roll into each other. They're not isolated. Very rarely does anybody simply say "no." People usually say "no," and add a story of some kind: "No, I'm not interested because this is what we're doing now."

My experience is that it's the second response that really matters. Once you understand that, you can start to see how well what you're suggesting is going to work. The key is the second response, not the first.

Once you understand this premise, you'll be much more effective in getting appointments. The approach I'm suggesting can be applied to a whole range of potential responses.

My company has a salesperson in London who gets so many appointments it would make your head spin. No matter what a prospect says to her on the phone, she says: "Oh, well, that's okay. Why don't we get together anyway?" Of course, that strategy only makes sense if you use it intelligently and judiciously. Consider the following:

Prospect: Well, you know, really we're not interested.

You: Oh, that's okay. Why don't we get together anyway?

Prospect: Well, we just signed a contract with a major competitor.

You: Well, that's okay. Why don't we get together anyway?
Prospect: Uh, well, we hate your company.
You: Well, that's okay. Why don't we get together anyway?
Prospect: Because I hate you.

The point is, though, that fighting with a prospect over the first response (or any response, for that matter) is foolish. Often, I ask salespeople, "What do you say when the person on the phone says he's happy with what he has now?" You know how they respond? "Well, Mr. Prospect, I sure could make you happier!" That's a challenge, and a pointless one.

If the potential client says, "No, we're not interested," many salespeople offer a different equally pointless challenge: "Well, I don't know what exactly it is that you're not interested in; I haven't told you what I'm calling about yet." Not the best strategy. If a potential client says, "I'm too busy to talk," many salespeople, as we've seen, will say, "Well, what's a good time to call you back?" That approach isn't going to work, either. And when people say, "Send literature," some salespeople respond, "It will only take five minutes. Please, sir, let me come in. I'll get on my hands and knees and I'll do a very quick presentation. If you don't like it, I'll be out in five minutes." I've had salespeople tell me they actually put a watch down in front of the person. "Here's my five minutes," they say, "You let me know when it's up." What foolishness.

You and I are professionals. We should be treated as such. What's more, we need to behave like professionals if we expect to be treated like professionals. The person who's subservient or submissive to the prospective client is not going to be perceived as professional.

Many years ago, I said to a prospective client, "This will only take me five minutes." I'll never forget what happened next. That person said, "Okay, you have five minutes." I went in to the appointment and I started speaking. After five minutes, he stood up and walked out. Foolishness. I created that for myself. But I never will again.

You're a professional. Never forget that as you deal with the responses you hear on the phone.

The Ledge

THE CONCEPT OF THE LEDGE in a cold call is unique to my company. As the name suggests, the Ledge is something you can step on—something you can use to regain your footing. A Ledge allows you to handle an extended conversation during your call. It doesn't limit your conversation. You use the Ledge to support your conversation as you're uncovering what it is that they do, how they do it, when they do it, where they do it, who they do it with, and why they do it that way. Then the Ledge lets you take that information and you turn it around to say, "You know something? That's why we should get together."

Welcome to the Ledge

A Ledge uses the first question or negative response as a foothold to turn an extended phone-prospecting conversation around.

Probably every salesperson in the United States has had an occasion to over-talk, to get so involved in a conversation that he or she forgets the reason for the call. Remember: The number one reason you're calling is to set the appointment. But it's easy to get involved in everything but an appointment discussion. Let me give you an example of how that happens.

When I make a cold call, I sometimes hear the prospect say, "Really? I might be interested in that. Tell me about it now."

These are truly terrible words, because you don't know enough to make any meaningful recommendation, and you can't simply refuse the prospect's request. You can't say, "No, it's a secret. I won't tell you about what we do." (I guess you could, but it probably wouldn't help you move the sales process forward.) So you can't really say no. And yet your aim is not to sell, but to set an appointment. So you have to prepare.

Ask yourself: What are you going to say when somebody you've never sat down with says to you, "Tell me about it right now. Tell me everything about your widgets. Go."

What are you going to do? Well, first and foremost, you're going to answer the prospect. That's your instinct, and that's fine. But that can't be all you do. Why? Consider the following exchange.

Prospect: How long has your company been in business?
You: We've been in business for the last seventeen years.
Prospect: No kidding! Well, tell me how you did that.
(So you elaborate on that. You pass along a couple of success stories. Then your contact says:)
Prospect: That's a very impressive story. Tell me how you did that.
(Now you elaborate. You offer all the specifics about that success story. And all of a sudden the person says:)
Prospect: Oh, well, that may have worked then, but we don't really need that.

And the conversation is over, because the person you're talking to is right. You started talking before you knew anything of consequence about the other person. The result? What you've just described doesn't match up with this prospect.

How do you avoid this outcome?

Here's an example of a prospecting call I made recently that will prepare you to use and understand the Ledge.

Steve: Good morning, Mr. Jones, this is Steve Schiffman from D.E.I. Franchise Systems, Inc. We're a major sales training firm here in New York City . . .

Mr. Jones: No kidding! You know, we're thinking about doing training. So tell me—what do you guys do?

(Again—I can't say to him, "I can't tell you what we do.")

Steve: Well, we've been in business for about twenty-five years. We've trained more than a half million salespeople. I've written more than a dozen books.

Mr. Jones: What kind of programs do you do?

Steve: Well, I do cold calling, prospect management, and . . .

Mr. Jones: Really! How do you train cold calling?

I give a brief answer. The call is going well. Then, somewhere in the conversation he says to me, "Well, what's your price?" And I have to deal with that.

We've had a friendly conversation, so I can't say, "Our pricing is classified." Instead, I say, "The range is between X and Y." I answer the question. And Mr. Jones responds by saying, "Wait a second, that's way too expensive."

Instead of defending myself, instead of fighting him on that, I simply say, "Mr. Jones, a lot of our customers initially had the same reaction until they actually got a chance to see the benefits. You know, we really should get together."

In other words, I use his response, his negative response in this case, as a reason we should get together. Look at it again:

Mr. Jones: Gee, I'm not sure that fits what we're doing here.

Steve: You know, that's what other people said who decided to work with us. We really should get together. How's Tuesday at 2:00?

Or:

Mr. Jones: Gee, I'm not sure that's right for us.

Steve: Some other people we work with now had the same reaction at first. That's why we should get together. How's Tuesday at 2:00?

No matter what he says, that's why Mr. Jones and I should get together. Once you understand that principle and implement it, your appointment total will improve.

Using the Ledge to Get an Appointment

The salespeople we train use the Ledge to regain control of a conversation by asking a question. This is an extremely effective tool; take a look at how it works.

I called a potential customer recently; the person told me that his organization didn't use sales training.

> *Prospect:* Steve, we're not interested in sales training. We don't believe in it here.
>
> *Steve:* I'm just curious . . . if you don't use sales training, what is it that you do? What do you do with your new salespeople? Just how do you work with them?
>
> *Prospect:* Well, we don't really train them. We simply have them work with the managers and when they're ready, they go out on their own.
>
> *Steve:* That's great, Mr. Jones! Then we should get together, because we work with a lot of other companies that have done the exact same thing. How about next Tuesday at 3:00?

And I got the appointment. That "I'm just curious" question allowed me to gain a foothold, to resume control of the conversation. That's the Ledge in action.

I used the information he gave me about what he does as a reason to get together. People who are successful at scheduling appointments understand the power of this simple concept.

Here's another example of how to use the Ledge:

> *Prospect:* Headquarters makes that kind of decision.
>
> *Steve:* Okay. I'm just curious, what do you do? What's your role there?

When he answers, I respond, "That's interesting. Based on what you've told me, I think we should get together."

Recently, I called up the New York City office of a major company located in Ohio. The person who answered the phone happened to be the branch manager. The conversation went like this:

Branch manager: Steve, I'd love to meet with you but we don't make any decision here. All the decisions are made in Ohio.

Steve: Oh, well, I'm just curious. What kind of training do you do?

He responded to this by telling me about three different types of training he does. Then I said, "You know something, we should get together, because we really complement those programs."

We ended up scheduling a meeting. When we got together, he said to me, "Steve, I can't make these decisions myself, but I can get them made." That meeting turned into a half-million-dollar sale, and it was generated by my use of the Ledge.

Here's another example. When I called the prospect, the conversation went something like this:

Prospect: Steve, we're really not working with any other outside trainers. We just signed a contract with someone.

Steve: Oh, that's interesting. I'm just curious, who'd you sign with?

Prospect: Well, we signed with XYZ Company.

Steve: You know what? We should get together, because we complement their program.

As you get more experience in cold calling, you'll start to learn more sophisticated approaches. For example, I called another company and got an appointment like this:

Prospect: Look, we just signed a contract with another training company.

Steve: Well, are you using the Brand X Selling Solution?

Prospect: No, we're not using Brand X. We're using Brand Y.

Steve: Oh, then we really should get together, because what we do complements Brand Y.

I can throw out any company, any kind of training program. He will respond to me in kind by correcting me and telling me who his company uses. (Prospects love to correct salespeople.) I always say, "Then we should really get together."

You've got the basic principle now. No matter what the person says to you, you're going to say, "We really should get together."

Talking to the Wrong Person

Another mistake salespeople make involves the way they respond when somebody says, "I'm the wrong person to talk to." Most salespeople then ask, "Who's the right person?" Never ask that. Instead, when the other person says, "I'm the wrong person," you should say, "Gee, I'm just curious. What is it you do?" And no matter what they say to that, unless you're absolutely sure this is the wrong person, you're going to say, "Oh, then you know what? We should get together."

If they're really not the right person, they're going to let you know. They might say, "I'm in charge of bricklaying here at the foundry." If you're selling video postproduction, then that's really not the right person. Then you should ask, "Oh, then who should I talk to?" And then you can take that name and use it as part of a referral call, which I'll explain later.

A Real Conversation

Once you start using the Ledge, you'll soon realize that you're really having a conversation with your prospect. At this point it's not a sales call, it's a conversation. Initially, my conversation happens to revolve around my desire to get an appointment, while the prospect's conversation is about what they're doing, how happy they are doing it, and why they see no need to change. Often, the Ledge is where the two conversations become one.

So first, most people would be "happy" if I never called in the first place. Think about that. If I didn't call Tuesday, but called Wednesday, would it matter to these people? They're still doing business. The world is still spinning. They don't "need" that call.

If you understand these basic ideas, and use the information you get from your conversations with prospects to create a Ledge in your cold call, I promise you that you will become more effective.

More Examples of the Ledge in Action

A while back, a sales representative who was in one of my programs said, "Steve, we have a problem. This cold calling stuff won't really work for me. You're good at it, but that's because you train it for a living." What he meant, I believe, was that the program is second nature for me, and that, for people who are unfamiliar with it, it isn't second nature. And he was right.

At this point in my career (I've been doing this for more than a quarter century), cold calling is relatively simple to me. It does come very naturally. For you it may be more difficult. The reason I told you the golf story at the beginning of the book was to make the points that certain aspects of cold calling are not going to be comfortable, and that, initially, you're not always going to like some of the parts of the process.

Whether you're comfortable with the program at first or not, you can honestly say, "I can improve my odds. I can get one more appointment a day if I simply employ these techniques." And if you give it an honest try, you're going to do that. When you hear resistance on the phone, you're going to ask a question, and then you're going to say, "That's great. You know something, we should get together." That's how the Ledge works.

Let's take a closer look at some more examples of the Ledge in action.

Example 1

Prospect: I'm really not interested.

You: A lot of the people we work with said the same thing before they had a chance to see the way in which we complement what they're presently doing.

Prospect: Yeah, but you know, we've had a difficult time with your company before.

You: Can I just ask you a question? Who presently supplies your light bulbs?

Prospect: Well, we use the XYZ Company. We went to them instead.

You: Oh, no kidding. Then we really should get together.

Prospect: No, I really don't think so. Why don't you send me information. I'll take a look at it.

You: Can we just get together? How about next Friday at 3:00?

Prospect: No, I'll tell you the truth, I'm really not interested.

You: Okay. Thank you.

(Hang up! You gave it your best shot. Call someone else.)

Example 2

Prospect: You know, we really don't have any kind of budget for that.

You: No kidding. Well, just out of curiosity, are you working with anybody right now?

Prospect: Sure we are. We have the 123 Manufacturing Company right here.

You: Are you using their ABC product?

Prospect: No, we're actually using their BC2 product.

You: Really? Then we should get together. How about next Friday at 5:00?

Example 3

Prospect: Why don't you tell me something about your product? *(Note: Remember that you must give a brief, direct answer to a prospect's question.)*

You: Well, you know something, Mr. Jones, we've been in business for the last forty-two years and we've developed a number of ways in which we can substantially reduce wear and tear in the manufacturing process. I'm just curious though, what does your company do? *(Instead of rambling on, you pose a question of your own.)*

Prospect: Well, we manufacture customized widgets. We use the ABC product line here.

You: Really? Has that been working for you?

Prospect: Sure it has.

You: Oh, that's great then. We really should get together so I can show you the ways we can complement ABC.

Example 4

Prospect: You know, why don't you put something in the mail. Let me take a look at it and I'll give you a call back. I'm really kind of busy right now.

You: Actually, the only reason I called is to set up an appointment. Would next Tuesday be okay?

Prospect: Well, not really. You know, I'll tell you the truth. This is my busiest time of the year.

You: I have an idea. What are you doing four weeks from today?

Prospect: Let me check—nothing.

You: Well, why don't we get together Friday the eleventh at 2:00?

Prospect: Okay.

You've now succeeded in scheduling the appointment. Confirm the address and politely conclude the conversation! Don't try to sell, and don't get involved in a long, drawn-out discussion.

Be Prepared!

Remember, in each case you're creating a Ledge. You're finding a foothold you can use to turn the conversation around.

Sometimes, though, you won't even need the Ledge.

> *Steve:* Good morning, Mr. Jones, this is Steve Schiffman from Widget Management here in New York. I don't know if you know who we are, but we're the major supplier of widgets in the area. We've worked with ABC Corporation and 123 Company. Anyway, the reason I'm calling you today specifically is to set up an appointment so I can tell you the way in which we've been successful with other companies. How's Tuesday at 2:00?
>
> *Mr. Jones:* You know, that sounds great. Come on over.

You know what? There *are* calls that play out like that. Be ready for them!

9 Mastering Third-Party and Referral Calls

THIRD-PARTY AND REFERRAL CALLS are variations on the standard script. Study them. You'll need them!

The Third-Party Call

First, let's look at the third-party endorsement approach to cold calling. It's very easy, and it may even complement the way you're now selling. This is the variation I use, and most of the salespeople we train say this is a very easy model to adapt. I think you're going to enjoy it.

The Basic Steps

The first thing to remember about this approach is that it uses the same basic steps we've already discussed:

- Get the person's attention.
- Identify yourself and your company.
- Give the reason for your call.
- Ask for the appointment.

These are key points that will increase the effectiveness of your calls—no matter what kind of call you're making. Let's examine how they apply to the third-party call.

Get the Person's Attention

I've already told you that the way you get the person's attention is not by saying something gimmicky (like, "Are you interested in making a million dollars?") but by saying the person's name. You can decide on your own approach here. Do you like to say, "Hi, Bob," "Hi, Joe," or "Hi, Jill"? Do you like to say, "Good morning, Mr. Jones"? Whatever you're most comfortable with, that's what you can use. I happen to like to say, "Good morning, Mr. Jones," or "Good afternoon, Mr. Jones." That's going to be my attention statement. I don't need anything more than that.

Identify Yourself and Your Company

I've already indicated that if I said to you, "This is Steve Schiffman from D.E.I. Franchise Systems, Inc.," the odds are you would not know who that is. So that statement, on its own, is not going to be entirely appropriate in getting an appointment or letting you understand who I am. I need to give you a chance to understand exactly what I'm talking about.

Why? Because when we telephone somebody, that person is not prepared for the call. We're the last thing on that person's mind.

What we're doing, by its nature, requires us to get people to think about something that they weren't thinking about before we called them. In other words, the call doesn't follow the natural course of the person's day. Your prospects are doing what they're doing, and you telephone them and say, "Stop, I need you to do something else." Well, why should they?

We have to give them an opportunity to understand what we're talking about, and then paint a picture for them so they can visualize the process. Here's how to do that.

So far I have "Good morning, Mr. Jones"; that's my opening. Here's my second step:

"This is Steve Schiffman, I'm the president of D.E.I. Management Group. I don't know if you've ever heard of us, but we're an international sales training company here in New York City. I also have offices in Chicago and Los Angeles. I do a lot of work with . . ."

And now I mention the XYZ, the ABC and the 123 companies in the context of cold calling and prospect management. This is painting the picture. I said key words. I've said sales training, cold calling, prospect management. I've mentioned the XYZ, the ABC, and the 123 companies, which are major players, not necessarily in Mr. Jones's area, but still major players in the United States. They're going to be familiar to him.

So I've painted a picture for my prospect. I've allowed him to imagine what it is that this call is about. My prospect can think, "Oh, this is in reference to sales training." Why should I make him wonder, "Huh? What? What's this about?" With this approach, I don't need a gimmicky opening.

Now you focus on a specific success story. You can choose your own references to call just about anyone you want to talk to.

A number of years ago I was working with a major bank. I had trained about 500 of their sales managers to be more effective on the phone. (I got the account because I gave a free speech at a Chamber of Commerce meeting, and a woman came up to me afterward and said she thought I could help the bank she worked for. It happened to be the number three bank in the United States at that time.)

About six or seven weeks after completing the program, I decided that I'd call another bank. It occurred to me that, since one bank was doing something about sales, another bank would probably be trying to do the same thing. If I could help one bank do that better, I could help another. It really had nothing to do with the fact that the organizations were competitors. Once this approach crystallized in my mind, I realized I had a means of entry into virtually any bank or financial services organization I wanted to call.

The next day I took a directory, found the name of a senior vice president of another bank, called him up, and said:

"Hello, Mr. Smith. This is Steve Schiffman. I'm the president of D.E.I. Management Group, an international training company here in New York City with offices in New York, Los Angeles, and Chicago. I've done a lot of work with ABC Bank in the areas of cold calling and prospect management." He listened—and he agreed to meet with me!

Take a look now at the third and fourth steps.

Give Reason for Your Call and Ask for the Appointment

Continue by saying, "The reason that I'm calling you today specifically is that I just completed a very successful sales training with the ABC Bank here in New York City. In fact, it increased their appointments by one-third. I'd like to stop by next Tuesday at three and just tell you about the success I had with the ABC Bank."

(By the way—in seminars, I tell salespeople that they can and should adapt the wording of their scripts to their own situation, but that they should leave certain elements intact verbatim. "The reason I'm calling you today specifically" is one of those elements. Don't alter it; it works just as written. Similarly, you should ask directly for the appointment by specifying a date and time: "How's Tuesday at 2:00?")

The beauty of this call is you never say, "What we did for ABC Bank will work for you. You're simply saying that you've worked with another company in this person's industry, and you were successful with that company. That's the heart of the third-party endorsement approach.

This approach can work very well across industry lines, too. Look at it again:

"Good morning, Mr. Blank, this is Steve Schiffman from D.E.I. Management Group, an international training company here in New York City. We're also in Chicago and Los Angeles. We've worked with the XYZ, ABC, and 123 companies in the areas of cold calling and prospect management. The reason that I'm calling you today specifically is I just completed working with U.S. Delivery, a major courier in the

Louisville area. I was very successful in showing them ways in which they could increase their sales by actually getting more appointments, which they did. They got 30 percent more appointments. Anyway, what I'd like to do is stop by and tell you about the success I had with U.S. Delivery. How's Tuesday at 3:00?"

The key to this call, once again, is that I'm not telling prospects I can do the same for them. I'm mentioning my success with other companies and asking for an appointment. I'm not making empty promises.

Here's another way I can make this call:

"Good morning, Mr. Jones, this is Steve Schiffman from D.E.I. Franchise Systems, Inc. I'm doing a lot of work with the XYZ, ABC, and 123 companies in the area of cold calling. The reason I'm calling you today specifically is that I just completed working with the Blankety Lumber Company here in the area. I was very successful in showing them ways in which they could increase their lumber sales by getting more appointments. What I'd like to do is stop by next Tuesday at 3:00 and just tell you about the success that I had with the Blankety Lumber Company."

I can also make this approach generic. I can say:

"Good morning, Mr. Jones, Steve Schiffman, from D.E.I. Franchise Systems, Inc. I'm doing a lot of work with the XYZ, ABC, and 123 companies in the area of cold calling. The reason I'm calling you today specifically is that I just came back from a sales meeting where I learned about the success we've been having in the Philadelphia area. I'd like to stop by next Tuesday at 3:00 and just tell you about our success with other companies in the Philadelphia area."

This allows you to tailor your call to the city in which the prospect resides.

Whatever works—whatever you need! You can also apply this approach to specific kinds of businesses:

> "Good morning, Mr. Jones, Steve Schiffman from D.E.I. Franchise Systems, Inc. We're a sales training firm that does work with firms like Acme Widget and Widget Co. The reason I'm calling you today specifically is that I've been very successful in showing them ways they can increase their widget sales. What I'd like to do is stop by next Tuesday at 3:00 and tell you about the success we've had with those companies."

Once again—I'm not saying that I can do for them what I've done before. I'm simply saying that I've done it for somebody else, and therefore it makes sense for us to get together. This method is utterly different from the approach most salespeople take. Typically, a salesperson calls up and says, "Good morning, Mr. Jones, Jack Smith here from ABC Widgets. The reason I'm calling today is that we have ways we can save you money."

Well, you're not sure of that yet. You don't know anything about this person's business!

"We have ways that can make you more efficient."

You're not sure of that yet, either!

"We have something that could help you."

You're not sure of anything yet!

When you pretend you're sure about how you can help the person, all you do is create a response in kind that allows the other person to say, "Well, I don't know whether you can really do that. That's not right for us."

That means you now have to defend yourself. What a waste of everyone's time and energy!

Still, suppose you take a completely wrong approach for some reason. Suppose you do get sidetracked because the person responds: "Well, you've just said you do X, and here are twelve great, detailed reasons X will never work for us."

You know what to say, don't you? Of course you do.

"Oh, no kidding! Mr. Jones, I'm just curious, what is it that you do?"

Regardless of the way you opened the conversation, his or her answer will give you the Ledge that will enable you to turn the conversation around.

Or suppose you don't get a detailed objection or a direct question (two situations where the Ledge is extremely effective). Suppose you hear:

> *Mr. Jones:* Well, you know, we're really happy with our long distance company. We have no interest in changing.

You can then say:

> *You:* Gee, I've got to tell you, a lot of people we work with have said the same thing before they had a chance to see how what we do complements what they're presently doing.

Or if you hear:

> *Mr. Jones:* Well, I don't know, why don't you send me some literature?

You can say:

> *You:* Oh, Mr. Jones, can't we just get together? How about next Tuesday at 3:00?

Don't defend yourself. Anticipate the responses, use the techniques I've taught you, and ask for the appointment.

There are variations on the third-party approach. I know someone who is a very successful life insurance agent. He calls people and says, "Good morning, Mr. Smith, this is Mike Jones from the XYZ Life Insurance Agency. Have you heard of us?"

Inevitably people say "no." Then he says:

> "Oh, well, let me tell you why I'm calling you specifically. I am an agent with the XYZ Life Insurance Agency. We've been very successful working with small business owners

in Boston, and what I'd like to do is stop by next Tuesday at 3:00 and just tell you about the success we've had with other small business owners."

Often, the people will say they have life insurance. Then he says, "Oh. Just out of curiosity, are you with ABC Insurance?" The prospect corrects him. (Good salespeople love getting corrected.)

Mr. Smith: No, we're not with them, we're with Brand X Insurance.

Mike: Oh, then we really should get together, because I can show you some ways we can complement that program. By the way, have you done any kind of estate planning?

And then, no matter what the answer is, he says, "Oh, that's great. Then we should get together. What about next Friday at 3:00?"

I'm not going to tell you that he gets an appointment every time. But the fact is he has become one of the most successful agents in the entire country by using the third-party approach and the Ledge.

Referral Calls

You can use the referral call when you have called someone in the organization, and that person has referred you to someone else. This approach helps you make the most of that opportunity to get an appointment.

Now you already know that when you telephone somebody and that person says, "I'm the wrong person to speak with," you're not going to ask, "Okay, who's the right person?" Instead, you're going to say, "Oh, what do you do?"

This is where you have to be ready to think on your feet. Sometimes, you'll realize you really are speaking to the wrong person. Sometimes, you'll ask the person you're talking to for an appointment.

Assume you're able to confirm that you really are dealing with someone who is the wrong person. Assume too, that you ask your contact for the name of the right person to meet with. Usually the contact will say something like "Why don't you get in touch with Pete Smith."

A side note: I prefer to ask, "Who would I be meeting with?" rather than "Who handles so-and-so?" At this point in the call you've shared some information about your company with the person and (this is important) asked what he or she does. If you keep the discussion on a personal, one-on-one level, you may get better information.

How should you use that information? Most salespeople call and say the following:

> "Good morning, Mr. Smith, this is Joe Johnson from XYZ Company here in New York. The reason I'm calling you is that I just spoke to John Jones, and he suggested that I call you and tell you about the work that we're doing. He thought you'd be interested in knowing more about my company."

Don't do it!

Instead, use what you've already figured out. You call Mr. Jones; he tells you he's the wrong person. You get the name of the right person, then you call him. Call the right person and say:

> "Hello, Mr. Smith. This is Jane Smith from XYZ Company here in New York. We're one of the top three widget companies in America. The reason I'm calling you today specifically is that I just spoke to John Jones. He suggested that I give you a call to set up an appointment. I wanted to know if next Tuesday at 3:00 would be okay."

You don't need to go through a full explanation. All you need to say is that your referrer suggested you give a call to set up an appointment. If you follow the system I've set up, your statement will be completely aboveboard. You will have asked for the name of the person you'd be meeting with.

At some point in my conversation with Pete Smith you're going to get a reaction. The typical reaction is, "Oh? Why would he want me to meet you? Well, what's this about?" Of course, Pete Smith doesn't know anything about why you're calling.

You can then take a step back and say, "Well, the reason I called John initially was that I had just worked with the XYZ Company. We were very successful in training their salespeople to be more effective on the phone. And when I told him that, he said that I should talk to you to set up an appointment."

Now the person has to react. He can react by saying, "Well, we don't do anything like that." To which you're going to say (you know it already, right?), "Oh. So what do you do?" And no matter what he says next, you're going to say, "Well, you know something, we should get together. How about next Thursday at 3:00?" So even with a referral call, we can still use the response turnarounds and the Ledge effectively.

The Ledge, I cannot overemphasize, is the technique you must, without fail, become familiar with. I tell salespeople to take a piece of paper or an index card, write the word "Ledge" on it, and keep it in front of them at all times when they make calls. Use the Ledge just as I've outlined it here!

You can use the referral approach in any number of situations. I recently met someone in Cincinnati who told me that I ought to call a friend of his in Indianapolis. I called the friend and said: "Hi, I met with so-and-so in Cincinnati and he suggested I call and set up an appointment for us to get together. I'm going to be in Indianapolis next week." (This was, in fact, the case.)

It worked—and we got a significant account from that visit!

CHAPTER

10   Leaving Messages That Get Results

I'M ALWAYS A LITTLE BIT MYSTIFIED when I run into sales-people who tell me they "don't believe" in voice-mail messages when it comes to making prospecting calls. Nowadays, that's a little bit like saying you don't believe in the planet Earth.

All the same, there are a good many salespeople we train who swear that it's a waste of time to leave messages for prospects. I have a sneaking suspicion that these salespeople simply don't like making prospecting calls in the first place. Reaching someone's voice-mail box is common now. Excluding all those potential contacts is, I think, basically a rationalization for the bad idea of focusing your calling efforts on "warm calls" to people who are already familiar to you. The problem is, there usually aren't enough people in that category to support your revenue goals.

Let's face it: A huge number of decision makers use voice mail to screen virtually all of their calls. Why would you want to simply hand that group of potential customers over to the competition?

I also talk to a lot of salespeople who take the opposite approach. They overcall cold contacts, and leave two, three, five, or even more voice-mail messages per week.

All that time, effort, and potential annoyance for people who have not yet set any kind of Next Step!

This method of using voice mail is not only a huge waste of time, but also a poor way to initiate a business relationship. Think back on the last time you received three or more consecutive voice-mail messages in a single week from someone you didn't know. Were you more or less likely to return the person's calls at the end of the week?

There's another potential danger with abusing voice-mail systems in this way when reaching out to new contacts: You may be tempted to distort your own calling numbers, and that can make identifying correct ratios and targets difficult. I can't tell you the number of salespeople I've worked with who've informed me that they make "fifty calls a week," but who actually make calls to just ten new contacts over a five-day period. They leave a message a day for each of those contacts, and consider each of those messages to be a separate call!

In this book, when I talk about making a certain target number of prospecting calls per day, I'm talking about reaching out to—and, if necessary, leaving voice-mail message for—X number of brand-new people you haven't tried to reach in any way, shape, or form that week. That's the standard to use. It implies, of course, that you should leave no more than one voice-mail message per business week when trying to establish connection with a new contact.

The situation is different, of course, once you've established some kind of Next Step with the person in question. At that point, you're dealing with an active prospect; it's quite common for people with busy schedules to exchange three or four messages before connecting in person or by phone, and some business relationships will actually unfold almost exclusively by means of voice mail or some other messaging option. The point is, there's a different standard once you've gotten the contact to agree to meet with you in person.

On the whole, I've found that good salespeople actually prefer delivering a solid, professional message to a voice-mail system, and dealing with the resulting return call. Here are five reasons for that.

1. The dynamic of the call is likely to be much more favorable, and a conversational tone will often be much easier to achieve.
2. When the person calls back, you're somewhat less likely to be interrupted (because you're less likely to be perceived as an interruption).
3. When the person calls back, he or she is more likely to actually listen to what you have to say.
4. You can easily leave messages for people who are difficult or impossible to reach directly on the phone.
5. You can make prospecting calls to voice-mail systems at just about any time of the day or night, which gives you more flexibility in scheduling.

In the age of voice mail, you must know how to leave a message that can increase your chances of having the person get back to you. I'm going to give you two specific, very effective ways to leave a message. The first way will give you between 65 and 75 percent return calls. The second way is almost 99 percent effective!

Calling with a Company Name

Here's the first way, the way that most representatives we train leave messages.

Let's say I'm calling someone, and the secretary or receptionist tells me I'm going to have to leave a message. If you recall the phone scripts from earlier chapters, the central reason for my calling is the success I had with the XYZ Company. Therefore, my referring comment or my reference point should be the XYZ Company. So my message will sound like this:

"This is Steve Schiffman from D.E.I. Franchise Systems, Inc.; my telephone number is 212-555-1234. Would you please tell him it's in reference to the XYZ Company?"

Or, for a voice-mail system:

"This is Steve Schiffman from D.E.I. Franchise Systems, Inc.; my phone number is 212-555-1212. It's regarding XYZ Company."

So when he or she calls me back, I'm going to say: "Oh, I'm glad you called me. The reason I called you is that we recently did a project with the XYZ Company."

And then I immediately go into my call about being successful with the XYZ Company. I have to carry that through. If I don't, then the calls will not be consistent.

You can't lie or mislead. You must leave your company's name as well as the referring company's. You must be precise, and you must make sure that the secretary or the assistant gets the name of your company. Be careful not to give the impression that you represent the XYZ Company. If you do that, you will have trouble later on. Maybe not on your first call or your second call, but eventually someone's going to say you misled them, and they'll be right.

The interesting thing is, you don't have to use a huge company for this strategy to work. It doesn't matter whether or not the person even knows the company, as long as you get him or her on the phone. You can use a company that you're familiar with or a company that your contact should be familiar with, but isn't. If the person says to you, "Well, I don't know anything about the XYZ Company," you can start by saying, "Oh, well they're the biggest widget company in the area. They do A, B, and C. Anyway, the reason I was calling you . . ." and then you can go right into your opening.

It doesn't even matter if the person tells you that he doesn't really care about that company, because now you're on the phone together. You can say, "Oh, that's all right. I'm just curious, though. What do you do?" And you're going to use their answer to create the Ledge for yourself. So it doesn't really matter how people respond to the message you leave, whether that response is positive or negative—as long as they call you back.

We get between 65 and 75 percent of our calls returned using this method.

Calling with an Individual's Name

The second method of leaving a message came to me in an interesting way.

Every once in a while, it's necessary to terminate someone, and sometimes people just leave. That's just the way things go. Some time ago I had a representative working for me who didn't work out—I'm going to call him Bob Jones. After Bob left the company, I started thinking that, as president, I really should call everybody Bob had ever talked to in order to see whether I could start the conversation again.

The first company I called was a huge telecommunications company that Bob had met with; the headquarters were not far from our office in Manhattan. I asked to speak to the president of the company; the secretary got on the phone and said to me, "I'm sorry, he's busy. What's it in reference to?" Now remember, I usually say that my name is Steve Schiffman, my company is D.E.I. Franchise Systems, Inc., my telephone number is . . . and I go on to mention the referring company. But in this case, I had Bob Jones on my mind. I had been thinking about him for some time, because it was a little bit frustrating to me that he hadn't worked out. So I simply said that Bob Jones was my reason for calling. The secretary took the message.

About twenty minutes later, the president of the company called me back and said, "You had called me in reference to Bob Jones."

I said, "Oh, yes. Bob Jones worked for our company a number of weeks ago. He's no longer with us, and the reason I was calling you today is we've been very successful working with the ABC Bank. I'd like to stop by next Tuesday at 3:00 and tell you about our success with them."

He gave me the appointment, and we eventually started a business relationship.

I started thinking about that, about how many other people Bob had met with. And so I called everybody and nearly every single person—almost 100 percent—called me back. I used the same message every time, referring to Bob Jones. Now, I don't know whether or not they really remembered Bob Jones, nor do

I care. I never asked that question. And when I showed up for an appointment, sometimes he would come up in conversation, and sometimes he wouldn't. But they virtually all called me back. So I asked myself: How else can I use this approach?

Maria, a sales rep who's been with us for about a year, was very frustrated because she had gone on a major sales call, and the person she had met with decided to stop returning her calls. I called her contact's office. Here's how the conversation went:

Steve: Can I speak to Brian Smith?

Secretary: I'm sorry. He's busy right now. What's it in reference to?

Steve: No problem. My name is Steve Schiffman. My company is D.E.I. Franchise Systems, Inc. My number in New York is 212-555-1234. Would you please tell him it's in reference to Maria. *(And I gave Maria's last name.)*

Thirty-five minutes later he called me back.

Prospect: You called me in reference to Maria?

Steve: Yes, you had met with Maria a number of months ago.

Prospect: Oh, yes.

Steve: Anyway, I wanted to find out what happened.

And he told me the story. I found out that the sale was over, but the fact is I got him on the phone in under an hour. (Maria had told me that was impossible.)

My point is, you can use this technique in a lot of different situations. Have your manager call contacts at those organizations where the sale did not happen. Remember, the status quo is your number one competitor. If that's true, and it is, then the odds are that your contact did nothing after your visit. So, therefore, your manager can say:

"Mr. Jones, I understand that you worked with Jan Smith, one of our representatives, and nothing really happened.

I just wanted to know if there was something that we did wrong."

In other words, your boss should make the assumption that your organization did something wrong. That's a lot better than saying the prospect did something wrong! Virtually every time, this is what your sales manager will hear:

Prospect: Oh, no, Jan was great! It's just that we had these three problems, A, B, and C.

Your boss can then say:

Manager: Oh, then we should get together, because we've been working with other companies who've had the same situation. How about next Tuesday at 3:00?

Working as a Team

Another way to use this technique is for two reps to trade off names. We have a number of salespeople in our office who do this. Ross will make the initial call. Sometimes, for whatever reason, he does not get through, and the person he's trying to reach doesn't call him back. Now, Melody uses Ross's name to call. Her message will be, "This is Melody from D.E.I. calling in reference to Ross."

This is all perfectly legitimate. Ross had called, and the contact never called him back. We don't know why not. When she gets the prospect on the phone, Melody simply says, "Ross from our office had called you. I'd like to stop by."

Typically, they'll call back and she'll get the appointment. So does Ross. But he does it in reverse, using Melody's name. You can use this method with your colleagues, or your manager can work with you.

There are many different ways to use this technique. For example, you can call all of the companies that other representatives in your company have called and have not been successful with.

Let's say two years ago Jimmy Jones picked up the phone and called the Umbrella Company of America. He never got through. You want to call again. Simply use Jimmy Jones's name in your message:

> "Hi, would you please tell him I called? My name is Chris Smith from the XYZ Company. My phone number is 555-1212. Would you please tell him it's in reference to Jimmy Jones."

When the prospect calls back, you're going to say:

> "Hi, you had spoken to Jimmy Jones from my company a number of years ago. The reason I'm calling is that we've been very successful with the ABC Widget Company. I'd like to stop by . . ."

The strategy I've outlined makes it easy to get return calls almost 100 percent of the time, and it virtually eliminates problems with gatekeepers.

Every once in a while, a secretary asks me what my call is in reference to. I simply reply that it's a long story. If pressed, I ask the secretary whether he or she wants to hear the whole story. Most secretaries say no.

I always leave a message, either with a human being or a voice-mail system.

If They Still Don't Call Back . . .

I do not persist in calling people after a certain point. My approach is simply that once I've called, I assume you're going to call me back. If I don't hear from you within a week or so, my assumption is you didn't get the message, and I'm going to call you again. As a general rule, I make no more than four attempts to contact a decision maker at a particular company in a given month.

You should follow the same rule.

I meet salespeople who say, "Steve, I call a hundred people a week." In reality, they call ten people ten times each. That may add up to a hundred, but really it's a very different number.

Years ago, a salesperson at a major company told me that she had called a decision maker over 400 times, and still had not gotten an appointment! That's like calling somebody fifteen times a day, every single day, for a month straight. Why would anybody do that?

Dealing with Telephone Tag

Telephone tag has to be the scourge of all salespeople. We call somebody over and over again; they call us, but we can't seem to connect. How do you handle that?

Salespeople face this obstacle every day. We probably won't reach up to one-third of all the people we actually call simply because they didn't answer the phone. They're busy, or they're away, or they are in a meeting. You trade calls back and forth. This can be very frustrating.

My whole approach to appointment making is based on the assumption that the prospect and I ought to get together. After all, why would I doubt that? So I'm going to use that assumption in dealing with telephone tag problems.

I've called the prospect, I've expressed interest in our getting together, and in making an appointment to meet. The prospect has also expressed some interest. Whether or not this person directly said, "I'm interested," the contact has not said to me, "No, I'll never see you," or, "No, never call me again." Once in a great while you do get such a response, but let's be realistic. Most people respond—in kind—by either saying, "No, this is not the best time," or by making an appointment.

What's really happening in telephone tag? The problem is that you have not really connected with a prospect. If you do connect, then you're going to set up a meeting. But do you really have to connect, or can you simply use the resources at hand to set the appointment?

Consider this sample call:

Steve: Mr. Jones, the reason I'm calling you is to set an appointment.

Mr. Jones: Please call me back.

I call Mr. Jones back in three weeks or in six months, depending on what his time frame is. What do I say? Listen:

Steve: Mr. Jones, the reason I'm calling you specifically is that when we spoke in May you suggested I give you a call today to set up an appointment. Would next Tuesday be okay?

That's a highly effective follow-up call. Use it! (By the way, much more about follow-up calls appears in Chapter 11.)

But let's say that, for whatever reason, I don't get to talk to Mr. Jones when I call back, so I leave the following message on Mr. Jones's voice mail.

"Hi, Mr. Jones—Steve Schiffman here from D.E.I. The reason I called is that when we spoke in May you suggested I call today to set up an appointment. I looked in my schedule and I see that I'm going to be in Philadelphia next Thursday, and I wanted to know if next Thursday at 2:30 is okay. My number is 212-555-1234."

That's the entire call. The approach uses the assumption that this person and I are in fact going to get together. (Again: Why not assume that?) This approach can be used with voice mail or with a secretary. You and the prospect have simply missed each other.

So refer to your first call in your follow-up call. (Never skip the first call or make untrue statements about whether you've called in the past.) Give a reason to set the appointment that day—because you're going to be in Philadelphia. (Never say, "I'm going to be in the neighborhood." That makes it sound like you're driving around Philadelphia with time on your hands. I don't think that's the message you want to send!)

Be specific. Say, "I'm going to be in Philadelphia next Thursday. I'm meeting with the XYZ Company. I could see you at 2:00, is that okay?" That kind of call will get a better response. Anything specific you can add usually gets a better response: "I'm going to be in Los Angeles a week from Friday to see the XYZ Company. Could we get together right after that?"

That's the kind of call you want to make. It sounds professional, organized, and respectful.

Cold Calling Messages

Now let me show you how to use this method without any previous contact. Let's say that I'm calling a company that I want to do business with. For whatever reason, the contact is not taking my call. Perhaps he's not interested. If that's so, I want to know that.

I just simply call up and say, "Hi, this is Steve Schiffman." Whether I've reached voice mail or a secretary doesn't matter. The message should sound something like this:

> "This is Steve Schiffman. I just looked at my schedule. I realize I'm going to be in Philadelphia next week to see the XYZ Company. I'll be about twenty minutes from your place. I'd like to get together. Would next Thursday about 2:30 work out?"

Now the person has to react—you've put the ball in his court. He's got to deal with you, either by making an appointment or not making an appointment. Obviously, you're not going to go over unless the person agrees to see you. And I'm not suggesting that you go on an appointment simply for the sake of putting mileage on your car. I am saying, though, that you can often set up a good appointment through voice mail or by leaving a message with a secretary using the strategies I've outlined.

Suppose you've just set up your first appointment in Philadelphia. You can think to yourself, "Okay, now that I've set up this appointment in the Philadelphia area, why don't I begin to set up more meetings for Philadelphia?" Now you can call all the prospects you have in Philadelphia, all the people that you're talking with in Philadelphia, and all the people you've ever called or anybody in your office has ever called in Philadelphia. Use the methods I've given you to make those calls and set up more appointments.

Now your calls sound like this:

"I'm going to be in Philadelphia, let's get together."

Suddenly you have a good reason to call a prospect back. You have a reason to make follow-up calls. You can now set up a major sales effort in Philadelphia!

Telephone tag problems are easy to solve if you understand the big concept: The person has asked you to call back and, therefore, you're calling back. You don't necessarily have to speak to the individual directly—you can simply set the appointment.

Sometimes it's easier to understand this process by looking at the entire sequence of events. Consider this series of calls, for instance.

The first time I call, I don't get through, so I leave a message: "Hi, this is Steve Schiffman. I'm calling in reference to Jim Jones." Or, "I'm calling in reference to XYZ Company."

Either way, the person calls me back. If I miss the call because I'm busy going on appointments, I call the person back again. Now they call me back. So: I've called them, they've called me; I've called them, they've called me. On the third call I leave my message:

"Hi, Mr. Jones, this is Steve Schiffman. The reason I was calling you is to set an appointment. Would next Tuesday at 2:00 be okay?"

Again, I can do this either with voice mail or I can do it with a secretary. I can use the same message if I happen to get through to the person I want to talk to. The fact is, I've shortened my message. I don't need to leave a longer message because I've already called. My assumption is that the prospect is going to see me, so I ask: "Can we get together next Tuesday at 2:00?"

This is the single best way to defeat telephone tag. It's breathtaking in its simplicity. And it works!

More on Voice Mail

Ironically, in earlier versions of my program, one significant idea put forth was to avoid voice mail. You wanted to work with a secretary or administrative assistant or anything that was actually alive. People, me included, weren't used to working with voice mail. Very often, first generations of it were unreliable. And just the idea of talking to a machine seemed somehow very *1984*-ish. (I mean, of course, the book, not the year.)

But all that's changed. Experience has taught me that it is very often the gatekeepers who are unreliable. They'll certainly deliver your name and phone number. And sometimes they may even deliver your entire message.

But what they don't deliver is your passion, your sense of humor, your belief in your product. So now when a secretary asks me if I want to be switched to voice mail, my answer always is a resounding "yes, please." In fact, there are some salespeople I know who think voice mail is the best way of cold calling.

They've found that they don't actually get through to prospects very often. And they waste a lot of time talking to whoever answers the phone before they're put through to voice mail anyway. So they place a lot of calls on weekends or later in the evening when they're likely to go directly to voice mail. They've found—and I can't argue with this—that a lead is likely to listen to their entire message (assuming it is relatively brief and not off target) without interruption.

Now the question becomes, what kind of message do you leave? Based on my experience, if you use the techniques from this chapter, you have a 65 percent of getting a return call. Remember, you can't get an appointment unless you eventually speak to the prospect. And using voice mail is a good way to do that.

Follow-Up Calls

FOLLOW-UP CALLS are what you make when someone asks you to call back in order to set an appointment.

For example, I call up John Jones and ask for an appointment, using one of the script formats in this book. But Mr. Jones says to me, "Steve, I'd love to talk to you but I'm really busy right now." So I use my turn-around by saying to him, "Other people have said the same thing . . ." or "Can't we just get together next Thursday. . . ." But he insists, saying, "Look, I'm very busy right now, and this is simply not the best time. You're going to have to call me back in the fall."

There are always going to be people who won't want to talk to you. Please remember: We're not looking to get every appointment, although we'd like to get every single appointment where we have a reasonable chance of doing so.

With follow-up calls, the objective is simply to build our competitive edge—to improve our ratio of success.

When the prospect says, "You're going to have to call me back," I assume that when I do call him back, I'm going to talk with him to set the appointment. That's an important point. I'm not calling him back next Thursday because I have nothing else to do. I'm calling him back because he asked me to call him back when I first called him to set up an appointment.

Remember That People Respond in Kind

The only way that you can accept this premise is if you remember that people respond in kind. After all, I said to him, "The reason I'm calling you is to set an appointment." Then he said to me, "Steve, I'm busy right now. You'll have to call me back." My assumption, unless I hear otherwise from him, is that I should call back to set the appointment. After all, that's what he is responding to. That's what I've asked for. So that's what I'm basing the follow-up call on. Look at it again:

> "Good morning, Mr. Jones, this is Steve Schiffman from the XYZ Widget Company here in Madison, Wisconsin. The reason I'm calling you today specifically is that, when we spoke last June, you suggested I give you a call today in September to set up an appointment. Would next Tuesday at 3:00 be okay?"

This is very different from what most salespeople do. Most salespeople do this:

> "Good morning, Mr. Jones, this is Steve Schiffman from the XYZ Widget Company here in Madison, Wisconsin. When I called you a while back, I explained that I worked with the 1234 Company. You were interested at the time but you said it wasn't a good time. So I'm calling you now and I just wanted to know if you might be interested in the possibility of hearing more about us."

I can't say it enough: People respond in kind! This opening is begging for a response like, "No, I'm not interested," or, "No, I'm too busy." But it's extremely easy to make that call! It takes practice to make a better call. This is why your scripts and your choice of words are so important. This is why we teach people to tape-record themselves making calls so that they can listen in on the calls and improve on their mistakes. I've recorded a number of people during role plays at our training programs. Once these people hear their own tapes, they understand why they haven't been getting appointments.

If you start in with, "The reason I'm calling you is that we had spoken a long time ago and you had expressed some interest then and I wanted to see if now is a better time," all you're doing is encouraging the person to say, "No, it's not a better time." Guess what? It will never be a better time!

Here's one more example of what your call should sound like:

> "Good morning, Mr. Jones, this is Steve Schiffman from XYZ Widget Company here at Anytown, USA. The reason I'm calling you today specifically is when we spoke in June, you suggested I give you a call today (you can mention the date if it's appropriate to do so) to set an appointment. Would next Tuesday be okay?"

Now the person has to respond to you. (Does that sound familiar? Good!) You know the person's going to respond to you. In fact, you're prepared for the response. The person could say:

> "Well, Steve, the fact is this is still not a good time to talk. I'm really busy right now."

As an expert cold caller, you now understand how you're going to work with this response. You're going to create a Ledge by saying something like this:

> "Gee, Mr. Jones, I'm just curious, what are you doing now? Who are you using for your widgets?"

The person will respond to you. They'll say something like: "We're using Acme widgets. And you know what? We're really happy with what we've got."

If you know your competition, you might decide to respond by saying, "Gee, are you using the Red Velvet model or the Blue Velvet model?" Then the person might say, "Neither. We're using the Green Velvet one."

You can then say, "Oh, that's great! You know something, we really should get together. We really complement Green Velvet very well. How's Friday at 3:00?"

Give it a shot, even though you know you're not going to get an appointment every time. But I guarantee you that at least 10 percent of those people you talk to during follow-up calls are going to see you. And that's 10 percent that you would not have gotten otherwise.

When to Call Back

As to when to call somebody back, I don't like to give someone three months, six months, or a year before I call them back. I think that's foolishness. And yet—how do you break down that time barrier? What reason do you use for calling earlier? There are probably a million reasons you can call people back. Here's my favorite:

"I was just thinking about you yesterday."

Not long ago, I was teaching salespeople at a major telecommunications company. The company was going through a major merger at that point. I told everyone in the room that they should pick up the phone on Monday morning and call every single person they were supposed to call back at any point in the next three months.

I asked them to say something along these lines:

"Good morning, Mr. Jones, this is Steve Schiffman from Data International Company here in Blank, Texas. The reason I'm calling you is that I was thinking about you yesterday. We were at a national sales meeting where I learned about a major merger that now puts us in a unique position, and I'd like to get together to tell you about some of the new things I've just learned."

The results? A lot more appointments!

The key to any call like that is the phrase, "I was just thinking about you yesterday." People respond to that, of course, and they're usually quite positive. I've had people say to me, "No kidding! I was thinking about you, too." Or, "It's a funny thing you called, we were thinking about doing X." Whatever the person says, the point is that you now have a reason to call, and you've eliminated that three-month waiting time.

I'm working with a company right now that I'd once had great difficulty getting business from. When I called I was told, "Why don't you call me back after the summer?" Of course, I didn't wait until after the summer. I called back thirty days later, and the call went like this.

> *Steve:* You know something, I was driving past a building, and I looked up and saw a billboard that advertised one of your products, and I thought of you, and I thought I'd give you a call.

That's all I said. My contact came right back with:

> *Prospect:* You know something, I was actually thinking about you the other day.
> *Steve:* No kidding?
> *Prospect:* Yes.
> *Steve:* You know what, we should get together.
> *Prospect:* Sure, come on in.

And that did it. Eventually, I got that business.

Do you understand the concept behind this approach? Your opening line is, "I was just thinking about you," which is absolutely true. Even if you weren't thinking about the person before you made the call, calling will certainly make you think about that person!

Once you start to think about it, you'll realize you can use this approach for almost any call you want to make. You can call anybody up and say:

"You know, I was looking through my list and I was thinking about you."

"You know, I just happened to be in Jackson, Mississippi, yesterday. I was thinking about you."

"You know, I was driving on Interstate 88 the other day and I was thinking about you. I'm going to be in Indiana; I thought we could get together."

This brings us to another approach you can use for follow-up calls. Consider this true story. I was looking at my schedule one day and I saw that I was going to be in New Albany, Indiana. New Albany, Indiana, is a very small town outside of Louisville, Kentucky. The point is that I was going to go to New Albany, Indiana, because I was visiting a client there. I called somebody who's in Atlanta, Georgia, and I said, "You know something, I was looking at my schedule the other day, and I realized I'm going to be in New Albany, Indiana, next Thursday and I thought maybe we should get together on Friday." And my contact said, "Okay, that makes sense."

Not much later, I used the same technique again! I called somebody in Texas. He said to me, "Look, I'm really busy this week. I can't see you." So I said, "Gee, I'm just looking at my schedule. On the 13th (which was about two weeks from that day), I'm going to be in Charlotte, North Carolina." Do you realize that Dallas and Charlotte are nowhere near each other? But that's what I said. "I'm going to be in Charlotte, North Carolina. I have to give a speech there. Why don't we get together the day before?" He said, "Okay." And all of a sudden there's a reason to meet. Somehow it makes sense. You're closer than you were before. If your budget accommodates this strategy, give it a try.

Part Three

Basic Selling
Skills

CHAPTER 12

A Tale of Two Conversations

I WALKED INTO A RADIO SHACK the other morning to buy a calculator. The lady there said to me as I stood at the counter with my purchase, "You know, we've got this great sale on batteries today. They're only a dollar ninety-nine for a four-pack."

When she said this, she was fully engaged in the conversation. She made eye contact with me, she smiled at me as she rang up my purchase, and then she said her piece.

Here's my question: If she says that to 100 people, do you think 10 of them might decide to throw a package of batteries onto the purchase total? If she did that every day, what do you think that the outcome would be for her store? If every Radio Shack store did that for an entire year, what do you think the results of the effort would be, and how do you think the effort would play out across the chain?

By contrast, later that same day, I went into a hardware store and asked the clerk, "Hey, how much is this?" I held up a snazzy carpenter's level. The guy checks his book, looks up for a split second, and says, "Thirty-nine ninety-eight." And then went back to his business.

That's all he said: "Thirty-nine ninety-eight."

Which of these two conversations . . . which of these two guiding philosophies . . . is driving your organization's selling and upselling efforts?

In this part of the book, you will learn how to have more money-generating conversations, in more situations, than you're having now (along the lines of the lady at Radio Shack). You will also learn how to avoid dead-end, low-revenue conversations (like the one the guy at the hardware store routinely finds himself in the middle of). If that seems like a worthwhile goal, read on.

13 The Yellow Pages

WHEN I AM TRAINING SALESPEOPLE during our company's seminars, I tell the story of a young salesperson who came to meet with me to try to sell me advertising space in the yellow pages. I asked him to wait in the lobby while I completed a few tasks in my office. But before he sat down in the lobby, I asked him, "Before we begin, what's the first question you plan to ask me when we get together?"

By making this query, I was, of course, beginning the meeting.

But he nodded enthusiastically and said, "Well, before we get started, I guess it does make sense for me to think a little bit about the first question. Usually, what I ask is, are you happy with your advertising?" "And," I asked him, "what do people usually say when you ask them that?"

"Well," he said, "usually they tell me that they're happy with their advertising."

"And what happens then?"

"Well, at that point, I usually ask if they have any questions, and if they don't, I move on to my next meeting. After all, I've qualified them."

I will not bother sharing with you the rest of our discussion, except to say that I did not end up buying yellow pages advertising from that salesperson. But notice how much information about his sales process I was able to elicit "before we began" the meeting!

I think that is the way a lot of good sales strategy works. You find a way to get some kind of meaningful information out on the table "before you begin"—and that is the way I want to start this part of the book. There is a lot to look at, but before we even begin, I want to share with you some important information . . . information that might just help you to take an approach to selling that is a little bit more constructive than the approach that yellow pages representative took during his meeting with me.

So—before we begin—here are twelve simple, career-changing pieces of advice I have been sharing for years with salespeople.

The list, which is the culmination of more than a quarter of a century of experience, may be brief, but I've noticed that those who follow all twelve rules always seem to outearn those who don't.

1. Always respond to customer queries within forty-eight hours.
2. Schedule sales appointments for early (8:00 A.M.) or late (4:00 P.M.).
3. Follow through immediately on thank-you letters, letters of agreement, and internal paperwork.
4. Set two new appointments every day.
5. Strategize with your sales manager on a regular basis.
6. Don't kid yourself.
7. Create a sense of urgency in all your communications.
8. Be honest.
9. Know ten client success stories.
10. Decide on your opening question for the meeting.
11. Decide on the Next Step you want and ask for it directly.
12. Always try to get the other person to do something.

Here's my challenge to you: Put these principles of effective selling into practice each and every selling day.

14 Selling Is a Conversation

WHETHER WE REALIZE IT OR NOT, selling is based on relationships. And the only real relationships we can count on are those that arise out of intelligent conversations between two people. Conversations are the foundation of selling.

I wish I could give you some spell that you could cast over your prospects that would instantly allow them to see the benefits of buying your product (or buying more of it), but no such spell exists. In the end, we will sell, or fail to sell, based on the quality of our conversations with our prospects and customers. If we display genuine curiosity, and ask appropriate do-based questions, we will sell more of our products and services to our customers. If we don't, we won't.

You may well ask, What are do-based questions?

Do-based questions are questions that focus, not on what we think the other person needs, or what we think his or her problem is, or what we think the potential pain is, but on what the other person is actually doing. If we focus only on what we consider the need, the pain, or the problem, then we won't get the whole picture of what's happening in the other person's world. We may get part of that picture, and we may close an initial sale, but to build a relationship for the future, we have to be willing to ask questions about what the other person does. For instance:

> "Hey, we've talked about your current salespeople—but how are you handling your training for your new hires right now?"
>
> "How long have you been trying to sell your motorcycle? What have you been doing to sell it so far?"
>
> "How did you handle this kind of staffing problem the last time around?"

All of these are do-based questions. And all of them are substantial improvements over silly questions like, "What would you change about your current so-and-so?" or "What don't you like about your present situation?"

Effective selling is an extended conversation that allows you to find out what the other person is doing and plans to do, review key objectives, and make those objectives your own.

If you never learn, or even bother to ask about, what this person is doing, or what this person's objectives are on the job or in other realms of his life, then you will not be in much of a position to initiate or expand the relationship.

15 Selling by Not Selling

WHEN IT COMES TO MOVING TOWARD THAT ELUSIVE GOAL—perfection in selling—we sometimes find that less is more.

Each and every interaction with a customer we hope to sell to or sell more to—especially those interactions that are not directly sales oriented—is, in fact, a selling opportunity. How's that for a paradox? These nonselling discussions are chances to deepen the relationship, expand our knowledge base about what is going on in an organization and in the other person's life, and pass along relevant suggestions that parallel our own experience and ability to add value.

The bottom line: You sell when you don't sell.

Let's say, for the sake of argument, that I am attempting to review the yearly training plan with a major account of my company. This contact is someone who has done a lot of business with our firm, and someone who has in the past had no problem sitting down with me to review what his training plans are for the coming year. Let's say we have been working together for three or four years. Now, all of sudden, the person vanishes off of the radar screen. I want to upsell to this person—that is, sell even more training to him—but my e-mails have gone unreturned, my voice mail messages have vanished into the ether, and my attempts to reach out to other people in the organization have gone nowhere.

What can I do?

The best answer, in my view, is to give the person a reason to take my call that does not have to do with selling. In other words, I might send the person a book or article (that is, physically send an actual book, not e-mail an excerpt or chapter) with a personalized note. At that point, I would allow three or four days for the mail to deliver the book. I can then call and leave a message asking what the person thought of the book or article.

I am giving the person an easy way to respond and giving him a conflict-free context for future conversation. If there's something there, I'll probably hear back from the person—or be able to reach him more easily the next time around.

I'll do anything to avoid the call that sounds like this: "Hi John, haven't heard from you in a while—just wondering whether you had the chance to look at my proposal."

Far better to call a current customer to add value to his or her day—and let the "selling" emerge of its own momentum during the conversation through "do-based" questioning!

Here's what I say at the end of the conversation about the book or article I sent along: "Just out of curiosity, John—can we get together for lunch next Tuesday at 2:00? I have an idea I want to bounce off you."

Some years ago, Robert Morse starred on Broadway in a one-man show entitled *Tru*. In that show, he offered a dead-on performance of the author Truman Capote. Capote was, as you may know, a brilliant, ultimately self-destructive literary genius. One of the more remarkable sections of the play came when Morse, as Capote, offered his advice on how to get anyone—repeat, anyone—to fall in love with you.

The advice, according to Capote, was actually very simple. Simply pay attention to the other person as though he or she were the only person on earth. Do that consistently, day in and day out, and regardless of the other obstacles in the relationship, you will find yourself united with this person.

It's a fascinating piece of advice, advice that is relevant to the business world as well as the world of personal relationships. Ultimately, the guiding principle for good sales conversations, or upselling, and for all aspects of person-to-person selling, is simply to pay a heck of a lot of attention to the other person. Not "sales" attention. Real attention.

Be absolutely certain that, when you are in a meeting with your contact, interacting with him or her on the phone, or sending an e-mail, you are sending the message that this person really is more important than anything or anyone else on earth. Forget about selling. Just focus on what the other person is doing with incredible focus and attention.

If you can follow through on that type of commitment, genuine interest, and unapologetic attention, you will attract interest, you will build a relationship, and you will be able to sell more.

"It Makes Sense!"

IN ORDER TO UNDERSTAND how people can buy more from us, we have to understand how they decide to buy from us in the first place.

To get an idea of how that process works, I want to ask you to think about the last purchase that you made that involved more than $100. (The same principles are at work in just about any purchase, but they are a little easier to see and remember if we focus in on purchases that require more than $100.)

Have you got that recent purchase in mind? Great. Now, let me ask you something. Why did you decide to make the purchase that you did?

Whatever your answer is, I am willing to bet that the underlying reason for your decision to make the purchase that you did was actually very simple: it made sense for you to do so.

There are any number of variations on this "makes sense" reasoning. It made sense for you to purchase a car for your family because you needed to be able to get the kids back and forth from home to camp and from camp to band practice, and so on. It made sense for you to buy the particular car that you did because the car you looked at was rated highly for safety, was available at a good price, had good recommendations from your relatives, and so forth. Whatever the actual reasons were, I think if you look closely at them you will find that they really do emerge as footnotes or elaborations on the statement "It made sense for me." If you buy a piece of exercise equipment, you do so because it makes sense for you based on your goals in terms of personal fitness. If you buy an insurance policy, you do so because it makes sense for you in terms of the protection you want to give to your family. That is how purchasing works. We only do what makes sense to us. And conversely, if it does not make sense to us, we are not going to do it. There is no way anyone will ever purchase anything based on the conviction that the purchase really does not make any sense.

So, let's think of the final step in the sales process as this decision that something makes sense. That is from the buyer's point of view. From the seller's point of view, we think of this as a "close"— although, in fact, there is very little that is actually closing and, given the focus of this book, it might be better to think of it as an "open."

We are not really closing up the relationship as much as we are opening it to the whole universe of possible future decisions to buy. The term closing is so prevalent in the sales profession that it probably makes sense for us to use it here, if only for clarity's sake.

And by the way, our formal "closing technique" is rooted in this "makes sense" principle. Here's what we train people to say when they want to close a deal, whether it's the first piece of business they get from a contact or the hundredth piece of business:

"Makes sense to me—what do you think?"

That's our whole closing strategy!

Now, from the salesperson's point of view, it is nice when someone decides on their own that it make sense to purchase something from us. But, as we know, it just does not happen often enough for us to be able to count on that revenue. So we have to go out and make something happen. We have to get in front of people and help move the process forward to the degree that we are capable of doing so. Otherwise we are basically taking orders.

There is nothing wrong with taking orders, but in terms of one's responsibilities as a professional salesperson, simply waiting for the phone to ring and doing nothing but taking orders really does not fit the bill.

So how do we get the person to decide that it makes sense to buy what we offer?

This is a simple question, and it brings us to the step immediately before the closing step, which is what I call the presentation or proposal step. Actually, even though this phase involves, from our point of view, a presentation or proposal, from the buyer's point of view, it is nothing more or less than the reason that it really does make sense to buy from us. So, to go back to the example of the car that we purchased to get our kids from point A to point B, the reasons for my decision to purchase a car could be that I want it to cost less than $25,000, that I want it to have a high safety rating, and that I want to get good gas mileage. Those might be my three "hot button" reasons for purchasing an automobile. The problem for the seller is, of course, that he will have no idea what my reason for purchasing a car might be. It is entirely possible that I have not even articulated the reasons effectively myself. But I will respond positively or negatively to certain reasons that are proposed to me.

Consider this question: How many possible reasons to buy a car could there be? Actually, there are quite a few, but most of them will not actually match up with my own personal reasons for buying one. In other words, if the salesperson at the automobile showroom insists on talking to me about the fact that the car can go 120 miles an hour, that is not going to be a motivator for me. If he tells me that the car is going to enhance my sex appeal as I am cruising up and down the boulevard, that is not going to be a big motivator for me, either, as the main reason I am trying to purchase the automobile is to get my kids from point A to point B. You will notice that there are many, many potential reasons that I could buy a car, but only a very narrow set of actual reasons that I would purchase a car.

The question that arises is, How does somebody who is trying to sell a car to me determine which are the right reasons and which are the ones not to bother with?

This very important issue brings us to the steps that precede the presentation or reason phase of the sale. It is with this issue that we come face-to-face with the most important part of the selling process—namely, the information-gathering step. Take a look at this graphic:

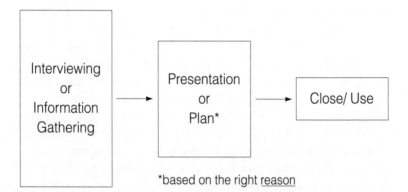

*based on the right <u>reason</u>

You will notice that the information-gathering piece is significantly larger than the presentation or closing in our ideal sales model. This is because I strongly recommend that approximately 75 percent of the salesperson's time and effort be invested in information gathering and presentation preparation. In other words, three-quarters of the work has to come before we make any formal recommendation. And it is in this information-gathering phase that we determine which motivators precisely are likely to be the ones that will resonate with our perspective customer. So during this phase, we would expect the salesperson in the showroom to find out a little bit more about me and my family, what made me decide to walk into the showroom that day, how many kids I am responsible for shuttling around, and so forth. If he or she manages this portion of the sales process intelligently—and that might well mean not trying to close the sale in the first visit, but reaching out to me by phone after I have spent an initial visit in the showroom—the interesting thing is that the salesperson will not only develop the appropriate information about my auto buying requirements, but he will also establish a certain amount of rapport with me as a person. He will get to know how I make decisions, what my preconceptions about automobiles are, what my speaking style is, and so forth.

Now, from a salesperson's point of view, we might like to think that these three steps are all that is involved in selling effectively. But the hard facts of human nature suggest otherwise. If I walk into the showroom and the car salesman instantly pounces on me and starts peppering me with questions about my family, my past history of purchasing automobiles, my reasons for walking into the showroom, and so forth, he is not going to close many sales. In fact, there is a precursor to all three of the steps that we have outlined here, and it is a very important one that we call the opening or greeting phase.

This is also known sometimes as the qualifying phase. It is an initial portion of the relationship where the salesperson establishes some kind of commonality or rapport with the person he or she has identified as a prospect. It can also be the part of the relationship where the salesperson makes a quick assessment as to whether or not this is a realistic prospect or a prospect at all. Both of these things basically happen at the same time, and if you put that phase of the relationship on the far left-hand corner of the model, you can see the entire process, at least for the initial purchase:

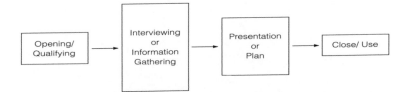

In the initial phase, on the far left of the description, you will find the opening of the relationship. And as I say, commonality is a big part of what happens. You studied such-and-such in school—what a coincidence, so did I! You made a certain career choice recently—and that's genuinely interesting to me, because I made a very similar choice a few years back.

So, in the initial discussion with my prospect, I am going to find elements that he or she has in common with me.

After a while, you learn to build up commonality with just about anyone. Honestly, I don't care who you put in front of me, I can find something I have in common with that person. If you bring me a tribesman from Nigeria and sit him down across from my desk in midtown Manhattan, I can find something that I have in common with that individual. We might, for instance, have a shared interest in making sure that the environment is protected, and that local agriculture be allowed to flourish in harmony with it. The point is that a good salesperson finds reasons to discuss things that he or she has in common with other people. And perhaps just as important, a good salesperson finds a way to discuss these things in a communication style that matches that of the prospect.

So if the other person speaks quickly, I am going to try to match that person's tone and rate of speed. If the other person is slower and more sober and reflective, I am going to try to find a way to match that as well.

Verification

THERE IS ONE ADDITIONAL SUBSTEP that we need to add to this process for purchasing something, and it is what is known as the *verification* substep.

Verifying is an important element of the sales process, because our information tends to improve in quality as the length of the relationship with a person increases. What this means is that the information I share with the automobile sales representative in the first five minutes of my conversation with him is not necessarily going to be as meaningful, or as accurate, as the information I share with him a week and a half later during our third conversation—or even half an hour later, during the same conversation.

As we get to know people better, and as we open up to them more fully, we fill in the blanks, offer additional facts, and even correct misperceptions that we may have, for various reasons, left in our initial conversations with the person. The bottom line is that we trust people with whom we have had an extended series of conversations more than we trust people whom we have just met. As a result, not every single solitary piece of information that a salesperson writes down in his or her notebook is going to be technically accurate by the time the interview phase is complete.

In fact, the interview can look complete when, in fact, it is not complete. And that is where the verification substep comes in.

I strongly recommend some kind of "replaying" of basic information before you make any attempt to close the sale or make formal recommendations. This verification can take any number of forms, but it is important.

Consider the example of the automobile dealership. If the product is right, and the quality is high, and if the reasons for suggesting the purchase really do match up with what I am actually looking to make happen in my life in terms of transport for my family, then that auto dealership has the right to hope and expect that I will come back to them for the next car. And, in fact, this is exactly how the best dealerships and the best automakers function. They build up high degrees of trust and communication with their prospects, they deliver on the promises that they make to their sale prospects, and they assure that their customers' satisfaction with their products is high both in terms of initial product quality and also in service and repair. So that after four or five years or however long it takes me to decide I need a new car, it would be much easier for me to return to that same dealership and that same manufacturer, and move up the ladder to the next model of car that seems appropriate for me.

So, you can see that the sales process itself does not operate in a vacuum, but is, in fact, geared toward repeat purchases if you do it correctly.

In any selling conversation, whether it is for a multimillion-dollar piece of construction equipment or a $2.99 monthly commitment to a magazine, there is a powerful sentence you can use to get a clear sense of precisely where your customer stands in relation to your offer: "Here's what I'm getting so far . . ."

This statement is one that has to follow some kind of intelligent questioning that features genuine curiosity of what is happening in the other person's world. Once you have done that, try to determine precisely where you stand by replaying key information and how you interpret it, by saying, "Here's what I'm getting so far . . ." You can then say, "Based on what you're telling me, this is what I'm thinking of recommending," and then ask, "Are we thinking along the same lines?"

Remember Why People Buy!

I WANT TO EMPHASIZE that the decision to buy from us in the first place does not happen out of thin air. It happens because the person decides to buy into our plan and use what we have to offer. Why would somebody do that? The answer is simple. They only choose to use what we sell if it makes sense to them to do so. Whether they call us up and ask us to come in and solve a problem, or we call them up and eventually make a presentation that they sign off on, the only reason the person ultimately decides to buy from us is that it really makes sense for them to do so—from their point of view. So what causes that decision to happen?

The answer in many cases is the proposal or plan or reason that we have given them for deciding to buy. If that reason is strong enough and compelling enough, and if we have elucidated it correctly, we are going to get the sale. If the reason that we give helps the person to do what he or she is already doing, we are going to get the sale.

But how do we get that reason or plan? Well, that goes to the step before the presentation. That is, the information-gathering stage. Notice that it is impossible to deliver a good presentation, a presentation that wins a sale, if we do not have the information we need. In my training sessions, I emphasize the important point that one must, realistically, expect to spend 75 percent of the sales process in the information-gathering phase—notice how big that phase is in the model I have given you.

Nevertheless, it is a fact of life that we cannot simply barge into the process office and begin asking questions. We must qualify or open the sale. That means developing a little bit of rapport, usually by means of some kind of small talk.

Notice that all four of these processes are interrelated, and that each one must unfold out of the previous step. This is the microcosm of the sale. This is a map of what happens when we do not know someone and we turn them into a customer.

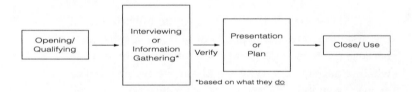

Offer, Timetable, Price

AT ANY GIVEN MOMENT during the selling initiative you may be presenting, there are three items that may be under discussion. They are:

1. *The offer itself.* This means the specifics of the equipment, service, or program that you want the customer to consider as an additional purchase.
2. *The timetable.* This is the point in time at which you would deliver or implement your additional sale.
3. *The terms.* This is how your customer would end up paying for the additional purchase.

There is an interesting rule of thumb that you may want to consider once you have identified these three elements of your sale. It is really amazingly simple, and it is one of those ideas that lead people to wonder why they did not think of it, once they encounter it for the first time. Basically, it is this: If you are having trouble dealing with one of these three elements, simply change gears and try to focus on one of the other two.

In other words, do not let the fact that the person has grave doubts about your payment schedule keep you from discussing the specifics of the offer or the possible timetable. Get as much buy-in as you can on those other two items, and emphasize the points that are most in line with what this person is already doing. Rather than hammering on whether or not you can get a special deal on the payment terms, step back and find a way to focus on your common interests: the benefits that the person will receive from your offer, and the timetable that makes the most sense for him or her to receive those benefits.

Far too many salespeople lose the opportunity to add revenue to their sale by focusing on the "letter of the law" with regard to one of these three key points. They will say things like "I can't change the specifications" or "I can't change the timing" or "I can't change the pricing." Whether or not that is true—and in most cases it turns out not to be true—you really do not gain any rapport or additional information by harping on such points. Focus on what is working in one of the other two areas, and move on to the minor detail of working out the issues in that third category.

Essential Selling Principles

To be a successful seller:

1. You must convey excitement about what you do.
2. You must know when to be quiet.
3. You must Keep It Simple, Stupid (KISS).
4. You must have an open mind at each step of the sales process. (No preconceptions!)
5. You must have a defensive sales strategy and anticipate what could go wrong. (Think one step ahead.)
6. You must temper zeal with pragmatism.
7. You must never minimize the role of the administrative staff at the target company, particularly executive assistants.
8. You must avoid keeping the wrong prospect in play for too long. In other words, you must know your own time cycle, and you must learn when to recognize that you are spending too much time, energy, and attention on an opportunity that is not moving forward during that average selling cycle. There really is an average period of time that it takes a current customer to move from the "initial discussions" phase to a decision to do more work with you. Your job is to find out what that average period of time

is—and honor it. If you consistently invest significantly longer periods of time than that in your selling, there's a problem, and you need to take a close look at your time choices.

9. You must learn to develop a realistic sense of what the target company wants to do with you. (Don't overvalue!)

10. You must maintain control of the meeting and the sales process as a whole.

11. You must monitor how much time you spend developing outlines and proposals.

12. You must learn to charge what you're worth. (Don't undervalue yourself; don't sell yourself short when determining the value you bring to the organization.)

13. You must remember that each relationship you build will stay with you over the long term.

14. You must think positively—and think big!

15. You must be an effective interviewer.

That last item is particularly near and dear to my heart. Bear in mind that a good interviewer is:

- Genuinely curious
- Interested in what the other person does
- Interested in how the company makes a profit
- Interested in how the company holds off competitive challenges
- Not product focused, and not eager to move into what he or she wants to say
- Willing to ask "how" and "why" questions
- Curious about what makes this person unique
- Willing to ask questions to which he or she does not always have the answer

Here's another important principle to remember about interviewing: *Don't ask, don't sell.* What do I mean by that? If you do not ask any questions, you cannot expect to gather any meaningful information. And if you do not gather any meaningful information, you cannot expect to expand the relationship.

Key Communication Principles

THERE ARE SOME FUNDAMENTAL communication principles that can support your effort to sell more to your customer. I've touched on some of these concepts briefly in the Cold Calling section of this book, but now it's time to go into more depth.

Principle #1: People Respond in Kind; We Create the Flow

As we have seen, selling is a conversation, and effective sellers must learn to master that conversation. An essential first element of mastering the art of the conversation, especially the upselling conversation, lies in understanding this first principle.

When Katie Couric secures an interview with an extremely important figure—the president of the United States, say—do you think she simply sits down and improvises her way through the conversation without any preparation at all? Does she allow herself the luxury of a long game of tennis the day before the interview, contenting herself with the knowledge that the president will certainly think of something interesting to say?

My guess is that Katie has a set of very interesting questions all ready, a list that she has reviewed many times, before she steps into her interview with the president. In fact, I would even go further and propose that Katie very likely allows herself a couple of different roadways for each question, depending on the response that she gets from the president! (More on this idea in a moment.)

My point here is that there is no point in winging it in your discussions with customers. They are every bit as important to you as the discussion with the president of the United States is to Katie Couric—if not more so. So, instead of wondering what is going to happen during the conversation, it makes much more sense to understand the vital role your choice of a question will play in setting the dynamic and the flow of the conversation. The reason your question is so important is that people will respond to the topics that you raise, just as the president will, of necessity, say something about the topic Katie Couric raises during her interview with him. Mind you, the president may not answer with precisely the same level of specificity that Katie might like, but the topic she raises will, without fail, influence the direction in which the conversation goes. If you want the conversation to proceed along a path that is beneficial to you, you will first need to identify what that path is, and then follow through by posing a series of questions that will point the conversation in that direction.

For example, when I am meeting with a representative of a company whom I wish to do more business with, my initial question is absolutely clear to me. Depending on the client, I might ask what the person has decided about expanding into a certain market; I might ask how the competition is doing in a new product release; or I might ask, "Where do you see us being able to add value in your South American operations?"

After the handshake and the pleasantry phase, I always have some specific question that I will use to determine the direction of the conversation. And I know I will be able to point the conversation in that direction because people will respond in kind to what I ask. After all, if I ask you, "How are you feeling today?" you are not going to respond by talking about peach ice cream.

Principle #2: Some Responses Can Be Anticipated

I said a little earlier that, when Katie Couric prepares for her interview with the president of the United States, she thinks about where her questions will go. This is another way of saying that she knows ahead of time that any president or presidential candidate—or, indeed, any politician worth his or her salt—will probably not give a direct answer to the question that she asks. For instance, if she were to ask a sitting president the question that his or her challenger during an election year would most want answered, the likely outcome would not be a direct response to the points in the question. Instead, she would have to expect a certain amount of rhetorical dancing, bobbing, and weaving. But here is the point: If she is really doing her job, she will know that ahead of time and prepare a follow-up question or response of her own in order to put the president's response into some kind of context for the interview.

What Katie Couric and any other good interviewer knows is that a discussion with a public figure, a colleague, or a sales prospect should not simply be a series of memorized questions. You cannot walk in the door and assume that the same questions that you have identified for your interview are going to be the best structure for that interview. You cannot simply rattle off all of those questions in sequence. Instead, you have to be ready for responses. And even one step further than that, you have to know what you will say back when you hear those responses.

Now, as a salesperson, your job is considerably easier than that of a journalist. For one thing, you are not out to "get" your interview partner, and you are certainly not out to prove him or her inconsistent in the same way that a good reporter may try to highlight any inconsistencies in a discussion with a politician. However, the central dynamic of knowing that a response will be coming, and being able to prepare for it, is exactly the same. In fact, this dynamic is a good deal more pronounced in the sales world, because the same kinds of responses come up again and again for people who have been selling for more than a few weeks. We have heard it all. We know the budget is too tight, we know that people have no time, we know that there are certain technical constraints that may prevent certain constituencies from deciding that it is a great idea to work with us . . . we know the drill. I am even willing to bet that if you took the time right now, you could identify ten objections—or, to use a more accurate term, initial negative responses—that you hear over and over again from your own prospects and customers. In particular, I will bet you could identify the types of questions, issues, and challenges that come up with your customers during your discussions about the best ways to extend your relationship with them.

If your sale is at all like mine, you encounter the same issues from customer A, in a slightly different form, or even in an identical form, as you do from customers B, C, D, and E. Here is the point: We can anticipate these responses. We can predict. We can predict and prepare for the responses we hear every day. And we can know exactly the right story or anecdote from our own experience or that of someone else on our sales team that will help us to address whatever issue has arisen.

For instance, suppose I am talking to someone who is eager to get more training from my company after having had a good initial program. It is common for us to hear that "the financing does not work." My contact will say, "Steve, we want to do the program, but our training budget is exhausted for the next two months, and we really can't make any commitment until June."

Now the first time I heard this, I could perhaps be excused for not having any intelligent response or story to share about it. But having been in this business for twenty-five years, I take some pride in being able to say, whenever I hear this response, that we have done a lot of work with customers who faced exactly this situation. And what we have done in the past, in order to address the problem, is simply schedule the date, allocate our own training time, get the company's people trained in the new processes they need, and bill against the next quarter. That is much better from my point of view, because I would rather get the business than not. And it is much better from the customer's point of view than leaving a team that has just been trained in one program without any further training for two or three months until the next program materializes.

That is an example from my industry, and I am sure you can come up with examples from your own without too much difficulty. The one point you do have to bear in mind, however, is that despite how similar some of the objections and responses and issues we hear may sound, they really are coming from a unique person and a unique organization. So you will want to be very careful not to assume that the dimensions of the problem are precisely the same as those of the last person you heard this issue from. Instead, you will need to express your understanding of what the person has said, replay what you have heard, and then share an interesting anecdote from your own history. You're going to express your opinion that you might be able to take a similar approach here, and then ask the person whether or not you are both thinking along the same lines.

Principle #3: People Communicate Through Stories

You will notice, in the way I explained communication principle #2, that I emphasized the importance of my sharing a story from my own company's history in response to an issue that had come up from the customer. That is obviously a great way to go, but it is not as powerful as getting the other person to share one of his or her stories.

People love to tell stories, and they often base their own decisions about whether to keep buying from us not only on the stories that we share with them, but also on the stories that they decide to share with us.

In fact, I think it is probably fair to say that one tangible piece of evidence of success in the information-gathering process is the ability to point to a story that the customer has shared with you. By asking questions like "How did you handle that?" or "What made you decide to work for the company?" or "What kind of place is this to work?" we are trying to get factual information, but we are also trying to get the customer to open up to us and share a story that is uniquely informative about his or her career or the organization's development.

You can make an argument that stories are what form corporate culture. In other words, if you were an employee at the company you are trying to sell more of your products and services to, you would know certain critical stories about the company's viewpoint and history. Some stories are all about the company's internal philosophy: how the founder drove through thirty-five snowy miles of rough terrain to deliver a shipment on time, for instance. Some stories will give you all the information you need about the internal politics that you face in dealing with a customer's internal communications challenges. For instance, you might hear a story about how difficult the legal team is to keep satisfied, and how important they are in the hierarchy since the company faced an unexpected series of product liability lawsuits. Whatever the story is, there is only thing you can be certain of: If you have not heard a story from your prospect about what his or her world looks like, you have not gotten all the important information yet. Consider it your goal to share your own relevant success stories with each and every contact in your own world . . . and also to ask the intelligent questions (and encourage the lengthy responses) that will lead you toward the stories that illuminate the world of the person to whom you are trying to sell.

Questions You Should Be Able to Answer

GATHERING INFORMATION IS A PROCESS that never really ends but that can, in my experience, at least be initiated properly.

Here are some of the questions I try to make sure salespeople can answer *before* they attempt to close the deal:

1. When are you going back?
2. *(If talking to a company)* What does the company do, and who are its customers?
3. Who are you talking to?
4. Why that person?
5. *(If talking to a company)* How long has your contact been there for?
6. *(If talking to a company)* What is this company doing now in an area where we can add value? And why aren't they using us already?
7. When was the first meeting or conversation?
8. Did you call them or did they call you?
9. How much is the deal worth?
10. In your view, what is the very next thing that has to happen for you to eventually close this sale?
11. When and how will you make that happen?
12. Who else are they looking at?

13. Why them?
14. What does your contact think is going to happen next?
15. When is that going to happen?
16. Do they want this deal to happen as much as you do?
17. What is your customer trying to do or accomplish?

And here are some additional "introspective" questions that I would encourage you to consider: The first seven are particularly important; their answers should be developed carefully, reviewed, shared with others, and rehearsed over and over again.

1. What do we sell?
2. What makes us unique?
3. What makes us better than the competition?
4. *Complete the sentence:* Even though our cost may be higher, people buy from us because . . .
5. Why do you work for this company?
6. How will you create the flow? (That is, what question will you ask to initiate the next conversation?)
7. What is your Next Step strategy?
8. If you could ask any question of your typical contacts, what would it be?
9. What information could you gather that would either increase the speed of your sales cycle or improve your closing ratio?
10. If you reached out to someone besides your typical contact, what else could you ask and what else could you learn?
11. How many initial discussions does it take you to develop a prospect? (For "prospect," think "Someone with whom I have had at least two good conversations and who is willing to set a time to talk to me again."
12. How many prospects does it take you to generate a sale?
13. How many upselling attempts does it take you to generate an upsell?

Part Four

Advanced Selling Skills

Four Phases of the Relationship

SOMETIMES WE THINK OF OUR SELLING and upselling efforts as though they exist in a vacuum, or as though they are being made with customers who are all identical. Actually, any attempt to bring a customer to a decision to purchase goods and services from us moves through a continuum. We can chart that continuum by looking closely at the level of the relationship that we have been able to develop with this person.

Let's look at first from the point of view of our customer. From the customer's point of view, we are likely to fall into one of the following four categories:

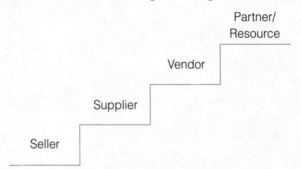

From the customer's point of view, there are four levels on the sales continuum. What we notice as salespeople is that the higher we move with the person on this four-step continuum, the better our information gets and the more valuable the relationship becomes.

At the lowest level, the customer simply considers us to be a seller. At this level, we have virtually no trust or information. The customer thinks of us typically as a one-time provider, and we may have that same mentality on our side. Most of the sales that "fall into your lap" come under the category of the low-level, seller relationship.

If we were move up a little bit on the scale, the customer would consider us to be a supplier. The supplier relationship features a fair amount of trust and information, but not a great deal. Basically, you're "in the Rolodex" when somebody considers you a supplier. When people look at what we offer this way, upselling is a possibility but not a sure thing. The customer may decide to contact us. We may decide to contact the customer. But in either event, there is a certain "prove it to me" mindset that must be overcome before the relationship gets particularly meaningful for either party.

The third level of connection is called the vendor level. When a customer thinks of us as a vendor, the relationship is marked by significant levels of trust and information. There is actually predictable repeat business here, and many people make the mistake of assuming that, if you upsell to a person regularly and you reach this level, you have hit the highest level possible. It's not at all true.

At the highest level is a partner/resource relationship. Here there are extremely high levels of trust and information and you function as a strategic partner/resource, and you and the customer are mutually dependent on each other for success. At the partner/resource level, you have easy access to all key players within the organization.

The Pyramid

You've seen how the customer perceives us, and the four steps in the relationship.

Now, we have a few more detailed ways of looking at this same process when we break it down from the point of view of the salesperson. Notice that the following pyramid encompasses all of the steps you just saw.

Here's what each of these levels tells you in regard to the type of relationship you have with the customer and how likely you are to be able to upsell with them:

Strategic Relationship
"Matching vision, values, mission, and ethics"—Positioning your company here sets you apart from the competition, makes upselling easy, and makes the relationship difficult to duplicate.

Strategic Supplier
"We help businesses do more business"—Upselling is comparatively easy here. By helping the prospect fulfill key objectives, we really begin to differentiate ourselves over time.

Future Direction

Your company emerges as a leader, with solid service and reliability. Upselling is a 50/50 proposition. The prospect looks to narrow the field of competitors here.

Product and Features

Feature, functionality, service quality, and application to fit are the big issues here. Upselling is not an issue, nor is it likely. If the prospect's decision is based on nothing higher than price and features, the competition may win this sale from us. If we win this sale, the competition may win the next sale with little difficulty.

Price: Commodity Market

Everybody is in the game here. The winner may not be your company. Upselling is not a realistic possibility, as future purchases are probably not on the prospect's radar screen.

■ ■ ■

Can you see that by the time you hit the top level, or even are moving toward it from the second or third level from the top, it is impossible for you to be at any of those levels *without knowing why the person decided to work with you?*

In other words, if you really understand the strategic purpose of the company and you understand the vision and you understand the major goals, you must, by definition, understand why the person is writing a check for you. You must understand where you add value. You must understand where, precisely, you help the company to achieve its goals and fulfill its mission.

The closer we get to the strategic vision and the further we move away from a commodity sale, the more likely we are to be able to understand the most important motivating factors behind the person's decision to buy from us. And the better we understand that, the easier it is to work with the person to expand the relationship.

Beware of Bad Assumptions

A NATIONAL SALES MANAGER I know was trying to expand his presence in one of his biggest accounts. He was not particularly successful, and he wanted my help in figuring out exactly why.

I asked him, "What are you selling them specifically?"

He said, "Well, among other things, paper—reams of business stock for use in copiers and printers."

I said, "Okay, how many people in the organization use paper?"

"Well," he said, "there are probably 15,000 people who use it, but there are only about 400 different work groups."

"Okay," I said. "There are 400 different work groups. How many of them are you talking to?"

"How many?" he asked.

"Yeah," I said. "How many of those 400 work groups are you in contact with?"

He went on to explain to me that he was "pretty certain" that they all bought through a single channel—namely, his channel. "That, at any rate," he said, "is my assumption."

I asked, "Why are you so certain of that?"

There was a long pause.

"I'll tell you one thing," I said. "If I had a company with 15,000 people using paper, I sure as heck wouldn't be channeling every single solitary purchase decision through one guy. My guess is that there are a lot more channels where paper is being sold than you're taking into account here. Have you ever asked them how they acquire their paper for those 15,000 people and those 400 work groups?"

"Well, no," he said.

We all can fall into this trap. We want to assume that the guy that we are talking to really is the guy who controls everything. We want to assume that the way that we have established a relationship really is the most efficient way to interact with our prospects. We want to assume that the work that we have done up front really is the only relevant work for us to do. But, in so many cases, those assumptions simply are not warranted.

The one thing that you can be sure about, especially in a major account, is that there is something going on behind the scenes that you can find out more about. So, in their situation, my instincts would be to go in to my contact, or to somebody else within the organization, and ask, "Just so I can be clear . . . how exactly do you acquire paper for your 400 work groups and your 15,000 people?"

That is the kind of question that a CEO or a senior executive will usually answer with confidence and authority and complete forthrightness in about a tenth of a second. By the same token, it is the kind of question that somebody who is placed a little bit lower on the chain of command would probably avoid, or he or she might spend forty-five minutes describing your terms back to you. So, sometimes, you have to reach out to other people in the organization.

When in doubt, ask, "Hey, how do you guys do X? Why do you do it that way?"

Raise the Hard Issues Yourself

WHEN I AM TRYING TO MOVE CLOSER TO THE TOP of that pyramid, trying to expand my relationship with a customer, I make a habit of identifying what I think the most difficult challenge in the relationship is going to be—and then bringing that problem up on my own, rather than waiting for the other person to do it.

You read right. What I do is try to put myself in the shoes of the other person, figure out what he or she would most likely object to in what I am proposing, and then talk about it first. You will recall, I think, what I said a little bit earlier in this book about the art of being more concerned about something than the prospect or customer is. This is exactly what you should do when you have an upselling initiative—or any selling initiative—that you feel could conceivably carry a problem for the person you are talking to. Your goals should be to say something along the following lines:

> I'll tell you the truth. I am actually kind of concerned about the price. I am not sure it is right. What do you think?"

"To be honest with you, I am a little concerned that the program might not be focused on the most important topics for your people. What do you think?"

"Here is where it fits together, but I have to be honest with you, I am a little bit concerned about how the schedule could work. I do not know if it is going to work for your organization."

"Here is the piece that we are not certain about. We are trying to find out whether or not this payment plan is right for your family. Help me out. What do you think are the pros and cons?"

"Let me tell you what is keeping me up at night. I think I understand what you are trying to accomplish here, and I think we can do it within your timeline. But I am not entirely sure that it is something you feel comfortable trying to share internally with your people, and I want to be sure that I get it right—help me out."

Whatever it is we are trying to sell or sell more of—a piece of equipment, a series of training programs, a newspaper subscription, whatever—we should identify a particular problem that could be waiting for us around the corner somewhere. We then try to raise that tough issue ourselves rather than wait for the customer to do so.

After all, what is the alternative? If we know we are going to get hammered on price but we do not have any meaningful feedback about what price the other person is looking for, why on earth would we wait for the person to give us an objection—or even worse, an objection that is not truly an objection that still stalls the sale completely? You know the response I am talking about:

"Gee—this is interesting, let me think about it."

I will do just about anything to avoid "Let me think about it." When it comes right down to it, I would much rather understand the true dimensions of the problem that is keeping the other person from deciding to buy more from me. I would rather get that information straight than hear some vague brushoff about needing more time to think about it or having to talk to somebody else.

By raising the most difficult issue ourselves, and not waiting for the prospect to either bring it up or, even worse, fail to bring it up, we get a much better sense of exactly where we stand when it comes to the initiative of getting this person to buy more from us.

Returning to the Plan

LET ME RECAP A CRITICALLY IMPORTANT POINT. Each and every person who has bought from us did so because it made sense for him or her to buy at that point in time—because our organization laid out a plan that connected to his or her interests. But here's the flip side of that (seemingly obvious) fact: People who *don't* buy from us again usually *decide* not to buy from us again because of our failure to follow through on the plan we laid out to them originally.

Whether we were aware of it or not, and sometimes we're not particularly aware, there is always some kind of plan or reason that guides these decisions of people who decide to buy from us. That initial plan or reason should be our compass in any selling or upselling initiative.

Let's take the example of someone who purchases sales training from my company. You might think, if you're not particularly familiar with the sales training industry, that the only plan or reason that would guide someone to purchase sales training is the desire to increase sales. The truth, however, is a little more complex.

I really can't assume that each and every person to whom I speak during the course of the year is, in fact, simply interested in increasing sales. Sometimes people work with us because the actual plan or reason is usually a good deal more personal than that, and increasing sales may be only part of the picture, or may not enter the equation at all.

Consider the case of someone who has recently inherited responsibility for a training department, a department that has been using our company to deliver its training for the past six years, with good results. Now, this new person has been told that he or she is responsible for selecting the training vendors—or even for eliminating the training budget entirely, if he or she chooses.

The actual circumstances are likely to vary, but in this situation, it's quite possible that the driving plan, or reason, for a decision to work with my company is not simply to increase sales, but to avoid changing a model that is already working, and sidestep or avoid entirely any problems with morale or performance that can be attributed to this new decision maker. In other words, he or she is very likely to want to avoid being held personally responsible for any change in the training regimen. That's a very different personal objective for a decision maker than simply wanting to increase sales.

If the person's job is dependent on his or her performance during the first year—which is not an uncommon circumstance—it's entirely possible that this person would completely overlook sales training in order to avoid the perception that he or she had advocated for something new and changed "what was already working."

I'm not saying that everyone would make a decision in this way, but that one should expect to run into certain decision makers who approach the issue in this way (and indeed we do). For such people, the objective is to avoid rocking the boat, to ensure continuity, and to avoid spending internal political capital they may need for other initiatives within the organization.

This is just one example of a situation where the perceived benefit of the product or service—increased sales—wouldn't necessarily match up with the actual plan or reason that the person might use to justify a purchase decision.

I'm not trying to be cynical about the underlying reasons to purchase sales training, but rather to give you a sense of the

importance of identifying the *individual's* plan or reason for deciding to do business with you. We cannot assume that that plan or
reason revolves around our own preconceptions; we must do the
work necessary to *identify what was originally most important to this
decision maker.*

And as long as that decision maker remains in the same place,
is facing the same situation, and is focusing on the same goals, that
plan or reason is what should drive our efforts to retain and upsell
to the customer.

The Six Mindsets of Change

HAVE YOU EVER NOTICED that some customers keep doing things in an old, inefficient way, even though they "know" there's a better way of approaching the task in question?

Why does that happen?

In order to facilitate constructive change for a person or an organization, you have to know where people are to begin with. Simply demanding that someone "do it the new way" will often make the situation worse.

Here's why. Change happens in certain predictable stages. Any time we human beings are challenged to develop a brand-new skill set, we are unlikely to adopt it instantly. To the contrary, we are likely to go through a developmental process with six distinct mindsets.

Mindset #1: Immobilization

We simply don't know what to do—and we are frozen in place. Typically, in this mindset, we say things like, "I don't believe in doing X. It just doesn't work for me." We don't even address the issue of whether change is in order. When dealing with people who are at this stage, it's a good idea to begin discussions with questions they will not perceive as threatening or attacking: "Why do you say that?" or "What makes you feel that way?" When we're in this mindset ourselves, we need support from other people.

Mindset #2: Denial (false competence)

We actively deny that any new approach is necessary. We try to improvise our way "around" the problem, or pretend that we have skills that we don't. Typically, in this mindset, we say things like, "It sounds interesting, but the way I'm doing it now works for me." When dealing with people who are at this stage, it's a good idea to begin discussions with an analysis of what their current activities will actually deliver if they keep doing what they're doing. When we're in this mindset, we need evidence that it's time to make a change.

Mindset #3: Incompetence

We encounter serious problems in absence of the skill. Typically, in this mindset, we say things like, "Yikes—I'm not going to be able to finish so-and-so in time." When dealing with people who are at this stage, it's a good idea to begin discussions with an evaluation of what the most important goal is, and look at all the options that will get us from point A to point B in the time frame we require. When we're in this mindset, we may need help identifying the alternatives available to us.

Mindset #4: Acceptance

Finally convinced that a new way is necessary, we admit that we have a lot to learn and start from scratch. At least we're attempting to develop new abilities! Typically, in this mindset, we ask for help: "Can you show me how you . . . ?" Obviously, the best strategy here for managers is to make sure the person gets the help he or she needs. When we're in this mindset, and not before, we're ready to try out new ways of doing things.

Mindset #5: Testing New Behaviors

We explore the limits of the skills we are now actively developing. Typically, in this mindset, we say things like, "I think I'm getting the hang of it." At this point, managers and trainers should celebrate any success—no matter how small—and minimize the long-term importance of any failure. When we're in this mindset, we're hungry for reinforcement!

Mindset #6: New Applications

We start to apply the newly acquired skills to new situations; we start to ask unique questions based on our own experience and capabilities. Typically, in this mindset, we ask questions like, "What if I do thus-and-so?" or "Could I use this same idea in a different way by changing such-and-such?" This is where managers and trainers need to support brainstorming sessions on either the small or large scales and also need to make sure great new ideas get recorded, reviewed, and implemented!

Tales of a Cable Installer

ABOUT A YEAR AND A HALF AGO, a cable installer came by to fix your cable box.

"By the way," he said, pulling stuff out of his toolbox, "do you have any kids?"

You said that you did.

"How many?"

You told him that you had two boys and a girl.

"What kind of stuff do they watch?"

You explain that they liked cartoons.

"Well that's interesting," he said. "Did you ever think of . . ."

At this point he reeled off half a dozen possible channels that were in a premium service package that he offered.

You had to admit it sounded very interesting.

"By the way, you like boxing?"

You said you didn't like boxing, but you were a golf fan. You had a long talk about golf, and while he was fixing the cable box, you each shared stories about triumphs and tragedies on the green.

"Did you know they have a special channel devoted just to golf now?"

"No, I didn't know that," you answered.

You share a pleasant conversation. At the end of twenty minutes, during which time he was supposedly only fixing your cable box, he had learned enough about your family—and you about his—for the two of you to consider each other something more than acquaintances, but something less than close friends.

Business acquaintances, if you will.

All of a sudden, he was your cable consultant.

"Well," he says, putting stuff back in his toolbox, "I'll tell you what I would do if I were you. I'd take a look at . . ."

And at this point, he shows you a brochure for three premium-channel packages.

Before he leaves, you've signed up for all three.

Upselling 101

When we talk about upselling, it is tempting to think of the process as requiring some—or even a great deal—of our time as salespeople each week. But what if you were able to make a very tiny investment of time up front, an investment that would pay off and deliver additional sales to you and your organization for weeks, months, and even years and years to come?

That is exactly what you can do by developing an upselling letter. Actually, I prefer to think of this letter as a modified thank-you letter, because it really serves as an excuse to upsell though its formal purpose is simply to thank the person for his or her business.

This letter will take you—or someone in your organization who is good at writing this kind of thing—no more than an hour to put together. But it will deliver astonishing results to you in terms of expanded sales from your customers and clients.

Here's what it looks like:

Dear [name]:

Thank you so much for your recent order. We appreciate your choice to do business with our company, and know that you have a choice when it comes to purchasing sales training.

I will be acting as your personal contact for the upcoming program. It is now scheduled to take place on January 5, (year). The topic of the program, as we discussed, is "Getting in the Door."

I know it will be of great value to your sales team.

If you need to contact me for any reason between now and the scheduled date of the program, I hope you will reach out to me using any of the numbers below:

My business number: (212) 555 1212

My personal cell phone: (212) 555 1213

My number at home, where I can be reached after 7:00 P.M.: (212) 555-6868

You can also reach me by means of my e-mail address, which is *joesmith@deisales.com.*

By the way, [name], you may be interested to learn that we are also offering a special this month on our e-learning programs. These are self-teaching diagnostic tools that your salespeople can use to sharpen their selling skills after the training. You can find an overview of the e-learning programs we offer as reinforcement to the main program at www.dei-sales.com. If you are interested in exploring this option for your sales team, please feel free to contact me at any of the numbers above.

Thanks again for choosing D.E.I. Franchise Systems, Inc.

Mike Ryan

D.E.I. Franchise Systems, Inc.

You see how it works? The point is to send out a thank-you letter that identifies you or someone in your organization as a critical touch point following the order. In the same communication, you will casually mention whatever special you or your organization is offering that month, and encourage the contact to reach out to the touch-point person for further information on ordering it. You can change the offer month by month, expand it, or even revise the entire letter. But my advice is that for people who purchase from you for the first time, you always send out some kind of letter that follows the general outline of what you see above. It is a time investment of such minimal scope that you may not even notice how long it takes. But if you make a practice of sending this out to each new customer, you will certainly notice the inquiries that come your way from people who have just decided to buy from you.

When You Work for a Large Organization

THE FOLLOWING IMPORTANT SELLING RULES will be of interest to people who work in companies that sometimes present bureaucratic obstacles to their customers. You really can solidify your relationship and improve your commission by adopting each of these principles. My general rule of thumb is that, if the prospect or customer calling you cannot reach you directly within one hour, you need to implement all of these ideas.

Principle #1: Make Sure You Are Reachable

No ifs, ands, or buts. If that means investing in your own cell phone or BlackBerry unit, and paying for that out of your own pocket, then do so. Your customers must be able to reach you no matter what. If they have difficulty doing so, you will lose out to the competition.

Principle #2: Share the Easter Eggs

You know what Easter eggs are. They are the secret parts of DVDs that you find out about only after somebody who really knows all the ins and outs of the fan club newsletter shares them with you. So, let's say you are looking at the DVD for *Citizen Kane*. You might have the DVD around for six months or a year before you realize there is a special feature that is not on the main menu—something that you have to access by positioning the cursor on a graphic that did not look like it was part of the formal user interface. Well, if you know somebody who is a big *Citizen Kane* fan, he can point you toward all the Easter eggs on the DVD, and show you how to get to the cool stuff quickly without waiting six months or stumbling across it on your own. The same principle applies to your own customers. You should make a point of listing things that are of added value that you can deliver for your customers—all the things that nobody else within the organization is likely to tell them. It might be a Web site that has the answers to critical questions. It might be a special toolkit or premium that your president has authorized for distribution to a select few key accounts. It might even be your own expertise in resolving typical challenges and opportunities that your customers face—a Frequently Asked Questions page of your own, if you will. Whatever it is, come up with at least three things that you can help your customers access within your organization. Make sure each and every one of your customers, at least the ones you want to hold on to, receives your "Easter eggs."

Principle #3: Introduce the Family

Do not just dash off to the Caribbean for three weeks and leave your customers high and dry. Pick someone you trust to handle their inevitable questions, crises, and suggestions. Schedule a conference call or even a face-to-face meeting to introduce the person who will be covering for you in your absence.

Principle #4: Build Your Own Company

It sounds crazy, but it really is how things get done in big organizations. There are subcompanies that emerge within larger companies. These are not formal business entities, of course, but they are loosely or not-so-loosely arranged alliances and communication networks. If you do not know who the four most important people you work with in your organization are, you should—and your clients should, too. Identify your own mini organization chart and share it with your key contacts.

Principle #5: Get Them a Meeting with Your President

If you cannot arrange a meeting with the company president, then get the highest-ranking person you can find. Look the person in the eye. Say, "It will help me hold on to this account if you spend half an hour with me today at lunch." If that person turns you down for whatever reason, work your way around your own organization and find someone else.

Principle #6: Give Them a Tour

Salespeople are very big on touring the facilities of our prospects, but it probably is just as important that your most important customers see how your operation runs, too. Anyone who is critical to your sales success should have a clear sense of how your company operates, and that means firsthand experience. This is one situation where face-to-face really does make a difference. The bigger the account, the more trouble you should go to in order to arrange for face-to-face interaction.

Principle #7: Send a Book

Whatever book you happen to be reading, if you think it is of interest to your prospects and customers, find a reason to send a copy inscribed with your own signature. Of course, if the book represents your company in some way—the autobiography of your CEO, let's say—that is all the better. But if this is not possible, and often it is not, just be sure to humanize your contact's relationship with your company by sending along a book that you have read and think the prospect will find interesting and valuable. One piece of advice: Keep it business related.

"Just Focus on Him"

THERE IS A SCENE in the movie *Sleepless in Seattle*, at the top of the Empire State Building, in which Meg Ryan is standing and staring at her costar, Tom Hanks. This scene took quite a long time to shoot. The director had to stop several times and ask Ryan to simplify her performance. Apparently, the first few takes were fascinating and filled with activity, but they were not exactly what the director was looking for. Finally, in effort to make sure that the all-important scene atop the Empire State Building came off correctly, the director gave Meg Ryan a very simple piece of advice: "It's really all about him. Just focus on him."

That simple piece of acting advice utterly changed the dynamics of the scene—and the entire film. By reminding Meg Ryan that the point of the scene was to focus with 100 percent attention on her costar, the director managed to capture that most appealing of all human decisions, namely, the decision to focus all of one's resources and listening power and experiences on another human being.

That is what made the movie work, as it turned out. That is what makes romance work. And that is, I submit, what ultimately makes upselling campaigns work.

I shared with you earlier a few thoughts on the importance of moving from the initial "vendor" stages of a relationship up to the "resource" stage of the relationship, and becoming a trusted business ally and a strategic partner in the process. I really do not think that it is possible for any salesperson to do that unless you are willing to focus on your prospect or customer with the same kind of relaxed, focused, accepting attention that Meg Ryan showed in that critical scene in *Sleepless in Seattle*. (Go ahead—check out the movie sometime and take a look. And while you are watching it, notice the factual error when Meg Ryan dashes into the Empire State Building and pleads to be let onto the observation deck. How she gets through without having to wait in line for a ticket, or how she manages to skirt the line to the elevator, are beyond me—but hey, these are the movies, and I'm just a New Yorker who knows how things really work.)

In real life, we cannot expect to make our relationships work by focusing on ourselves. That is true as we enter our marriage, and it is true as we enter any business relationship. The simplest and easiest prescription for succeeding in the all-important task of moving to the top of the pyramid is to spend as much time, energy, and attention on the other person as possible, and to make it a holy mission to fulfill that person's objectives—within the guidelines of your own ethical and business capacities, of course.

Pull Out Your Legal Pad

HERE'S ONE OF MY FAVORITE STRATEGIES for moving toward "strategic partner" status: start small and gather one fact at a time—with old-fashioned pen-and-pad technology.

We live in a high-tech world, and sometimes I think that that technology does not always serve us with perfect efficiency. Let me share with you what I mean. Most of the salespeople whom I train will begin a meeting with a prospect by saying, "Let me show you a Power-Point that we put together for the people we want to do work with."

At that point, they begin paging through a generic PowerPoint that is designed specifically for nobody and generically for everybody. This is basically a twenty-first-century equivalent of the common problem of "throwing up" all over the prospect by reading verbatim from the brochure, only it feels a little bit less like that because the person uses the PowerPoint as a tool to hold what could be mistaken for a conversation with the other person.

To my way of thinking, this is a huge mistake, and a violation of the rule that I have just shared with you here for success in upselling, namely, that we must be sure to focus every conceivable atom of our attention on the other person during our meetings. This point is particularly important in the first meeting, but it applies to all subsequent meetings as well.

Consider the advantages of the old-fashioned legal-pad-and-pen approach.

- By pulling out the legal pad and your pen, without asking for permission to do so, you make a subtle but important point. You are here in a professional capacity and you are here to do a job. That job is to take down information from this person or group of people.
- By maintaining eye contact with the key people in the room, nodding briskly, and then jotting down key points on the legal pad, you will be sending the message that you take seriously every piece of information the prospect is giving you.
- By having your legal pad out during the meeting, you can use it to develop impromptu sketches and diagrams and adapt as necessary when you receive corrections from the people you are talking to.
- By taking the time and trouble to actually write down notes by hand, you will be demonstrating that you are willing to do more than most salespeople do—and indeed more than most people in any field of endeavor do—and will be willing to make a personal commitment to get things right, even if it takes a little bit more time and effort.
- At the end of the meeting, you can review all of the key points that you have taken down by hand, and begin a recap of all of the essential information from the meeting, one that begins with a phrase similar to "Well, here's what I got from you so far . . ."

I am not saying that you should never use a PowerPoint presentation in your conversations with prospects and customers. What I am saying is that, if you do use one, what you must do—at least if you want to move forward into the "resource" phase of the relationship that I am emphasizing here—is build a customized PowerPoint deck that is based on the notes you take by hand. In all likelihood, you should save that for the second substantial meeting with the committee or person to whom you are trying to sell.

These days, of course, the first meeting may well take place by means of a conference call or other remote meeting format. In this case, your best bet will be to reach out by phone before the meeting, and do your note taking by hand then! Yes, you certainly can take notes over the phone, and you get most if not all of the benefits of doing so in person simply by mentioning to your contact that you are doing so. You can pull this off by using phrases like the following at key points in the conversation:

"Hold on, let me get my pad out—I want to take some notes."

"Let me be sure I've got this correct in my notes—what you're saying is . . ."

"So let me just recap what I've heard so far—this is what I've got down in my notes . . ."

What's the Next Step?

I BELIEVE all effective selling and upselling is based on developing urgency in the relationship. If someone isn't willing to make a time commitment to speak with you, meet with you, or put you in touch with other people, that's not a good sign. One of my cardinal selling rules is that we always want to get the other person to do something. Ideally, we want the other person to do something that results in measurable action that is scheduled for the short term.

That's a little bit of a cumbersome phrase, "measurable action that is scheduled for the short term," so I use a shorthand version, a term that's come up a few times in this book already: *Next Step*.

A Next Step is something someone puts in his or her calendar that shows a willingness to meet, discuss, or otherwise interact with you at some point between now and two weeks from now.

What's so special about two weeks from now? Well, one of the things we've noticed over the years in our company is that there are two very different types of time commitments. There is the kind of time commitment where I say to you that I'm willing to meet with you at some point, and then there's the time commitment where I say to you that I'm willing to meet with you at a point in time specifically between now and the next two weeks.

What's interesting is that even if I get specific and offer you a time slot that is for more than two weeks from now, let's say, the day after New Year's, and it's October, that commitment has a statistical likelihood to go unfulfilled. It starts to drop right after the two-week mark. And it's easy to see why. We live our lives in two-week chunks. If you talk to the average business person, and get a look at his or her calendar, what you'll find is that there's a great deal of specific information about what's happening on the calendar between now and the end of the period that's two weeks from now. You'll find much less specificity and much less competition for slots two weeks further and out. This is not a hard-and-fast rule, but it is a general guideline.

So think about the implications of this. The part of the schedule that we're focusing on is, inevitably, that which is on our horizon: whatever is happening within the next two weeks. The part of our schedule that we're not focusing on is the part that is two weeks or more ahead. What this means is that someone who is trying to put you off—but who really doesn't want to say, "I have no intention of meeting with you or discussing this with you"—can do so simply by saying, "Let's schedule it for four weeks from now."

It's even possible that someone who genuinely means to get together with us or speak with us or have a conference call with us, and simply is booked between now and two weeks from now, will innocently place us in the schedule for four or five or six weeks from now, simply because that's when most slots are available. But guess what? When the person finally gets that week into the two-week "horizon" of real-world commitments, there will be other priorities! Something that was important enough not to move six weeks out will find its way into that person's schedule, and we'll be bumped again or perhaps even forgotten about.

This phenomenon is familiar to virtually every salesperson on the face of the earth who's worthy of the name. If you've ever set a meeting with someone for four weeks ahead of time and then failed to confirm that the meeting was taking place and simply showed up on the person's doorstep at the appointed time, you have no doubt had the experience of having your meeting be supplanted by some other, suddenly more important, activity.

So when we say that a Next Step must take place at some point within the next two weeks, what we're really saying is that we're asking the people we're interacting with to make a clear assessment to us of exactly how important this discussion or meeting or conference call really is to them. That's not how we say it, of course, but it's how we can measure it. If the person is willing to set aside a specific chunk of time within that critical time frame that embraces the next two weeks, then we can rest assured that we are dealing with someone who's really interested in talking to us. If, on the other hand, the person puts us off time and time again or "schedules" time to talk with us that is a month or more down the line, we can make a realistic assessment that this person really isn't all that interested in interacting with us. That's not to say he or she couldn't be interested in interacting with us at some point, but it is helpful to us in prioritizing where we're putting our time, effort, and energy to know who's a real prospect.

"Based on What We've Discussed Today . . ."

HERE ARE SOME MAGIC WORDS: "Based on what we've discussed today . . ."

Okay, maybe they're not really magic. But they can be quite powerful. Take a look:

"Based on what we've discussed today, I want to come back here on February 4 at 10:00 and show you some ideas of how we might be able to work together on this new project. Before we get together, would you be able to . . ."

"Based on what we've discussed today, I'm excited about what we're talking about—but I'll be honest, I'm a little concerned about (the price/the timing/your budget/whatever). What's your feeling on that?"

"Based on what we've discussed today, let me ask you something—just between you and me, what do you think is really going to happen here?"

"If I came in and met all your criteria next week, could you see us doing business together again?" ("Well, it all depends on Mel, because Mel makes all those decisions with me. . . .")

"You know what? I'm thinking it makes sense for you and I and Mel to get together. Based on what we've talked about here today, does that make sense to you?"

When you have a Next Step, you have something. When you don't have a Next Step, you've got nothing. Among the reasons you can offer for getting together with someone are the following:

- A chance to strategize before a committee meeting
- A chance to debrief after a committee meeting (I am a big fan of setting these postcommittee sessions before the actual meeting takes place with my contact.)
- A tour of the facility
- A chance to meet the president of your company
- A chance to meet the president of the prospect's company
- A chance to meet with the prospect's team
- A chance to report back on what you think the prospect's team is doing right
- A chance to report back on what you think the prospect's team is doing wrong
- A chance to explain how you think you can implement the prospect's plan for the next month, quarter, or year
- A chance to explain why you think the prospect's plan for the next month, quarter, or year will not work.
- A chance for the prospect to see your product or service in action.
- A chance for the prospect to see you in action. (This is particularly effective if you are a trainer, technical expert, salesperson, or on-site consultant. If there is something you do and do well, feel free to invite the prospect to watch you do it, especially if there is any showmanship you can incorporate at some point in the proceedings.)
- A chance to see a product demonstration.

- A chance to visit or have a conference call with a happy customer of yours.
- A highly customized PowerPoint presentation delivered in person.
- A highly customized PowerPoint presentation delivered online.

Just be sure that you're taking plenty of notes and not missing the key points. And watch out for body language to make sure that the person is not drifting off.

This is just a few of the many, many, many things you can do to develop some sort of Next Step with the person you hope to sell more of your product or service to. It has been my experience that all that is really necessary, if there is a meaningful relationship in place already, and sometimes even if there is not, is for you to call your contact up and say, "Hey listen, I have an idea that I want to discuss with you, and I think we should get together in person to do it."

That is perhaps the most powerful test of whether or not you have got a real relationship going. If you do not, and if your prospect is not willing to make that investment of time and effort with you to discuss your idea, then perhaps you should try to reach out to somebody else in the organization.

35 The Art of Making People Look Good

COMPANIES ARE CONSTANTLY CHANGING. Not only our own company, of course, but the company we're trying to sell to, as well. But . . . not every single person in every company knows every change that is coming.

Generally, the higher up I sell my products and services, the more likely I am to find the one person who's familiar with all the changes on the horizon. However, there is a challenge. It's not enough for me just to spend time with a key decision maker; I have to add value, and I have to know how to make the person look good within his or her organization.

Don't confuse the quantity of time with the quality of the relationship. Just because you play golf with a person, that does not mean you have a partnership or a resource relationship going. If you are in a resource relationship, you have instant access to anybody within the company if you want it. If you are in a resource relationship, you can ask, "How come you are doing it that way?" and you will get a meaningful answer. If you have a resource relationship, you could ask the person who is buying your stuff, "How are you prepared to handle such and such a problem?" And the person would say to you, "We were coming to you guys tomorrow morning to ask about that. How do you think that we should handle it?"

You will know that you are not at the top of the relationship pyramid if the problem is one that you can solve, yet the customer does not call you first. In that case, you are lower down on the pyramid, and the question you should be asking is, "How come you are talking to them?"

For example, I could go to the CEO of a company that's already buying training from us and ask what changes are happening in his telesales department. He would probably have an overview of the kinds of missions that they're on. But he's not necessarily going to know what kind of software they're going to use.

So, my goal is to position my upsell properly—and the key to positioning the upsell is, on the most basic level, to find something that is going to help someone do what they're trying to do and look great in the process.

But what are they trying to do? That's the $64,000 question.

For most companies, it breaks down this way: what they're trying to do is . . .

- Gain market share
- Gain a competitive edge in the marketplace
- Improve/increase revenues
- Increase/improve profits

Those are the big four from the company's point of view. So, in order to do that, of course, companies do all kinds of things. They improve sales, improve the people, recruit better people, and try to retain better people. They try to improve their customer service, reduce attrition, and increase retention (which improves the profit per sale and reduces the cost of sale). They try to make their companies more attractive to investors by becoming more productive, more efficient, and less wasteful or by increasing their profit margin. Those are the ways companies carry out those four big goals. Basically, they're trying to make more money, keep more money, and position themselves right for the future.

But what companies do isn't the whole picture. What do individuals in the company try to do?

Well, typically, they're trying to change things in their own lives. Specifically, they're trying to . . .

- Get a raise and/or a promotion
- Change the amount of work they do
- Change the amount of perceived power and status they have
- Change the actual level of control they have over specific events in their department

So, with the individual—and ultimately, I believe, it always does come down to individuals—the goal is to make the person you're working with look so good that he or she makes progress toward one or more of these goals.

Help them look good in order to get a raise and a promotion. Help them look good in order to change their perceived power and status. And so forth. Do that through the person's own department/division, which is helping the company achieve its goals.

For example, this morning I had breakfast with the president and head of a major media company that had already purchased training from us for his field salespeople. My goal is to sell him training for his telesales group as well—a classic upselling situation, from my point of view. He bought A, and it worked out well for him. Now I think he should buy B.

He doesn't know (for instance) what specific kind of phone system they have, but he did tell me that what they're looking to do on an overall level is to improve every department—in fact, he told me, there's a department heads meeting going on right now. And they're all looking at getting more sales out of every department.

I said, "What's going on with your telesales department?"

He said, "Well, we're trying to get more sales out of that group."

I said, "Okay, why are you looking to get more sales out of telesales?"

He said, "Well, you know, we're just trying to get more sales out of everybody."

"Listen," I said. "Let me just tell you something. Companies that I know that improve their telesales and that also have a field sales group find that every dollar they can get out of telesales has a lower cost per sale. Every sale made by the telesales group is a sale that the field salespeople, who are more expensive, don't have to make. So, the higher the level of sale you're able to accomplish on the phone, the more the higher-profit sales are left for the more expensive salespeople. If you find the right balance, you could actually increase sales slightly through telesales and dramatically improve your margins."

What does that help him do? Look like a hero to the board of directors. This is obviously the kind of relationship we want to have. And notice that I put it into language that he can understand: improving margins.

If you stop and think about it, people are motivated by the desire to look good in front of other people. It is just human nature. They are also motivated by the fear of looking bad in front of other people. These are really two sides of the same coin. However you approach it, any upselling initiative that reduces the likelihood that somebody is going to look like an idiot, or that increases the likelihood that somebody is going look like a hero, is likely to help you build bridges and turn a onetime customer into a repeat customer.

The truth of the matter is, though, that you really cannot do this unless you have expertise or value that you yourself can add in a unique way as a representative of your company. Take a look again at what I was able to do with that CEO of that media company. I found the area where I knew a little bit more than he did—okay, maybe more than a little bit more—and I made a direct appeal to something that was true in my experience, namely, that telesales departments are there for a very valid budgetary reason. They are cheaper than field sales departments. This is not to say that field sales departments are unnecessary, but it is to say that in many situations, it makes just as much sense financially to train your telesales people to operate at peak efficiency as it does to train your field sales people to operate at peak efficiency. In fact, it makes far more sense!

So, this is a piece of value that I was able to deliver to him, and it ended up making him look great in front of his audience, his board of directors. As a result, we have gotten quite a lot of business from this company. Now the example I have given you sounds very high-end and very complex and very corporate, but I can tell you that the same precise relationship is in play every time you reach out to another human being and share some piece of value that you have about how what you offer impacts how good they are going to look in front of somebody else. Specifically, if you are selling exercise equipment, you do not go and spend your whole afternoon harping about how wonderful the equipment is because it has this feature and that electrical attachment and this conversion ratio. Instead, you want to share real-life stories or, better yet, your own real-life experience with using the equipment. How much weight did you lose? How much weight did somebody that you know lose? How did it affect your social life? How did it affect the way you were perceived at work?

Notice that precisely the same model is at work in the high-end sale—looking great in front of a board of directors because you have been able to reduce the cost of sales—and the low-end upsell—looking great because you have lost fifteen pounds in fifteen days. The point is, if you are credible, if you are enthusiastic, and if you are committed to making the other person look good, you really can get the other person interested not only in what you are offering this time around as an upsell, but also in all the other materials that you may be able to pass along over the next weeks and months and even years.

Well, let's return to my example. Suppose I had to approach the guy who's in charge of telesales and try to win new training business from him, rather than from the CEO. He's in charge of telesales and is trying to look good to his company so that he can get a raise and promotion. But I can't take the same approach with him that I would with the CEO.

What I could do with him is to say, "Listen, what I could help you guys do is this. Right now, you can't increase talk time, you can't increase the lead base, you can't increase the head count. But what I can do is help you to reduce the amount of wasted time your people spend on the phone. That will decrease your queue times, improve your customer retention, reduce attrition, and improve customer satisfaction. Basically, I can help you drive your numbers up. And I can show your people how to make an upselling presentation that will enable them to increase the average value of the call they close over the phone. And I can show you how to measure all that, and guess what? You're going to look like a hero when you have the numbers to show off to your CEO."

Managers must be given ammunition to prove that they are good managers. In this case, if I were approaching a manager to get him to buy into the idea of expanding my company's relationship with his, I am going to have to do so not by pointing out that his salespeople are paid less than other salespeople in the organization, but rather by giving him access to tools that will help him to generate a spreadsheet that proves what a great job he is doing with the resources he has. It is a different rhetorical emphasis, and it is a different piece of strategy.

When you are dealing with managers on the front lines, people whose job it is to deliver the results and keep the teams pointed in the right direction, think of the tasks they face in a world dominated by the obsession of cutting costs and trimming away "fat." This person is interested, first and foremost, in proving to the rest of the company that he and his people do not equate to "fat" in any way, shape, or form. So, as you approach these decision makers and advocates, remember that their take on what will turn them into a hero usually depends on your ability to prove that they are not only doing a job, but doing it well and nobly.

Now, suppose my job were to go to the telesales people and turn them into allies for the idea of purchasing another training program from my company, a program designed specifically for them. Here's what I would say to them: "Now, what you guys want to do is, you want to make more money, am I right? So here's how you make more money. You want to increase the average value of your call, and here's how you do that, by building this 'by the way' step into your closing process."

Notice that I'm talking about the same component of the training but *identifying a different benefit*. Here, when I'm appealing to the actual salespeople, my goal is to focus on increasing personal income. I have to keep repositioning my upselling effort to match the audience I've targeted.

The Follow-Through Campaign

IN MY COMPANY, which is a sales training company, we have a pretty simple strategy for developing new business from our existing clients. We tell them exactly what we want to do next.

Actually, as a precursor to that, what we do is, we take the radical step of being very honest with them very early on in the relationship.

When I am meeting with a decision maker who is considering purchasing things from our company, I will say something like the following to him: "I am going to tell you the secret of the sales training industry, a secret that most people do not want to share with you, but that we tell each and every person that we work with. Sales training does not work—unless you reinforce it. If you simply do two days of training this month, and then never do anything else, what you have got is a motivational event and results will trail off, even if the people you are training get some real benefit from the things that they have been taught.

However, if you do the program, you pass along the information, you give people the strategies they can really use, and you follow up a month afterward with a conference call and a face-to-face refresher session, then your results are going to be dramatically better. You are going to be able to sustain the improvement, and you will be in a much better position to build it into the way that people operate day after day after day. If you just rely on sales training, it does not work—because it does not permanently affect behavior. If, on the other hand, you rely on sales training and effective reinforcement, you can change people's habits and change the culture of the organization. And that is what we always recommend our clients do."

Now, every word of what I have just shared with you about what I said about clients is true. Strategically, it really does make the most possible sense to build policy programs into every sales-training event. But just as there is no effective training program without a follow-through, there is also (in my experience) no meaningful upselling strategy in our industry without a follow-through.

We have a number of training programs that we offer, but typically the people we work with come in looking to fix only one thing. So, they come to us for help in, for instance, setting more new first appointments. That is the main item on the agenda. We know it, they know it, and it is the only thing they want to focus on right at the outset of the relationship.

Well, as it happens, we can do both the training program and the reinforcement program that will permanently change the way an organization develops new leads and makes first appointments. However, we offer a lot more than that, too. So, what we will do, in the ideal situation, is establish both the training program and the reinforcement program for that initial appointment-making piece, and then during the reinforcement piece, the follow-through piece, the checkup piece, we will develop a strategy for sharing the *other* training programs that we have to offer with our prospects and customers.

When there is a reinforcement session to do the diagnostic work, that diagnostic session will allow us to point out where else we can add value. That is how we take a client who may otherwise be thinking about a single program, and extend that relationship into four or five or six or more programs over time.

The key to making this work is simple: the diagnoses we make are valid!

The teams who have learned how to set first appointments *really should* move on to the next programs in the sequence, and their overall numbers *really do* go up as a result of doing so! But they would never have gotten the chance to improve in that way if we had not scheduled the posttraining meetings to evaluate where the teams were.

37   The Mole

DURING MY SALES-TRAINING SEMINARS, I always make the point that when you are interviewing during the sales process, it is important to think in the long term, and to interview both in terms of the individual and also in terms of the company. Some people think this is just a bit of warm and fuzzy hand-holding that is meant to make our training sound accessible, but it really is a strategically important step to bond with the person as an individual and find out what is going on in his or her world.

I'll tell you why it's so important. If you focus only on corporate initiatives, and never focus on the goals and aspirations of the individual, not only will you fail to win the allies who can help you implement your products in the target organization, but you will also miss out on critical information and, ultimately, find yourself subject to the whims of decision makers you never meet.

I also compare the process of finding a corporate ally whom you understand as an individual and as a member of the target company to the process of getting good intelligence. In order to get good information about the enemy, you cannot simply pick up the newspaper and expect to learn what his or her next move is going to be. You have to have a "mole" on the inside. You have to have someone placed within the enemy's headquarters, someone who will keep you informed and give you a heads-up when something big is about to break.

That is exactly what you end up doing when you sell successfully to a single account over a long period of time. By connecting with a decision maker or highly placed insider within the target company, and establishing a personal bond with him or her, you not only win a friend, but you also have a mole within the organization. This is absolutely essential if you expect the accounts to grow over time.

Here are some strategies you can use to develop the one-on-one personal relationship necessary to "plant" a mole within the target company.

As a practical matter, in larger accounts, you should probably resign yourself to the fact that a lot of decision making is going to happen independent of your efforts to influence the decision. In other words, the larger the organization, the more likely that intelligence is going to be important for you to position yourself within that account.

What this means, in the real world, is that you'll be in a better position to upsell within that account if you have accurate information about what's actually taking place within the company. This can be, as experience has shown, extremely difficult to track down. The best advice I can give you is, build meaningful relationships with as many people as possible, and make as many people as possible look good.

What we're really talking about is the task of building alliances with people—with at least one, and preferably more than one—who can act as moles for you within the organization. I'm not going to kid you. At very large companies, you really do need someone, or a series of someones, who has heard the latest scuttlebutt and who is willing to share it with you. We live in the "information age," so it should not come as a huge surprise to you that your upselling efforts will benefit by gathering as much information as possible from as many different people as possible.

It follows, then, that your goal should be to build up a network, informal but meaningful, with as many people who are friendly, or even neutral, to your cause as you possibly can. Here are a couple of good ways to build up that kind of a relationship. You can use these strategies for building up your intelligence within the company—for creating moles in your network, people who will tell you what's really going on, at least from their perspective.

Strategy #1

When I get a call from headhunters, and I frequently do, I reach out to my key contacts at my best accounts and say, "Hey, listen, I just got a weird thing, would you call me back?" Inevitably, they call me back. Then I say, "Here's the thing. I got a call from a headhunter. I don't know if this is appropriate for you, or if you know anybody, or if you're looking—I don't know. It's none of my business. But if you are interested, this is a number, this is the situation. Here's the opportunity. Here's the phone number. Mention my name if you call them. I just thought you'd like to know." Suddenly, I'm a guy who's now connecting with you on a more personal level. And you're more likely to share information with me about what's happening in your world.

Strategy #2

Our company subscribes to an editorial service—we get leads via e-mail that tell us which editors want to do which stories, and what kinds of experts they're looking for. Some of the leads are appropriate to our business, but most of them aren't. So when I see a lead that seems right for one of my customers, I pass it on. I e-mail the person, and then I follow up with a phone call. I say, "Listen, there's an article here. I subscribe to this service. They're looking for an expert in such-and-such an area. It occurred to me that you might be that expert. You might want to respond to article number two." Again, when you get that kind of call from me, you're more likely to share information that *you* come across.

■ ■ ■

The principle is startlingly simple. Find a way to do something for someone else, and you'll eventually find that there's a pretty good likelihood that they'll do something for you at some point down the line. I think it was Benjamin Franklin who pointed out that the Golden Rule—"Do unto others as you would have them do unto you"—makes excellent business sense and is not merely a religious principle. In this case, the idea is to pass along critical information that you know will benefit your contact in the hope that he or she will pass you similarly critical information when it comes his or her way. It works!

And guess what? When your mole leaves company A to start a new job at company B, you've got a hot new prospect to call!

38   "I've Got an Idea . . ."

RECENTLY, I had a meeting with a senior sales executive who works for one of the world's largest manufacturers of industrial chemicals. His main customer was a major global manufacturing company in a fairly heavy industry that is one of the largest producers of engines, trucks, tractors, and so on. The senior VP is getting ready for a meeting with his contact at this heavy equipment manufacturer. So I asked him, "What are you trying to accomplish at this meeting?"

And the sales executive says to me, "Well, I'm always looking for ways to build new products into their order. I'm trying to upsell."

He has already got a relationship with this manufacturer, and he would like them to use more of his products. It is only logical he would want to develop an expanded relationship. So I said, "How are you planning on doing that? What are you going to do to expand the relationship?"

And the senior executive says to me, without batting an eye, "Well, I am going to go talk about product X, product Y, and product Z and show them all the specifics on how those products work. I'm going to give him the complete technical breakdown."

I just stopped and stared at him. He had made the classic sales mistake, in that he was planning to build his meeting around the idea of executing what we call a "products dump" on his contacts. That means reciting a long litany of technical details or advertising copy, and pretending it's a conversation with a customer.

Now, in my sales training programs, I warn people not to simply recite the contents of their brochure to a new prospect, not to deliver a monologue about all the technical specifications of their product, not to go off on a tangent about their own internal quality control program and all the similar programs. I warn people not to do this because it is a great way to turn people off and destroy the rapport of an initial meeting. And, here is a senior executive at one of the largest chemical products manufacturers in the world, planning on taking this exact same approach with a current customer—one who represents literally millions of dollars in sales!

I said, "Let me ask you something. Have you ever once gone in with an idea of how he could use one of these lubricants? In other words, not explaining how the lubricant works, but sharing your own thought about how he could use the lubricant to save money, increase his equipment life, and so on?"

"Gee, I never thought about that," he said. "That's a great idea."

Did you notice that, by *sharing* my idea—one that was about sharing ideas—I was able to move up the pyramid with my customer?

You remember the top of that relationship pyramid we looked at? This is what the strategic partnership looks like. The strategic partner is the guy who walks in the door to meet with his key customer and says, "Hey, I have this great idea. It kept me up all last night. I was thinking about your challenges with your equipment, and how you need to be able to extend the workable life of it, and I got together with some of my people, and here's what we came up with. Let me know what you think of this."

That's a strategic partner talking!

A strategic partner does not sound like this:

"Our model ZGL compound has been tested in sixty-five different regression analyses, with four different quality networks, and has been reinforced with the additive G239, which protects you from poor alignment of Neptune when the Moon is in the Second House . . ."

Remember, the point is to walk in the door more concerned about the person's challenge than he or she is. The point is to make it clear that you were up all night worrying about this, *and that you have an idea* that you are eager to be able to share with this person. That is the key to upselling . . . and, I think, the key to effective selling.

Getting the CEO on Your Side

Let's look now at a fairly complex upselling strategy that makes use of this "I've got an idea" approach. This strategy involves the CEO of a company that is already buying from us.

This is an interesting dynamic, because CEOs tend to have very short attention spans. This means they sometimes evaporate when you don't want them to. Of course, it's all well and good if the CEO calls a meeting, announces that you are the vendor or supplier of choice, and then orders everyone to carry out the details. Unfortunately, this does not happen very often. What is more likely to take place is that you will have an initial contact with a person at the head of the operation, who will then refer you to others with whom you will have to deal for some period of time.

If you are not extremely careful, what happens next is the evaporation problem: the CEO's initial contact with you is the very last you ever hear from the top. Basically, in the "default" setting, the CEO says that what you are proposing sounds interesting, and that he would like to consider doing more business with you, but that he needs you to work with people at other levels in the company before finalizing the purchase arrangements. And he then leaves you to the mercy of the rest of the company.

Six months later, nothing has moved forward.

Bad outcome!

The question is, how do we make sure that the CEO continues to work as an effective advocate for us even though he or she has a million other things to look at and is unlikely to try to make a conscious effort to be involved in our sales process? Here's one approach.

My goal in this situation is simply to schedule a series of breakfasts with the CEO. What I have to do is open up a line of communication and keep it open. Think of your contact with the top person as a pierced earlobe. I know that's an odd comparison—but think it through. If you pierce somebody's ear and you don't put an earring in there for a while, it closes up, and the person can't wear an earring. On the other hand, pierced ears that you constantly put earrings into will stay open.

So I want to keep my line of communication open once I establish it with the CEO. And here's how I do it. Immediately after my *first* breakfast meeting with the CEO, I send him an e-mail message right away. And by "right away," I mean, preferably within twelve hours of my face-to-face meeting.

This e-mail says, basically, "Thank you for meeting with me. This is what we talked about. This is what I'm going to think about. This is what I'm going to do. And I am going to contact you from time to time about new ideas that I have, and I hope we can discuss those."

Every time I get a thought now that might conceivably benefit his company, I send him an e-mail—whether he receives it, whether he does anything, whether he replies or not. If I come up with what seems to me like a good idea, I send it along.

My guess is that 70 percent of the e-mails I send to him get forwarded to other people, even if I don't know about it. Then periodically I call him up. Every six weeks or so I check in with him, and I say, "Hey, let's have breakfast again. I have an idea I want to show you"; then I schedule *another* breakfast meeting. And before the breakfast, I e-mail him: "Here's my thoughts about our upcoming breakfast; here's what I'm thinking of talking about."

He may reject my agenda completely, but at least he knows there's a plan. At a minimum, we have breakfast together. In a better scenario, we're talking about something that is of interest to one of us, and in the best-case scenario, we're talking about the things that I wanted to talk about—namely, how my discussions with his people are going.

Now, I don't necessarily have to make the sale through him. I could let him know what's going on with his own organization. I could say to him, "Listen, I've been calling somebody in your company and I just want to let you know what's going on. I call this guy, he talks to me, this other guy's talking to me, while this guy's been holding me up." I don't ask for help directly. But I let him know what I'm up to, and where I'm hitting brick walls.

I'm just bringing him up to date. I really don't drop his name in my discussions with his people. But by having regular breakfast meetings with the top guy, and by constantly passing along my ideas, I get his insights, his guidance, and, not infrequently, his quiet help in overcoming the obstacles that might otherwise keep us from doing more business together.

Selling to a Committee

FIRST, THE BAD NEWS. If your selling initiative requires you to make a presentation before a committee, you are already in trouble. Nine times out of ten, a committee will be most comfortable not taking any action whatsoever. It is basically part of their nature for committees to not actually do anything. If you allow nature to take its course, committees will study, discuss, deliberate, and ultimately abstain from taking any kind of meaningful action in a significant number of the cases involving a decision to buy more stuff from you.

That's the bad news. The good news, which a great many salespeople ignore, is that you can, with a great deal of hard work, counteract this tendency toward inaction. In this chapter, we will look at some of the ways you can do that.

Let's look at some of the specific elements that can kill a decision to purchase more products or services from you. First, you can fail to earn a place on the agenda. This is a favorite tactic within the organization that is eager to purchase from another vendor or perhaps simply even not to buy from you, but that does not want to have to navigate a long, drawn-out conflict over the matter. Instead of placing the question of whether to buy more from you on the agenda, it quietly makes sure the question does not show up in the first place.

The best way to counteract this problem is to tactfully ask to see a copy of the agenda for the meeting from one or more of your allies in the organization. It is not inconceivable that your ally thinks you are on the agenda, but your enemies have made sure that you are not.

Perhaps more subtle, but just as damaging, in a practical sense, is the situation where you are the last item on the agenda or are placed strategically late in the meeting. This is a recipe for being shelved indefinitely, and it requires basically the same strategy as the problem of not being on the agenda at all.

A third reason selling attempts can die on the vine is the problem of having the materials you need to deliver an effective presentation delivered too late for your meeting. In other words, there is some kind of logistical problem, and the stuff you need to be able to make a great impression simply does not show up or does not work. There is really nothing internally you can do to overcome this problem, except perhaps put everything into a package that you yourself bring to the meeting. But keep reading, as this, too, carries its share of challenges.

When it comes to any kind of selling to a committee, the real mistake is to imagine that anyone is going to walk into the meeting neutral on the question of whether to buy your product or service. People already have a bias before the meeting even begins, and there are always political issues to take into account. A fair number of people you run into will be opposed to any initiative that person A proposes, simply because their goal in life is to make person A look bad and to frustrate any of his or her initiatives.

So, looking beyond the obvious challenges that await you in preparing for your meeting with the committee, namely, those of agenda placement or lack of materials, there remains a whole category of internal politics and strategic information gathering that can, if you are not careful, eat up a good deal of time. So, please take this piece of advice: Be sure that the opportunity justifies a good deal of up-front work *before* you invest that up-front work. In other words, if you are confident that the resulting outcome is a

$2 million piece of business, and you are convinced that you have a realistic fifty-fifty shot at winning that business, go ahead and do everything else that appears in this chapter to win the additional business. On the other hand, if you are not convinced that you have a fifty-fifty shot, or if the deal is not worth the time and effort, then stop here and think about developing additional business with another of your customers.

Still with me? Good. Here are some basic principles to keep in mind when selling through committees.

Principle #1: Know the History

Find out what kind of committee you are dealing with. Is it a standing committee or an ad hoc committee? An ad hoc committee is something that is put together for the sole purpose of resolving a specific problem and may have a different chain of command than a standing committee does. It is common, for instance, for CEOs and other heavyweights to assemble an ad hoc committee and order it to report back with a recommendation. Whatever the situation is, you will need to know. If it is an ad hoc committee, you will quickly become aware of the fact that these people have never worked together. They may not actually be all that good at working together, and they may welcome your help as a facilitator. On the other hand, if it is a standing committee, there are, in all likelihood, already strong group dynamics at work, as well as a record of past decisions and strategies for implementing those decisions. Find out as much as you can about both by appealing to your contacts before the meeting takes place.

Principle #2: It Is More Important to Know Who Decided Who Would Be on the Committee Than It Is to Know Who to Target on the Committee Itself

This is a very important concept. Even on a standing committee, the odds are good that someone in the organization with a good deal of clout had the final say on which people would and would not serve on that committee. For instance, if you were contacting my company, you might well find yourself talking to a member of the committee that handles our franchising decisions. But—and here is the key point—your sales cycle would accelerate dramatically if you found out that I was the person who named each of the individuals to the committee! By contacting me directly, and convincing me that you are worth talking to, you would very likely get important information and position yourself much more effectively for winning the committee's approval than you would by contacting each of the individual members themselves.

Principle #3: Ask Intelligent Questions

If you are invited to make a presentation before the committee, that means, by definition, that you have a "champion." The champion is a person who wants you to make your pitch. It is all very well to receive this information, but just receiving it and then immediately acting on it shows a lack of foresight. Yes, you may receive additional business from this meeting—but why not improve the odds? Get as much information as you can. Ask your champion why he or she is allowing you to come. Ask him or her whether he or she is personally invested in the outcome. And ask him or her for help in setting up the Next Step. Say beforehand to your champion, "Okay, the meeting is this Friday—can you and I schedule a time right now to meet on the following Monday?" This is perhaps the most important question of all to ask your champion. Use this time to connect with your champion and debrief on what really took place after the meeting. After all, it is very unlikely that the decisions will be delivered to you immediately after you make your presentation.

Principle #4: Find Out the Real Agenda

With your champion's permission—or, if the meeting is your idea, with the permission of your most important ally—try to do an informal phone survey of all the people who will be on the committee. You might say, "Would you mind if I contacted some of the people who will be in on the meeting just to find out a little bit about what they are looking for?" In the vast majority of cases, your champion or ally will have no problem with this. It is then imperative that you get on the phone and identify, to whatever degree is possible, what each member of the meeting hopes to see from you. Your call will inevitably include some question like the following: "What do you think, Mr. Contact, that the key concerns of the committee members are going to be?"

Notice that you are not asking the committee member what his or her agenda is, only for his or her assessment of how the committee is likely to view the initiative under discussion. You do not want to put somebody on the spot unnecessarily, and asking the question this way will almost always give you whatever information you are likely to get about this person's agenda.

If you follow these first four principles, you will walk in the door and not be a stranger. You may not have succeeded in the goal of building alliances with everyone on the committee, but at least you will not be a complete unknown, and you will have a good sense of what the group dynamics are.

Principle #5: Focus on "How"

During the presentation, put the rhetorical focus on the question of how you will be doing more business with this company, and not on the issue of whether the company will be buying more products and services from you. Make the assumption that the logistics are what you are there to discuss. After all, you are not going to get a decision today anyway, so why not try to set the agenda moving toward the question of how to begin the additional work together?

■ ■ ■

One final thought on selling to committees. The ideas in this chapter are likely to be helpful to you if you find yourself in a situation where you are being asked to make the case for expanding the relationship and formalizing the decision to purchase more products and services. However, although this is a common situation, it is not the optimal one.

The optimal situation, which is relatively rare, is that you get someone who is very high-placed in the organization to make your case for you. In other words, if the CEO is willing to spend ten minutes explaining to others why he has decided to buy more widgets from your company, let him or her do that! You should, if possible, ask if this is a realistic option. Unless your champion is very highly placed in the organization, and is also extremely enthusiastic about what you are offering, the odds are good that it will not be a realistic option.

But over the course of time, you will run into situations where this type of selling can occur. When it happens, make the most of it.

You may want to suggest to your contact that you help out by creating a summary outline of key points—a draft of major issues. This document will help your champion stay focused as he sings your praises, and then moves toward the implementation schedule that both you and your champion feel is appropriate.

Take Responsibility

I'VE DISCOVERED ONE PARTICULAR TECHNIQUE for rescuing a blown presentation that has worked for me more times than I can count. I've taught it for years in my seminars and one-on-one training sessions and gotten nothing but positive reactions. This book would not be complete if I didn't tell you about it.

I call the method "taking responsibility." I know that may sound like a novel idea at first, because it's so easy to let someone else—the company, the production department, whomever—assume responsibility for the ultimate happiness of the customer or prospect. But I think if you stop to reconsider, you'll probably realize that your best customers now have come to rely on you in an important way, and that much of your relationship with these kinds of customers is based on trust. Earning trust is really the same thing as accepting responsibility, and assuming personal responsibility for the sale as it progresses is a remarkably effective sales tool. It works so well that, if you're like me, the first time you hear about the technique, you'll probably wonder why you didn't incorporate it into your sales routine long ago.

Convictions

So how does it work? Well, to begin with, you have to be utterly, completely convinced in your own heart that you can offer your prospect the best possible solution to his or her problem. If that confidence isn't there, the technique I'm about to describe simply won't work. If the prospect (or anyone else) asks you to talk about your firm, you have to be able to reply with sincerity that you work for a one-of-a-kind, customer-first company and are proud to do so.

Now then. When you're on a sales visit, and you come to the closing stage, you simply say something along the lines of "It sounds good to me; how does it sound to you?" (Again, that may seem audaciously simple right now, but this method of closing can be adapted to just about any close.) One of two things is likely to happen. Either the prospect will answer your question receptively—and thereby start down the road to becoming a customer—or the prospect will back off and say "No" flat out.

If you find yourself facing the second scenario, you take responsibility for whatever problem has arisen.

What do I mean by that? Well, at this point, the salespeople I know of who use this technique successfully are genuinely taken aback—even shocked. And it's no act. They believe in their company so completely, and know so much about the prospect by this stage of the game, that they are legitimately concerned to see any evidence of a negative response to the proposal they've made. And they state that concern in no uncertain terms. You can too.

What you say will sound something like this: "Mr. Prospect, I'm really not sure what to say. I am so convinced that we have the best service, the best pricing, the best customization, and the best reputation of any firm in our industry that I can think of only one reason for you not to sign on with us. And that's that I must have done something terribly wrong just now in giving my presentation. So I'm going to ask you to give me a hand, Mr. Prospect, and tell me where I went off course. Because, to be quite frank with you, I know this service is right for you, and I'd really hate to have made a mistake on something this important."

Getting the Information You Need

Wow! What do you think you'll hear in response? One thing's for sure. It's not going to be easy for the prospect to come back with a run-of-the-mill brushoff like, "It's just not up our alley, Susan." No, if you're Mr. Prospect, you probably respect the person who had the courage to say that to you, who believes so strongly in the service you're looking at. You're going to pass along information—information on exactly what the problem is with your firm's signing on.

In practice, you will find that the common response you'll hear after you take responsibility for the initial "No" will sound something like this: "No, no, no, Susan, it has nothing to do with you. It's on our end." And the prospect can then be expected to go into detail about the remaining obstacles. Then you have the facts you need to continue through the cycle.

Let me repeat: This can be a startlingly effective technique, but it requires absolute faith on your part that you can in fact deliver on your promises. There is another catch as well: You have to be willing to put aside the common fixation with "being right" we all share to a degree. But, hey, when it comes right down to it, would you rather be "right"—or close a sale?

Money, Money

YEARS AGO, at a meeting with the top brass at a large bank, I was following my own advice and encouraging my prospects (in this case, it was a committee) to help me compose the proposal I would eventually present.

When it came to money (as it often does, either here or at a later stage of the sales cycle), I started getting funny signals. I'd talked about the plan I wanted to develop for the bank, I'd tried to identify the major objectives of the people I was working with, and I'd stated a rough (read: negotiable) dollar amount that was appropriate for the work I was anticipating doing. I said, "Let me give you a feeling for what I think this is going to cost." I named a figure. The president of the bank looked at me, smiled, and told me he had no problem with the amount of money I had mentioned. But the chief executive officer saw things differently.

He said to me, "I'm not sure that we want to pay that kind of money." And then he stopped talking. A hush fell over the room. What to do?

Because I'd been attentive during the interviewing stage, I knew that the company, although large and profitable, was growing fast, and was experiencing the kinds of cash constraints common in a high-growth environment.

Companies that are growing rapidly tend to eat up a lot of cash. So instead of perceiving the chief executive officer's comment as a challenge to my program's viability, or as the first salvo in a negotiating war over my fees, I reacted to it as though it were simply an expression of concern about cash flow.

Which, it turned out, was exactly what it was.

I offered the chief executive officer the opportunity to pay off my fee over an extended period, explaining that I could make an exception to my standard payment terms this time around because of the size of the deal. The chief executive smiled broadly and said he thought that approach could work. A week later I made my presentation (complete with extra time to pay) asked the principals what they thought about what I had to offer, and closed the sale.

My point is not that you should always try to get around price obstacles by offering creative payment terms. Sometimes that will be the correct response; sometimes it won't. My point is that, if you truly listen to your client, if you avoid the temptation to assume that this prospect's price objection is the same as the last person's price objection, you'll be in a much better position to get the information you need to put together a presentation that closes.

After all, can you imagine what would have happened in that case if I'd assumed that their financial situation was exactly like that of the last prospect I'd met with? If I'd held off discussing the issue of price until the very end of the process?

I would have named a figure. The president would have said it made sense. The chief executive officer would have had his reservations. Everybody would have said that the committee needed time to think. I would have left. At some point the chief executive officer would have pointed to his (valid!) cash flow concerns, and someone could have pointed out, rightly, that I had not mentioned anything about any payment plans. The committee would have had to assume that I would require the standard terms that show up on my published price list—half on signing, half on completion. They could have felt uncomfortable asking me for other terms—if they'd thought about asking at all. And I would have lost the sale!

Know When to Move On

ONE OF THE GREAT NEGLECTED TRUTHS ABOUT SELLING is that the very best strategy is sometimes to recognize that there is no possibility to expand a relationship with a given customer.

That may sound cynical, but it is actually quite optimistic. There comes a point when your aim is to move on and find a better opportunity. Your goal is not, and cannot be, to try to find some system that will expand every budget, improve every relationship, and allocate every organization's dollars to your company. No such incantation exists, and you should not waste your time waiting for one.

The trick is to align yourself so well with the interests of your prospects and customers that you learn to develop a sense for whether or not the possibility really exists to expand your relationship in a way that benefits both parties. The last part of that sentence is particularly crucial, so please read it again. Notice that I said that your goal must be to develop a proposal or initiative that *benefits both parties*!

Inexperienced salespeople sometimes tell me that they do not see any problem in moving somebody from the prospect stage to the customer stage. Let's say they set an appointment with somebody with whom they have done business before. And let's say that they have got a new proposal they want to give that former customer, to expand or deepen the relationship.

When I ask an inexperienced salesperson about this kind of relationship, I generally do so by posing a question like this one: "So, why do you think they bought from you in the first place? You told me that they placed an order for widgets three months ago. Why do you think they did that?"

I will get any number of responses to this, but with inexperienced salespeople, the sad truth of the matter is that they will very rarely have any idea exactly why the person bought from them in the first place. As a result, their efforts to expand or upsell the relationship are statistically unlikely to bear fruit. It is not impossible that they could get new business from this customer, mind you, but it is, in my experience, unlikely that you will significantly expand a business relationship when you know absolutely nothing about the reason the person bought from you in the first place. You are still at the commodity level of relationship.

We do not like to admit it to ourselves, but a certain percentage of the people who buy from us buy from us at the commodity level, and will not ever buy for any other reason. We help them resolve a short-term problem or address a sudden crisis. We are not part of their long-range plans. The first decision is what I like to call a "one-off." That means that the person really is not supposed to buy from us again, and there is very little that we can do to change that. That is not the way it is in all the cases and with all the customers, but it is what we face in a certain percentage of the relationships. And when we do not do any meaningful exploration of the reasons that prompted the person's decision to work with us in the first place, we should not be surprised when we are not able to move the person up to the next level.

I've never met a sales manager who actually held on to the job for more than a year or so who couldn't develop a "sixth sense" for identifying which customers were "one-offs" and which customers represented a realistic chance for long-term business.

Let me give you an example of what I mean. The business I am in, the sales-training business, has a lot of different reasons that motivate people to buy. Sometimes people buy training because they want to hit a certain sales goal and they feel that the tools that their salespeople have are not sufficient for them to do that. Now you might think that a goal like that is the only guiding motivation when it comes to purchasing sales training, but that is not the case at all. Sometimes, believe it or not, the reason people buy training is that they have a certain number of dollars left in their budget and the end of the year is approaching and they want to be absolutely sure that they still get the same amount in their budget for next year, so they want to be sure to spend it—and quickly.

So, the people in a situation where they have come to the conclusion that their sales team is deficient in certain critical sales skills—say, for instance, setting first appointments—have one reason for calling me up and asking if I will train their team. The people who want to get rid of the $X,000 that is sitting in their budget before the clock runs out have a different agenda in calling me up and asking if I will deliver sales training to their team.

Here is the point: The first customer represents a better chance for repeat business than the second.

In other words, I cannot assume that I know that the person who is calling to get rid of the budget dollars has the same motivation or requirement as the person who wants to see measurable increases in first appointments over the next sixty days. They are two totally different situations. And the person who wants to maintain the same budget level next year, and as a result wants to spend money with me right now, is very likely to be what I call a one-off. This is the kind of sale that may, as a statistical fact, never be more than a single piece of business. That is not to say that it is impossible that I could not sell this person. It does mean, however, that I am not going to build up the same level of time, energy, and attention after delivering the program as I will with the other person—especially if I continue to get signals that the only reason that person wanted to work with me in the first place was to get rid of the budget money.

Simple lesson: Focus your efforts on a "high-percentage shot" rather than on a "low-percentage shot." I know that standard is more or less impossible to quantify, but it works for me. Some people really are one-offs, and after just a little bit of experience, you learn to recognize who they are. Don't bother investing large amounts of time and energy trying to develop an upselling campaign for them. If the initial deal closes within an acceptably short time frame, celebrate. If it doesn't . . . move on!

43 | The Special Challenges of Telesales

LET'S TALK A LITTLE BIT ABOUT SELLING in the telesales environment. I like to focus special attention and energy on the challenge of the telemarketers and training programs, because I honestly believe that telesales is one of the most difficult kinds of selling.

Why do I say that telesales is one of the most difficult selling jobs? There are a number of reasons. For one thing, you cannot see the person you are selling to. We know for a fact that the majority of human communication occurs through nonverbal signals, and yet the telesales professional must perform his or her job without any indication of the other person's facial expression, posture, gaze, or even whether the person is doing something else entirely unrelated while we are speaking! We have only the person's tone of voice to go on, and that really does leave us at a major disadvantage.

Another reason that people working in telesales have it so very difficult is that they usually have to be better prepared than a field salesperson does. I say that because the telesales environment is usually highly compressed. When a field salesperson closes the sale, it is usually as a result of two or three (or four or five or six) weeks' worth of work, and sometimes much more work than that. But while the payoff may—or may not—be higher, the telesales professional must close his or her sale typically in one or two or three telephone conversations. Sometimes the "sales cycle" is a single telephone call.

Another reason telesales is among the most difficult ways to sell for a living is that recognition and praise are a little harder to come by. This is another way of saying that the profession is fraught with stereotypes, and the task of selling for a living over the telephone often does not come with the same praise and recognition from friends, relatives, and even colleagues within the organization as the job of selling face-to-face does. I know a good many telesales professionals who sell highly specialized and very expensive technical solutions and who make a great deal of money doing so. What I find particularly interesting is that they always find ways to change the title of what they do for a living! They do not want to be confused with the "average" telesales representative. This is a stigma that makes the job more difficult. I will not even go into the social standing of those in this type of selling, and the media stereotypes that are perpetuated about them.

Probably one of the clearest indications telesales is a very difficult kind of selling is that people who sell in this environment hear more frequent—and harsher—*no* answers than just about anybody else who sells. If you set an appointment to meet with someone a week from now, and you walked in the door to talk to that person, it is very unlikely that he will look you in the face, ask you what the heck you are doing in his office, and order you out brusquely. But it is a very common occurrence, indeed an occupational hazard, for a telesales professional to be greeted with rudeness, obscenity, and hang-ups. In fact, for most people who sell over the phone, it is a very unusual day indeed when they do not encounter this demoralizing kind of response. As in any profession, of course, there are good telesales professionals and less skilled telesales professionals. Unfortunately, even those who do everything "right" and want to approach their jobs professionally are held accountable, within the first fifteen seconds of the conversation, for the perceived sins and shortcomings of all the others who have fumbled the assignment with that prospect over the past month or so.

Yet another reason that telesales is one of the most difficult kinds of selling is that telesales representatives are more closely observed by their managers. Whereas a successful field representative earns a certain measure of autonomy and is sometimes a beneficiary of the mindset that says "As long as you hit quota, I don't care how you spend your day," there are very few telesales representatives for whom this is the coaching model. (Whether or not this hands-off approach is a workable coaching model, of course, is another subject.) The fact remains that, whereas field representatives do not have the prospect of their sales visits being recorded and reviewed, or the number of discussions that they initiate evaluated from a computer bank, telesales professionals do. Whether this is a good thing or a bad thing is not at issue here. I am simply pointing out that this can be an added stress in the position, and that many telesales representatives are monitored by inept managers.

One special set of challenges makes telesales difficult for certain categories of telesales professionals, in particular those involved in the inbound sales process. Whereas outbound telesales people make calls to people on a more or less restricted basis, there is a time management challenge that is unique to people whose job is exclusively related to inbound selling, namely, that their daily workflow experience hits peaks and valleys. In other words, there are periods of intense activity and periods of dormant activity, when the phone is not ringing, and the question of how to manage and balance these cycles is sometimes poorly addressed by managers.

Last but not least, among the reasons contributing to the fact that telesales is a difficult way to make a living, and a difficult environment in which to upsell, is the fact that, as a general rule, compensation schemes tend to be lower—indeed, significantly lower—for the telesales professionals than for other people who sell for a living. This adds to the stress of the job and makes burnout and high turnover rates more likely.

All of these stresses affect the job of upselling in a predictable way. They make it much more difficult.

Monitoring Your Numbers

There is another reason telesales is a difficult job, but this one has to do with numbers and it is completely within our control. Most telesales teams that I know of do not monitor their numbers in any meaningful way. I will tell you a secret about my training program. There is nothing that is easier to implement, and more likely to generate a measurable increase in sales, than the act of getting your team to measure their own numbers. Mind you, I am not talking about instituting some Orwellian scheme under which the managers spy on the salespeople and compile numbers independent from them. What I am talking about is changing the culture in such a way as to make the salespeople in any telesales team—or, indeed, in any selling team—conclude, of their own accord, that it makes sense for them to monitor their own numbers because they will make more money if they do.

Take a look at the following graphic.

INBOUND SALES NUMBERS

proposals/ discussions	initial interviews	upsell presentations	sales	attempts	upsells
100	81	74	40	11	1

Notice that these are numbers for an inbound selling team, and that the numbers in question are for one sales rep. Monitoring inbound phone sales numbers is a good illustration, because it is in an inbound selling environment that we are also asked to upsell to the prospective customer who has called in to us. So, think of the following numbers as though they were someone answering the telephone at a call center, perhaps in response to an infomercial advertising exercising equipment. The total number of sales would be one figure; the total number of upsales, namely, a subscription to a company's fitness magazine, might be another.

In this figure, we have 100 total discussions during the course of a day, and 81 interviews. By interview, I mean an intelligent discussion with the person making the decision about whether or not to buy from us. This is a point at which we ask a key question that will help us to both gauge the person's interest and engage the other person in a conversation. Of course, as we pose questions, we are gathering information.

Those eighty-one interviews led to seventy-four proposals or presentations. That is to say, out of those eighty-one interviews, there were seventy-four times when the discussion led to a direct recommendation to buy the exercise equipment.

Of those seventy-four proposals, forty turned into sales. So a little more than half of the time, the inquiry about the exercise equipment turned into sales for us. Now watch what happens.

We make eleven upselling attempts in this scenario. Of those eleven upsell attempts, we find that one turns into an actual subscription. The point is that sales is a numerically driven process, built around the concept of *ratios*. Again, these activity totals don't exist in a vacuum—they relate to one another, and their relationships are something we can measure.

That is true in the inbound selling environment, and it is also true for outbound sales as well. Take a look at the following graphic:

OUTBOUND SALES NUMBERS

call attempts	discussions	interviews	proposals/ presentations	initial sales	upsell attempts	upsells
181	100	81	74	40	11	1

Notice that the outbound call process starts with one column to the left of the "discussions" box, which adds another element to the equation. In this case, we might make, say, 181 calls in order to generate those 100 discussions.

My point is not that these numbers are right or wrong. My point is that they are interrelated. I do not know if forty sales is a good number for you or a bad number for you. All I know is, it takes seventy-four presentations or proposals to generate those forty initial sales. And I know, too, based on our scenario, that of those forty initial sales, we are making only eleven upsell attempts and, by the same token, we are closing only one sale for the magazine subscription. So, here is my question: How could we increase the total number of upsells?

If you spend any time at all looking at the numbers, you will realize where the opportunity lies. We look at the chart again, notice that we have closed forty initial sales, and we have made only eleven upsell attempts. Of those eleven, we closed one. Why on earth would we not make forty attempts to match the forty sales that we closed? If we did that, the ratio of our upsell attempts, one to eleven, would almost certainly stay in the same ballpark. Let's assume it stays exactly the same. Simply by asking the twenty-nine additional people about an upsell opportunity, we could add two and perhaps three additional upsells to our day . . . and increase our income measurably. How long would it take to close off *each* additional conversation with the same request about whether the person would like to subscribe to the fitness magazine?

Notice I am not asking at this point what form that request should take, only whether it makes sense to ask it at the end of every conversation in which we actually sell something. I hope you can see through this simple illustration that, in this case, it definitely does make sense to ask forty, not eleven, people whether they want to buy a subscription to our fitness magazine.

What Telesales Numbers Mean

LET'S THINK FOR A MOMENT about what the numbers you just looked at could really mean to your career.

Imagine how they could change your relationship with your supervisor. Instead of offering vague advice like "you must do better" or "you have to close more sales," which only makes salespeople frustrated, imagine what would happen if you were able to track the total number of:

- Calls
- Sales interviews
- Initial presentations/pitches/recommendations
- Initial closed sales
- Upsell attempts
- Upsells

. . . and then strategize the improvements *you* wanted to see in your performance!

It's not enough for a manager simply to say, "You have to do better." It's not even enough for a salesperson to say to him- or herself, "I have to do better." Instead, we have to be willing to ask ourselves, exactly how many discussions with people does it take for me to reach my goal for a given day?

When we ask ourselves a question like "Exactly how many discussions with people does it take for me to reach my goal for a given day?" that presumes that we have a goal for that day. Where did that goal come from? Well, ideally, it comes from our own income goal for our own lifestyle. In other words, our activity is directly related to our daily routine, and it's that daily routine that delivers our income, and it is in turn that income that will determine our lifestyle.

Nobody disagrees with me when I make these points in the abstract, but making them specific is sometimes a bit of a challenge. Often, when I talk to a telesales group, I might say, "How many inbound calls did you take yesterday?" or "How many outbound calls did you make yesterday?"

Very often, they simply won't know how many dials or discussions they took part in just twenty-four hours earlier. If you think about it, that's really amazing. We live in an era where people know their Social Security number, the mileage on their car, their telephone number, even the batting average of the guy who just made the All-Star team. But they don't know how many dials or conversations they had yesterday with the people who will end up paying their salary!

It's a critical question because so many of the salespeople I work with are dissatisfied with their income. In other words, they want their income level to match a certain expectation, and they're not sure why it doesn't. Well, the income is determined by the activity, and if you don't know what the activity is, you're not in a great position to change it for the better!

So here's the critical question: What is the total number of dials you should make? When I ask our participants in the sales training programs what their total number of dials is, I usually get a quizzical look and then perhaps a guess: "I don't know . . . six?" As though I know the answer and they don't.

I'll continue bravely and say, "Okay, let's assume it's six. Why that number?"

And again, the person stares at me as though I were asking him or her to recite the Magna Carta.

If someone were to ask me why I make my fifteen dials each and every day, I would know the answer to that question. I wouldn't stare back as though I were being interrogated by some surrealistic figure in a bad dream. I would have the answer. I make those fifteen dials every day *in order to* generate the seven discussions and the eight meetings every week. I generate the eight meetings every week *in order to* close one sale per week. I close the one sale per week *in order to* have fifty sales over the course of the year. And I want those fifty sales because that's my lifestyle number. That matches my income goal. I know for a fact that my activity is related to my performance.

So notice that, in my case, I have a series of ratios that affect the total income I eventually earn. *Dials, conversations, appointments, and sales.*

Now look again at that graphic that outlines the ratios of the inbound total sales performer. Those are ratios, too. We have a total number of calls, which relates to the number of sales discussions that arise. We have a total number of presentations or recommendations, which arises out of those sales discussions. We have a total number of closed sales, which is intimately related to the number of presentations we make. We have a total number of upsell attempts, which connects to the closed sales, and a total number of upsells that we actually close.

These numbers all connect! And no, you can't simply expect your sales manager to track them for you. *You* have to track them for yourself, because it's *your* lifestyle that the numbers will determine!

You can't simply set a quota for the final element without setting a quota for the first element! Too many sales managers and salespeople focus only on the result—and not on the cause that will deliver their results.

The Outbound Side

We've seen what the ratios look like for inbound calls. What do they look like for outbound calls?

In this case, we want to track the total number of:

- Dials
- Completed calls
- Presentations, pitches, and recommendations
- Closed sales
- Upsells

In the outbound sales environment, upselling can happen in a couple of different ways. We can close the sale and sell our exercise equipment during the call, and then follow up immediately with a request or a suggestion that the person buy a subscription to our magazine. Or, we can follow up at a later point in time and suggest that the person consider subscribing to the magazine.

45 The Dynamics of the Call

LET'S LOOK AT THE DYNAMICS under which the inbound and outbound calls unfold. They are actually quite different—but they are both focused on the task of developing a conversation that will enable us to gather the information we need to help the other person better *do* what he or she does.

The reason that they are so different is that the mindset of the people whom we are talking to in the telesales situation is different.

Let's look at the inbound telesales call first. You're the caller; I'm the salesperson. In an inbound sale, you have perhaps seen a promotional piece or an infomercial, heard about my company from a friend, or had some other source of information that led you to me. So, you pick up the telephone and you call. Usually, you will be calling with a very specific purpose in mind. In many selling situations, the person who makes the inbound call will be trying to track down a quote or get an idea of the general price range for a certain product or service. In other words, they may not be ready to buy.

However, even if the person is not eager or willing to buy from us, he or she did initiate the call—and that makes a world of difference when it comes to strategizing the call from the salesperson's perspective. There are two critical points in the inbound selling model. Take a look at the steps in this model of a successful inbound sale:

1. Greeting/Hello
2. *Critical Point #1:* Segue to information-gathering phase
3. Interviewing or Information Gathering
4. *Critical Point #2:* Verification of information to close on presentation
5. Presentation or Plan
6. Close

Notice that the call opens with a greeting or some form of saying hello. After that, the first critical point is that we segue to the *information-gathering phase* of the call. We want to move out of the initial pleasantry phase and into the portion of the call where we are determining what is happening in the other person's world. So, the transition out of the first element and into the second one is extremely important. The inbound call will usually stand or fall on the person's ability to make this transition.

The second critical point is the *verification phase.* This is where we confirm what we have learned about the other person and try to get the facts straight so that we can build our presentation around it. I should point out here that this presentation may take place during this call or during a subsequent call, but regardless of how many telephone conversations it takes for me to get to that point, I do have to verify my information if I want to have a chance to close the sale. You see that the presentation itself follows the verification, and the closing element follows that.

So you can see the two most critical elements of that call are the point at which we are able to move the person out of his or her immediate questions or opening pleasantries, and into the information phase—and then whether we are able to confirm that the information that we have gotten really does reflect something that is happening in the other person's world.

The outbound call is quite different. In this situation, the other person is not expecting our call. In fact, he or she is doing something else entirely.

It will come as no surprise to you, I am sure, that the person we are calling not only does not expect the call, but even has a negative response all ready for us when we make it. In other words, we call our prospect at 11:30 in the morning, and he is preparing for a big meeting that he has to attend at 12:00. Guess what? Talking to us about our widget is the last thing on his mind. So this call has a different first critical point—it's the part where the person we're calling tells us, in one way or another, that he's really not interested in pursuing the conversation. Take a look at the steps in the outbound sales model:

1. Greeting/Hello
2. *Critical Point #1:* Getting past initial negative response
3. Interviewing or Information Gathering
4. *Critical Point #2:* Verifying of information to close on presentation
5. Presentation or Plan
6. Close

As we've discussed in the Cold Calling section of this book, that initial negative response is virtually always waiting for us when we place an outbound telesales call. It does not matter whether our widgets are the best thing on the planet, our price is the most competitive, or even whether the person has just been given the formal responsibility to track down widgets for the organization. The urge to get ready for that meeting (or to do whatever the person was doing before we called) means we are going to hear the negative response.

The response is typically something along the lines of "I'm not interested" or "I don't have time for this."

It is not a reasoned, intellectual response to what we've said. It is more like a knee-jerk response.

So, getting past that initial response is obviously the very first critical point here. If we do not find some way to turn that response around and develop some kind of conversation, nothing is going to happen during this call.

The second critical point is the same as in the inbound. In this situation, we also want to verify the information so we can close our presentation.

At this point, I want to challenge you to think of these two models as the means by which we can get to a basic or simple sale. In other words, think about these two models, with their two critical points, as the work that you need to do to get on the other person's radar screen and turn him or her from a prospect into a customer.

To do this, we'll use a calling approach, which might sound like the following in the inbound environment:

Greeting/ID self and company: "Thank you for calling ABC Widget."

Get basic information from caller: "Can I get your name and phone number, please? *(Gets this information.)* Thank you!" "And could I take down your address, too?"

"Great! And what can I do for you today?"

Transition to information gathering (What has CHANGED in the person's world?): "By the way, can I ask you what made you decide to call us today?"

And here's what the approach might look like in the outbound mode:

Attention statement: "Hi, Mr. Jones."

ID self and company: "This is Brian Marks from ABC Company. I'm not sure if you're familiar with us—we're the biggest supplier of widgets on the East Coast."

Reason for the call, built around a BENEFIT: "The reason I'm calling you specifically today is that we've been working with a lot of (homeowners/your counterparts in the _____ industry/companies in the _____ area) to help them reduce their widget expenses."

Transition to information gathering: "Just out of curiosity, what are you doing now to maintain your widgets?"

And we'll prepare and practice a turnaround, which might sound like this:

> *Turnaround:* "You know, some of our best customers told us that before they saw how we could improve their bottom line. Just out of curiosity, have you ever worked with a widget reconditioning service before? *(Any response.)* I see . . . well, that's why we really should be talking, because we've helped a lot of people in your situation. Would it help if I told you a little bit about what we do?" *(An extremely brief ten- to thirty-second commercial follows, permitting you to pose another question and continue gathering information.)*

Then we'll interview for information, using do-based questions. We'll replay what we've learned, and we'll verify our information. Then, God willing, we'll close the sale by saying, "Gee, based on what you're telling me, this really makes sense to me. What do you think?"

The question for us then is, how do we get the person to buy more?

"By the Way"

Three simple words will not only help you upsell, but will also help you to manage *all* the transitions you just saw in those two sales models, the inbound and the outbound. The words are: *"By the way . . ."*

There is a variation on this phrase that is almost as effective. It sounds like this: *"Just out of curiosity . . ."*

These are known as transitional phrases, and you should practice using them until they become second nature. Let's see how the phrases can help you to manage these four critical points in the telesales dialogue.

Take the inbound call first. You will remember what I said earlier in the book. Let's reinforce a key point here, namely, that information is what makes effective selling possible. If I do not have the right information, then I am not going to be able to connect with this person on anything more than a superficial level. If I do not have the right information, I can expect to get only the sales that "drop into your lap"—the sales that were going to happen anyway. My skill as a salesperson will not come into play when it comes to my developing a relationship with this prospect.

So, what is the most important piece of information that I want to find out about the person who is placing the inbound call to me or my company? Take a moment and think about the answer to that question. Please do not move on until you have come up with an answer.

What You Need to Find Out

Did you actually come up with an answer . . . or did you simply keep reading? You will only get the most out of this book if you make a conscious decision to *change what isn't working and replace it with something that does work.* So you should, at the very least, identify what you're trying to find out from people over the telephone right now, and compare it with what I'm going to suggest that you try to find out from this point forward.

Pretend I'm the telesales representative, and I'm taking an inbound call. My information-gathering priority is *finding out what made the person decide to call me in the first place.*

This is an extremely important principle, one that I hope you will build into each and every calling day.

"By the way, what made you decide to call us today?"

"By the way, can I ask how you heard about us?"

Or, if the person "knows" he "needs" widgets:

"Just out of curiosity, what made you decide you needed to order widgets?"

Or:

"Just out of curiosity, what made you choose to call us about this?"

By identifying exactly what made the person decide to get in touch with us, we do a couple of very important things. We start to uncover what's going on in the other person's world, and we make it clear that our job as a salesperson is to find out about the other person.

The caller could say to me that his equipment just broke down, or that his sales force has just had a huge increase in quarterly sales targets. He could say to me that he is pricing a number of different vendors in order to arrange for a presentation to his own CEO. He could tell me that his standard training vendor has canceled unexpectedly, and he is looking for a replacement for this Monday morning at 8:30. These are all very different situations.

Whatever the answer that comes back to me sounds like, I am going to find some way to place it in the context of what my organization has done before. So, if the person is calling because the sales training company backed out at the last minute, I can share a number of stories that illustrate how we have been able to come through in similar situations for some of our clients. We have found many ways to build long-term relationships with such "accidental" customers.

Look at it again:

"Just out of curiosity, what made you decide to get in contact with us today?"

You must—repeat, *must*—ask the other person at some point very early in the conversation *exactly what prompted his or her call.*

It really is imperative that you make an effort to learn what made an inbound caller decide to get in touch with your organization. If you are a telesales professional and you're hoping to use this book to improve your selling numbers, rest assured that this one simple step is the single most important piece of advice you're going to get on this subject. If you do this, you *will* gather more and better information, and you'll be in a great position to improve your telesales numbers.

The *mindset* you bring to this undertaking is all-important. If you believe you are constrained by the requirements of your manager, your script, your employer, the economy, or any other force outside yourself, you will have already lost most of the battle. The trick is to take whatever structure you're working under and *turn it toward* the task of learning what has changed in this person's life.

Sometimes I will work with salespeople who say, "Steve, I'd like to ask why the person decided to call us—what's different in his or her world, what made him decide to call me rather than go bowling or something. You're right. I should know that. But my hands are tied! They give me a script, and I have to follow it. When I answer the phone, I have to say the words, 'Hi, this is Jim Miller, thank you for calling ABC Company. How can I help you?'"

I always tell them, "Fine . . . so go ahead and say that. But then, at the very first opportunity, once you have found a way to deliver the opening portion the way you are supposed to, you should also find a way to get to the bottom of a very basic human question: How come you did this? Why did you decide to get in touch with us? What prompted your call?"

There are probably a dozen different ways you could phrase this all-important question. In the final analysis, it really does not matter how it is phrased, as long as it is phrased, and as long as it is comfortable for you. I have used the two phrases "by the way" and "just out of curiosity" in this book because these phrases have been proven to deliver good results for most of the people we train.

In case you had not noticed, the opening question, "What made you decide to call us today?" is, in fact, a relatively simple transition out of the opening portion of the call and into the information-gathering phase. We are asking an intelligent question about what the person does, and we are going to continue asking intelligent questions to follow up on our query about what made the person decide to call. As a result, we are going to be working from a much better platform when the time comes to upsell. We're going to have developed much more meaningful information than will the salesperson who doesn't know what has recently changed in the prospect's world.

(By the way, the turnaround strategies that we discussed in the Cold Calling section of the book are just as helpful in the tele-sales environment. The only difference is that, instead of redirecting toward a face-to-face meeting, the turnarounds typically point toward a "do"-based question about the other person's situation.)

Gathering and Verifying Information

You've seen how you can use the simple "by the way" or just "I'm just curious" phrases to get past the initial response, to develop a meaningful conversation, and to start moving into the information-gathering process. You can also use these phrases to verify your information. It might sound like this:

> "So what I'm getting from you is that A, B, and C, are important to you. By the way, a lot of our clients think D is important as well. Is that an issue for you, or have we covered everything with A, B, and C?"

This is a classic verification question, one that is likely to be used in a telesales call where the sales process is relatively short. We are just replaying what we have learned from the conversation and then adding that, by the way, the person's counterpart at such and such an organization or such and such an industry has experienced some other element as well. Does what the counterpart experienced match what the prospect has experienced, or do we need any more information?

Obviously, in more complex sales, the verification process can go into considerably more depth. I have worked in industries where the selling cycle is a year and a half to two years long! In those situations, verification becomes an extremely important and lengthy part of the sales process that usually involves several salespeople and technical experts at the same time.

The point is that you cannot simply move forward to offer your presentation until *you have confirmed or verified your information.* If that means the conversation continues for a while, so be it! Go into as much depth as you can with the customer. As long as you're uncovering relevant information, and the person is invested, as you are, in the process of moving the sale forward, keep asking questions and verifying what you've learned. Remember, you are supposed to do 75 percent of your work before you make a formal recommendation or suggest a specific plan.

WE CAN ALSO USE THE "BY THE WAY" PHRASE as a strategy for upselling during the call. And it is this use of the phrase that we must be absolutely certain to turn into a habit—because it is only by making a regular habit of what I call the "by the way" upsell strategy, that we can make significant improvement in our numbers.

If we only know that we *should* ask for additional business, but fail to do so, we're wasting our time and our company's investment in us as salespeople!

Let's say that the person has agreed to purchase the exercise equipment from us that we wanted to talk about. This can happen both as a result of an inbound call to us, or as a result of our call to the person, based on his or her having called us in the past or sent in a request of some kind. In any event, assume we have closed the sale by gathering the right information, verifying it, and then saying something along the lines of, "It makes sense to me—what do you think?"

So, at this point, the person is going to purchase our (for instance) exercise equipment. He or she has given us the credit card information and has confirmed all of the details for the order.

Before we close out the call, however, it is very important for us to make some kind of an upselling attempt, assuming that is something that is supported by our product or service offering. Usually it is.

Here, in my perfect world, is what that upselling effort sounds like. Notice how simple it is!

> "By the way, Mrs. Jones, we have a special on today for people who order the Power Riser Ab Cruncher exercise unit. If you wanted to, you could get our award-winning magazine, *Abs on Parade*, for just $9.95 today—it's usually $19.95. Should I put you down for that?"

Notice that the phrase "by the way" inoculates us against any sensation that we may be pressuring the person too much. If used properly, this phrase makes everything we say sound conversational and relevant to the person's situation. We are not pressuring, we are not pushing, we are just mentioning something of interest. By the way, we also have this special on.

If you are not comfortable with "by the way," or you are already using it and do not want to keep repeating it over and over, you could say something like this:

> "Just out of curiosity, Mr. Jones, we do have a special on today for people who order the unit that you have asked to have delivered. Our award-winning magazine, *Abs on Parade*, usually costs $19.95, but because you ordered the unit from us today, you would be able to get it for half off, only $9.95. The magazine shows you a lot of advanced exercises you can use in developing your muscles. Should I go ahead and lock in that low rate for you?"

Remember—if you don't ask, you don't sell!

Similar to the "by the way" opening, the "just out of curiosity" opening makes the upsell sound casual and conversational. The tone is just as important as the words you say. Keep it light, keep it human, keep it personal—and do not close the call without offering some variation on the phrases "by the way" or "just out of curiosity" in reference to an upselling offer that your company extends.

Two Basic Telesales Philosophies

In telesales, there are two basic selling philosophies. It is up to us to choose which one is right for our market situation. If we choose the wrong philosophy for the situation in which we find ourselves selling, we have only ourselves to blame.

- Philosophy #1: *Speak to as many different people as possible.*
- Philosophy #2: *Spend as much time with each person as possible.*

This is an extremely important, but typically overlooked, point about selling on the phone. Your telesales approach must reflect the right philosophy!

Identify which basic approach is more likely to lead to success in your business situation.

Here is the key question: How much information do you need?

If you need a large amount of information, you may need to spend as much time with each person as possible—and make plenty of follow-through calls to check in on the person's status, gather and confirm new information, and make additional "by the way" upselling appeals, based on your relationship with that specific customer.

If, on the other hand, you need a comparatively small amount of information, you will probably want to pile up as many contacts as possible, and probably make your upselling attempt at the conclusion of the call that terminates in a sale.

It is *your* job, as a telesales professional, to determine which philosophy is right for you.

Send the Right Message

For me, selling over the phone is basically built around an individual salesperson's creativity *and* the words "by the way. . . ."

We have already gotten something going with the person, and we know that we have that business. Before we imagine that the relationship is complete, we take advantage of the fact that we have built up a certain comfort level with the person, and we keep that casual tone going by saying, "By the way, we have this other thing you might be interested in. . . ." And we build the conversation creatively from there.

I want to share with you a few additional theories and concepts about upselling in the telesales environment. These are some concepts that will, I think, help you as you work to develop and expand your relationships with prospective customers.

First and foremost, remember that the *emotional tone* you set in the first few seconds of the call is extremely important to your upselling efforts. What you say—and how you say it—will have a tremendous positive or negative effect on the rapport you are able to build with your contact. So, be absolutely sure you do not sound as though you wish you were someplace else while making your calls.

Instead, send the message, both with words and in tonality, that you are having a great day, that you love what you do for a living, that any job worth doing is worth doing well, and that you are capable of taking good care of people that come into your life. These are all important messages that can be "said" in the very first few moments, indeed the first few seconds of your call. I have had calls with telesales professionals who communicated all these positive messages simply by means of a single word—*hello*—and saying their name. If you say your name with pride, with energy, and with optimism, you will go a long way toward establishing rapport with your prospective customer.

In addition, I believe you should identify, and become comfortable discussing, at least ten relevant success stories: These are important because you need to be able to give examples of how what your company does has benefited other people. Consider ten as a bare minimum. Learn them, become conversant with their details, and be ready to share their specifics—with enthusiasm—at a moment's notice.

Finally, be willing to use appropriate humor to lighten the mood of the call: it is possible to turn a difficult call around if you know how to use self-deprecating humor. If you can keep your poise and laugh your way through an awkward moment, you will be well on your way to establishing the one-on-one vocal rapport that makes selling—and upselling—over the phone possible.

Part Five

E-Mail Selling Strategies

A Tale of Two E-Mails

ONCE UPON A TIME there were two e-mail messages. The first looked like this:

Subject: Our implementation notes and related items

Good morning Mr. Miller:

I am Mike Conway, Senior Sales Associate for ABC Interactive Media, located here in New York City. I would like to have the opportunity to share with you some notes on assessment and implementation that we have assembled by means of a careful review of the existing prospective customer base that overlaps with your industry, a copy of which list is available in a variety of different formats for your review. We understand that you are a major manufacturer of widgets, and we wish to make you aware that we have a significant number of widget plants and widget-related businesses on our current customer list, all of whom have come to rely on us for widget retooling services. (One of these is Century Manufacturing, a supplier of yours whose operations manager, Ken Steiner, suggested that I give you a call.) You will find more information on this on our company's Web site, *www .retooler.org*, which is accessible and fully functional via both Microsoft Outlook and Mozilla Firefox. To access the list of companies with whom we have worked, simply access the site and click on the function bar that reads "client list," then work your way through the first fifteen categories until you reach the sixteenth one, which reads "Widget companies with whom we have worked." At that point, you will be able to click the icon and access the names of the firms in question. These, just to clarify, are the firms I wish to discuss with you in person. May I ask that you phone me as soon as possible at 606-555-5555 to discuss the possibility of our evaluating this list together?

Yours very sincerely,

Mike Conway

P.S. I would like to assure you that our client references are of the highest possible quality and that I can give you my personal assurance that you will not be disappointed by a decision to contact me by telephone, which I hope you will do at your earliest possible convenience.

Here's what the second e-mail message looked like:

Subject: Ken Steiner

Ken, as you know, works for Century Manufacturing, one of our clients; he suggested that you and I meet to discuss your widget retooling plans for the coming year.

Could we meet this coming Tuesday at 2:00 p.m. at your office?

Sincerely,

Mike Conway
www.retooler.org
978-555-0555 (office)
978-555-5550 (cell)
978-555-5050 (home)

Which e-mail message would you be more likely to read? Which e-mail message would you be most likely to respond to? If you were the CEO, which e-mail message would you be more likely to forward to your administrative assistants with the note "Set up a meeting with this guy"?

E-Mail and the New Sales Culture

E-mail has made it easier for salespeople to communicate than ever before. That's both a good thing and a bad thing.

It's a good thing because I, a salesperson just like you, can now contact virtually anyone in the world. For the first time in history, I can reach out to a prospect or customer and send that person a message that reaches them in just a few seconds.

It's a bad thing because I can also *screw up* that conversation in a millisecond.

The new sales culture, at least where e-mail is concerned, is one that is all too often based on instant actions, on rambling away, hitting "send," and seeing what happens next.

In the case of the two e-mails you just read, hitting "send" in the first example is a great way to make sure the person never opens another of your messages for the rest of his life. (I'll go further—it's a great way to make sure the person never even takes your call—assuming that he remembers your name from the long e-mail that you sent.)

By the way, did you notice how the one piece of information that the reader might conceivably have a positive reaction to—Ken Steiner—was buried in the middle of the message, where it was least likely to be read by a busy executive?

Notice, though, that in the second e-mail, that single piece of relevant information was in the subject line . . . the very first thing our executive (or whoever is screening his incoming e-mail) would be likely to see. Notice, too, that the second message didn't take all day to answer the reader's unspoken question ("What the heck do you want?").

Our sales culture may be priming us to hit "send" to as many prospects and customers as possible . . . but if our job is selling, we have a duty to increase the odds that the people we're trying to communicate with will actually open, read, and take action on the e-mail messages we send. If they do that, we will accelerate our sales process.

Way Back When

WHEN I FIRST STARTED OUT as a professional salesperson, more years ago than I care to remember, there was not only no such thing as e-mail—there was no such thing as a personal computer.

You could pretty much count on every piece of communication falling into one of two categories: People were either talking to you face to face, or they *weren't* talking to you face to face.

Nowadays, they may well talk to you face to face once, then conduct the rest of the relationship by means of e-mail messages and conference calls.

You're used to that. And I'm used to that. Now. Back in the 1970s, though, most of the important interaction would come about as a result of these quaint things we used to call "meetings." That's an old, out-of-date term, I know—let me define it for you. By "meetings," I mean situations where you and the prospect or customer could sit down, face to face, and talk things over. With *nothing else going on in the background.*

A wild idea, I know, but believe it or not, that's actually how we used to do business. People would say, "Hey, I'm going into a meeting, hold my calls, please." And then they would walk, with the salesperson, into a room without (gasp) any access to the Internet whatsoever! And then, having ushered the salesperson to his or her seat, the person you were talking to that day would actually stride over to the door, *close it*, and focus on you, and only you, for 30, 60, 90, sometimes even 120 straight minutes!

Yes, that was how it was back in the covered-wagon days of the Carter administration. It's a little embarrassing to admit that I was in fact alive back then, but the truth is, I was.

Meetings are still the lifeblood of the field sales force. They are not important for people who sell over the telephone, of course, but for those of use who still sell face to face, the advent of e-mail has profoundly changed the dynamic of the selling relationship. In some ways, it's made it much more difficult for us to sell in 2007 than it was for us to sell in 1977.

How, specifically? (That's not a hypothetical question. I'd really like to ask you to think of your best answer before moving on to the next section.)

The Information Equation

I just asked you how, specifically, the selling job is likely to be more difficult in 2007 than it was in 1977. I hope you came up with an answer of your own. Here's my answer. Compare it to yours and see how close we are.

Back in 1977, if you bought from me, you and I had a series of face-to-face meetings where I was pretty much the only thing happening in your world for a half-hour or so at a time.

In the twenty-first century, if you buy from me, I'm lucky if I get any one-on-one time with you, and during our (brief) face-to-face encounters, there are usually a whole lot of other things happening.

SCENARIO A: In 1977, I would ask you for a meeting, and you would either meet with me or you wouldn't. If you did, we would meet face to face, I would suggest another meeting, and you would either give me that one or not, and then eventually I would close the deal with you—perhaps after three or four face-to-face sessions.

SCENARIO B: Nowadays the cycle (in some industries, at least) might very well look like this:

- You e-mail me a message based on something you saw on my Web site.
- I e-mail you back asking for your telephone number so we can chat further.
- You e-mail me the telephone number and let me know the best time to reach you.
- I pick up the telephone and call you but reach, not you, but your voice mail system. (There is another piece of technology that was not around when I first started selling. But I digress.)
- You return my call and we actually speak, voice-to-voice. (Note that this is the point at which the relationship might have actually begun thirty years ago.)
- We agree to meet a week from now on Tuesday at 2:00.
- We do in fact meet face to face for the first time, and we have a good discussion about how we might be able to work together. I ask you for another meeting, and you agree that we should talk again—but this time it should be a conference call, one that involves your boss (who operates out of another city) and a member of your technical team.
- We set the date and time for that conference call.
- I try to confirm the conference call by sending everyone an e-mail message a few days before we are scheduled to "meet"—on the telephone.
- You and the others acknowledge receipt of your e-mail message. But there's a scheduling problem.
- We set up another time that works for everyone.
- I confirm the date and time of the conference call once again, and this time everyone's schedule is in agreement.
- We have the conference call, and we all discuss how we might be able to work together. You agree that it sounds good, and you ask me to draw up a formal proposal. We set a date and time for another conference call.
- I work up the proposal.

- I confirm the date and time of the conference call.
- Once again, the date and time doesn't work, and we have to reschedule.
- I reconfirm the date and time of the conference call.
- This time it sticks, and everyone is on the call. I go over the proposal point by point, and you love it. You ask me to draw up a contract.

Obviously, there are big differences between Scenario A and Scenario B. The main disadvantage of Scenario B in comparison with Scenario A, though, is that I have much less time with anyone face to face.

That's an extremely important fact, and one that's potentially quite damaging to me, the salesperson, because of something I call *the Information Equation*.

The Information Equation sounds like this:

The quality of the information I, the salesperson, get from you, the prospect, tends to improve with the number and quality of our face-to-face interactions.

When I explain this Information Equation principle to salespeople during our training sessions, they instantly "get it," and my bet is that if you've been selling for more than six weeks or so, you "got it" quickly too.

When I (the salesperson) meet with you (the prospect) in person, not just once, but for a second or third or fourth time, the quality of the information you share with me tends to get better. It's a reliable principle. People really do share things with salespeople they have back in for another meeting that they don't share on the first meeting.

And guess what? The quality of the information gets even better if the meetings you agree to have with me take place in different venues. First, you let me sit down in your office. Then, a week later, you walk me through your factory. Then, a week after that, you introduce me to your boss and show me her office. What I learn from you on that third visit is, as a general rule, going to be more meaningful on that *third* face-to-face visit than the information I got on the very *first* face-to-face visit.

That's just a universal principle of human relations as it applies to the sales process. You may occasionally run into an exception, but I guarantee you that in *most* of the situations where you have meetings with people, the information improves with the number of face-to-face meetings you have.

Now look again at Scenario B above, and you will notice that *our business culture is moving away from face-to-face meetings, and toward remote meetings.*

This trend seems likely to continue, which means that if you do nothing and simply keep setting up conference calls as instructed, the quality of the information you get from your customers and prospects is going to decrease over time, and you're going to close less business.

In fact, if you're like most of the salespeople I train, you can very easily think of situations where you played Scenario B through for weeks or months on end . . . and then lost the business for mysterious reasons that only became clear after the fact. You know what happened? Someone else was getting meetings while you were settling for conference calls. Someone else was building relationships while you were reconfirming people's schedules.

So—what do we do about that?

Wishful Thinking

HERE'S WHAT WE DON'T DO. We don't spend all day writing e-mails designed to get us into more conference calls when we could be finding ways to get in front of more people face to face.

I wish I could tell you that the act of writing a better "let's have a conference call" e-mail message than your competition will, in and of itself, guarantee you a better relationship with, and better information from, your prospect.

But I can't.

If I were to tell you that, I would be engaging in wishful thinking, rather than strategic thinking. And wishful thinking, alas, is the one syndrome I have identified over the years that has inevitably led to failure among individual salespeople and organizations as a whole.

Here's what I can tell you. If you're smart, and if you implement the principles in this book, you can use e-mail more intelligently than your competition is currently using it, and thus get *more in-person meetings* and *accelerate your selling cycle*. In so doing, you will improve the quality of your relationship—and thus improve the quality of your information and your likelihood of closing the deal with people who keep moving forward through the sales process with you.

Ultimately, I think you should be using e-mail as a tool to establish momentum with people who could conceivably buy from you. And I'm going to warn you ahead of time, if your job is to sell face to face, you're going to get the best results if you use e-mail to uncover reasons to get face to face with your prospects and customers.

If you sell over the telephone, your goal is going to be to have as many good conversations as possible with your prospects. The best way to do this is to establish commitments for a "phone appointment," as in, "Yes, I will agree to talk to you again tomorrow at 2:00 P.M." You must, unfortunately, accept as a fact of life that someone who manages to establish a face-to-face relationship with your customer, while you can maintain only a voice-to-voice relationship, is very likely to steal the account away from you. In any event, most of what follows in this book about using e-mail to support the sales process will be very easy for you to adapt to the telesales world.

To understand what I'm talking about, you have to have a little bit of background on what can go wrong in the selling process. Let's look at that more closely right now.

50 Screwing Up the Sales Process

ONE OF THE INTERESTING THINGS about the twenty-first-century sales process pattern that I called "Scenario B" is that it features many more possible "touches" with our contacts than "Scenario A" did. It also exposes us to more people than "Scenario A" did.

I'm not saying those facts are good or bad in and of themselves, just that they're worth understanding. They're part of the new selling environment we all face today. If we understand that environment and act intelligently in response to it, we will prosper. If we don't, we won't prosper.

So: You want more "touches"—or at least the opportunity for more "touches"—and more contact with more people within the purchasing organization. By "touch" I mean something that I, the salesperson, do to remind you that (a) I exist, and (b) you and I have a relationship that could be beneficial to you.

Back when I first started selling, there were only three ways to "touch" a contact: mail the person something, call the person on the telephone, or meet with them in person.

Now we have this technology that makes it much, much easier to "touch" the person to whom we are trying to sell.

But notice that a meaningful "touch" only takes place *after* I have already established some kind of relationship with the person. In other words, it is no good fooling myself into thinking that I am "touching" a sales prospect, or improving the relationship in any way, if my pattern looks like the following sequence, which I'll call "Scenario C," or "The Scenario That Screws Up the Sales Process":

- I e-mail you and ask you for a meeting, even though you have never heard of me before.
- I e-mail you again the next day, asking why you did not reply to my earlier e-mail message.
- I e-mail you again on the third day asking what I have done wrong and why you would ignore so many messages in a row.
- I go on your Web site and find your telephone number.
- I reach out to you by telephone—for the very first time—and leave you a voice mail message asking if you have gotten my e-mails.
- A week after that, I e-mail you again, reminding you of all the messages you have been ignoring, and suggesting that you be so polite as to call me so that we can set up a meeting.
- The following day I repeat the request, under the pretext that you may have missed my earlier phone message.
- The day after that I send yet another e-mail message that includes the text of all my previous e-mail messages to you. I once again request that we have a face-to-face meeting.
- Three months go by. I don't contact you during that time. Amazingly, you don't reach out to me, either.
- After that three-month period has elapsed, I e-mail you again and ask once again for a face-to-face meeting. The process begins all over again.

Obviously, the "touch" in this sequence is very different from the "touch" in the sequence that resulted in you actually buying from me.

In Scenario C, *there is no relationship*. There is no buy-in, no connection, and certainly no conviction on your part that you will benefit in any way, shape, or form by granting me your (divided) attention for fifteen minutes.

Let's be realistic. In Scenario C, I do not even have any guarantee that you know that I exist—much less that you have read my messages. And considering the possibility that my e-mail messages may have been blocked by your company's mail system, there is really no way for me to be certain that you ever could have received my messages!

If I'm committed to Scenario C, complete with that telling three-month gap, I'm committed to either bugging you to death or ignoring you completely.

Truth in advertising disclosure: There is no e-mail strategy you can employ—nothing outlined in this book or in any other book— that can possibly overcome the damage you can do by making Scenario C your default selling routine.

Can you use e-mail to initiate a productive relationship with someone?

Sure.

Can you *obsess* with e-mail and thereby initiate a productive relationship with someone? Sorry, no.

Let me tell you a story that illustrates what I mean. There was a guy awhile back who stumbled across my company's Web site and "decided" that he was going to become my business partner. Did he call me (or e-mail me) to ask for a meeting so we could discuss this potentially huge step, in person? No. He blizzarded me with "ideas," day after day after day, as though the fact that he had my e-mail address meant he *already* had a business relationship with me. He didn't. I got every newsletter, every article, every quote, every media mention this person could muster. And I got literally dozens of personal e-mail messages from him. There was this massive wave of e-mail that I was supposed to read (or maybe memorize) based on . . . let's see . . . *nothing* that he and I had ever agreed to do together.

You know what my first reaction was when I heard that he was on the phone and wanted to talk to me?

"Not the crazy e-mail guy!"

You know what my reaction would have been if he had left a voice mail message on the same day, asking for a conference call with me, him, and one of his people?

"Not the crazy e-mail guy!"

You know what my answer is now if anyone, anywhere, asks me what I'm looking for in a business partner?

"Not the crazy e-mail guy!"

51 Relationship = Commitment

ANY MEANINGFUL BUSINESS RELATIONSHIP is built on the principle of commitment.

As salespeople, we get little commitments first—like "Yes, I'll agree to meet with you," or "Yes, I'll take your call on Tuesday at 8:00 A.M." And we build our way up to more meaningful commitments—like "Yes, I'll give you a tour of our plant," and "Yes, I'll introduce you to my boss."

Along the way we gather information, and if we're lucky, that information improves in quality and depth over time. Why? Because we've made suggestions about things we could do together that are

- *Perceived as helpful* to the other person
- *Easy for the other person to agree to*

I want to ask you to take a very close look at those two criteria. They're extremely important for anyone who actually wants to practice and implement e-mail selling techniques that really accelerate the sales process. (As opposed to e-mail selling techniques that constitute wishful thinking.)

Let's say I want to get a commitment from you to buy from me. I can't do that without the right information from your side. Agreed? The information you give me, if I do my job right, should improve in quality and depth as time passes.

Well, that will only happen if I suggest things to you that are (all together, now):

- Perceived by you as helpful
- Easy for you to agree to

If my suggestions meet those criteria, we may—*may*—end up doing business together.

If my suggestions don't meet those criteria, we definitely—*definitely*—will not end up doing business together.

You've just read the basic philosophy I'm going to ask you to apply, not only to all your e-mail messages with prospects and customers, but to all of your communications of any kind, and in any medium whatsoever, that involve prospects and customers.

No Magic Wand

Granted: E-mail really does give salespeople the opportunity to have more frequent, and more widely distributed, contact with more prospects and customers than I ever dreamed possible back in the mid-1970s. At the same time, e-mail is a trap.

It's a trap because we, as salespeople, are often sorely tempted to consider the medium of e-mail to be more of a "magic wand" than it actually is, or can be. We want to write some snazzy copy, wave the e-mail wand, hit "send," and make hordes of willing customers appear. To my mind, that's not selling, but rather order taking. And it's not what this book about.

E-mail is a tool for moving a relationship forward, and a very good tool. It is not the best tool for *initiating* a relationship, though it can serve this purpose occasionally. Not very often, though, in my experience. (When was the last time you actually built up a meaningful business relationship based on an e-mail you received from somebody you did not know?)

The vast majority of the blind e-mails that I get, I automatically delete. My guess is that you do the same. So it would be both dishonest and impractical, in my view, for us to pretend that blind e-mails are really the answer to the array of selling challenges that most field salespeople and telesales professionals face.

Sending out huge volumes of blind e-mail isn't the answer, and most salespeople I run into already understand this (even though some marketers have tried implementing the blind e-mail approach on a large scale).

The reality is this: e-mail is part of your tool kit. If you are incapable of communicating effectively with your prospects and customers by means of e-mail, you are probably not going to do very well as a professional salesperson in today's marketplace. These days, salespeople simply can't say, "I'm not comfortable using e-mail." It's a little bit like saying you don't feel comfortable talking with your prospects and customers on the telephone. If you were to say that, you would be granting a huge competitive advantage to everyone who competes against your company and goes to bed at night dreaming of turning *your* customers into *their* customers.

So in that sense we really are looking at a radically different selling environment. We can no longer say, "I'm just not good with computers; don't bother me about e-mail." But, at the same time, some salespeople are under the impression that they can e-mail their way *around* the task of making cold calls or networking at public events in order to generate leads. And I think that's just as big a mistake.

Believe me when I say that I know how tempting it is to believe that e-mail has rendered prospecting obsolete. After all, nobody really enjoys making cold calls, and we're always on the lookout for evidence that some technological advance has rendered obsolete something we really don't like to do. But the sad truth of the matter is that even superior, seasoned, experienced salespeople find themselves in an income crisis when they neglect prospecting for extensive periods of time. That was true in 1977. It's true in 2007. And I will bet you my fifty-dollar bill against any box of doughnuts you choose that it's going to be true in 2037.

So my first and overriding message to you is this one: Learn how to use e-mail to support your sales process—but do not expect e-mail to replace the prospecting that is a natural part of your sales process.

Mass E-Mail Ticks People Off

I MENTIONED A LITTLE EARLIER that attempting to use huge volumes of blind (that is, unsolicited) e-mail to create or initiate a relationship is a mistake.

Making this your central prospecting strategy might seem like a good idea at first. After all . . . the process seems simple and straightforward enough, doesn't it? Buy a blind list, write a message, blast 40,000 people at a time, wait for the fan mail and inquiries to come back.

In fact, there are a whole bunch of reasons for you *not* to do this.

The first and most important reason is that you are a professional salesperson, and a professional salesperson is, by definition, someone who is focused on the development of personal relationships. Making vast numbers of anonymous, remote, identical appeals is what a billboard does, not what a salesperson does.

I should say, too, that my personal experience indicates that mass e-mail *lengthens* your selling cycle rather than shortens it. It also *increases* the amount of time you have to spend doing boring, fundamentally unproductive things like dropping people's e-mail addresses from your list.

There is, in addition, one more great reason not to use mass e-mail as your primary strategy for developing new relationships with prospects. It is this: Doing this invariably gets a certain percentage of people really, really furious.

Now, don't misunderstand me. There are plenty of businesses built on the principle that it makes a whole lot of sense to send out thousands (or even millions) of unsolicited, unauthorized e-mail messages every single day. I'm not saying those companies don't exist. What I am saying, though, is that those businesses are, quite frequently, operating one step ahead of a pack of furious e-mail recipients—people who have gotten so sick and tired of (a) receiving stuff they didn't ask for, and (b) having to delete all that junk that they do things like call their senator, the Federal Trade Commission, and, for all I know, the Knights of Columbus in order to complain. Not surprisingly, a fair percentage of the businesses we are talking about are also operating one step ahead of the sheriff.

The federal government has passed important and far-reaching legislation that severely limits the nature of unsolicited e-mail that a business or a person representing a business—that is, *you*—can send out. The legislation is called CAN-SPAM, and its stated goal is to reduce the seemingly overwhelming tidal wave of unsolicited e-mail with which virtually everyone who uses a computer nowadays is already all too familiar.

Be honest. You yourself are no fan of the spam that you receive from people who try to sell you various prescription medications or car insurance deals, not to mention steamier or perhaps less ... ethical business propositions that may come your way by means of spam. Think, then, about how angry a prospective customer (or an actual client!) might be upon receiving a similarly unsolicited e-mail message from you or your company.

I will assume that you are reading this book because you want to do business responsibly, promote a positive image of your company, and create and sustain responsible business relationships that benefit both parties. Sending out waves of unsolicited e-mail is simply not the way to do any of these things.

What Makes E-Mail Different

THERE ARE LOTS OF WAYS THAT E-MAIL DIFFERS from other methods of communication, but the chief distinction I want you to bear in mind is that e-mail is, at its foundation, remarkably easy to ignore.

In fact, it is so easy to ignore that people routinely get in trouble for ignoring it!

The tide of e-mail we each have to do battle with these days is so vast and covers so many possible topics and is presented in so many different environments that we often miss extremely important e-mail messages from people we are striving mightily to impress!

Isn't that true in your world?

Think back on your own workplace relationships. At some point within the last year, haven't you accidentally overlooked a really critical e-mail that a customer, a prospect, your sales manager, the CEO of your company, or maybe even a member of your family sent along? Didn't you, at some point during the past year, have to make an excuse like the following: "I am so, so sorry I missed your e-mail—I was working on yada yada yada, and I did not notice that your message had come in. Please forgive me."

What about times when you even forgot to acknowledge a message from one of these important people that was marked *urgent* or had a red flag next to it? Has that ever happened? Ouch!

If you're like me, and the vast majority of people who write and read business e-mails, you have in fact missed important e-mails from customers, clients, or other important business allies . . . even though you did not mean to.

So what does this mean for us as salespeople? Well, for a start, it means that we should build in an assumption that a lot of our e-mail is going to go unread.

Yep. You read right. The odds are quite good that the person *will not* read your message. This is one reason that I am not a big proponent of spending hours and hours crafting the single most perfect e-mail message possible for somebody who does not yet know, or may not remember, that I exist. If this person may well, without meaning to, ignore a message from his mom, there is a decent chance that my message is going to get ignored, too. I'm not saying we should never send a message to such a person, mind you, only that we should recognize that sending it is, in basketball parlance, a low-percentage shot.

But there is another implication, one that I want to share with you here, that I think too many salespeople lose sight of:

We gain absolutely nothing by reminding people that they have missed or ignored our e-mail. And in fact we only do ourselves a disservice when we do this.

Top of the Mind

WHAT IS THE SINGLE MOST PRESSING QUESTION on your mind when you evaluate whether or not to open an e-mail message? If you're like me, that question is, "Do I really have to look at this?"

Now—why do we ask ourselves that question before we even open the message? For a very simple reason: You and I and everyone else in America with access to the Internet and an e-mail account are constantly struggling to keep track of a sea of e-mail messages, most of which are totally irrelevant to our world.

Our prospects and customers are in the same boat.

Even if we have the world's best spam filter, and even if we somehow manage to set our e-mail preferences in such a way as to prohibit messages from reaching us unless we actually know the person they're coming from, we are *still* likely to receive messages that have absolutely nothing whatsoever to do with us or our workday.

Why?

Because large numbers of people find it satisfying to "copy" just about everyone on earth with their own e-mail messages. Because the guiding principle in business communication today sounds something like this: When in doubt, copy somebody on the message. That seems to be the approach, doesn't it?

So between the commercial messages that we have absolutely no interest in and the latest update from the people in human resources on what they are having for lunch three weeks from now, we generally have far too much e-mail to keep track of . . . and too little time to keep track of it.

If that is an everyday reality for people in sales (and it is), we can rest assured that it is an everyday reality for the people you are trying to sell to. We have an overflowing inbox. So do our prospects and customers.

So, why do so many salespeople assume that this is not the case? Why do they write e-mail messages that assume that people have all day long to read what they want to pass along? Why do they assume that the person who is evaluating the message has been waiting breathlessly to receive the latest update on what has just happened in the salesperson's world?

Our job is to increase the odds that our e-mail does not get lost in the shuffle. To do that, we have to make certain that we are putting *only* relevant information in front of the other person.

That's the driving principle. Make sure the information we convey by e-mail to our prospects and suspects features *only* relevant information. (A "prospect" is someone who's actively playing ball with us; a "suspect" is someone we want to sell to who *isn't yet* playing ball with us.)

These days, salespeople ask me at just about every training event whether, and how, they should use e-mail as a prospecting tool. As you have no doubt gathered by now, my feeling is that, because most unfamiliar e-mail messages are ignored, e-mail is simply no replacement for prospecting by phone. Therefore, it shouldn't distract you from prospecting by phone.

Even so, e-mail may occasionally be useful for reaching out to specific contacts with whom you otherwise couldn't connect. Some people really will react more quickly to an e-mail message than they will to a telephone call. And they will react positively—if the message reaches them in the first place, if they open the message, if the message has meaning to their day, and if the message is perceived as helpful. If you do all of those things, the message will stand a decent chance of attaining what the marketing people call "top of the mind" awareness.

I believe that any e-mail you use to try to set up an initial meeting should be crafted in just the same way that the opening of a face-to-face sales meeting or discussion should be prepared: with skill, care, and foresight.

Let's look at some strategies for doing that now.

CHAPTER 55

Nine E-Mail Strategies for Accelerating the Selling Cycle

HERE ARE NINE WAYS to increase the odds that the e-mail prospecting message you send will accelerate your selling cycle.

1. **Choose a heading that gets you noticed.** In the subject line, try using a reference name, someone you can list as a referring party or someone they might know. Consider referencing a company that will be familiar to the reader, one that you have worked with in the past. You can then build your message around your work with that company.

2. **Get to the point.** The message should be no more than two to three sentences long. The shorter it is, the more likely it is to be understood and acted upon.

3. **Use the person's name in the body of the message.** Otherwise, he or she may assume that this is an e-mail that a thousand other people are receiving.

4. **Emphasize commonality.** If you can, point out that your company has been doing business

with other firms in this person's industry. Another way to emphasize commonality is to reference the name of someone you have in common, preferably in the subject line of the message.

5. **Don't try to sell.** Don't include long monologues about how great your company is. Say clearly that the reason for the e-mail message is to set up an appointment. Offer a specific time and date that you want to get together.

6. **Don't hound the person.** Send one message a week, maximum. If the person says she doesn't want to get any more e-mail messages, don't send any more messages.

7. **Don't make getting this particular individual to answer your message your life's work.** After three e-mail attempts, move on.

8. **Don't try to turn an appointment into a prolonged premeeting correspondence.** Once you have set the appointment, there is no need to turn the exchange into a protracted discussion. Send a polite, short message of thanks and confirmation and then show up at the appointed day and time.

9. **Include the name and the physical address of your company, as well as a way for the recipient not to receive unsolicited messages in the future.** This, as it happens, is a requirement by federal law.

56 Establishing the Relationship

OBVIOUSLY, I cannot just walk in the room for my first meeting with a prospect and start shooting off questions; the prospect and I have to establish some kind of a relationship.

There really must be some kind of give-and-take, eye-to-eye or voice-to-voice contact with the other person before we start imagining that we can move through the sales process and gather the information we need. So that is what our first step of the process is really all about, the opening of the relationship. This is where we are going to connect, do a little bit of building commonality and establishing some rapport with the other person. Obviously, we cannot gather any more information until we have actually done that.

So here is what we are looking at, the four-step sales process we first discussed in Chapter 4: the *Opening*, the *Information Stage*, the *Presentation Stage*, and the *Closing Stage*.

So what does all this have to do with e-mail? Well, the point is that once we make the effort and invest the time to sit down face to face with a person and open up the relationship, once we get to that first step, we can hasten the progress as we make our way through the other three steps by means of e-mail. We can stay on the person's radar screen, remind her or him of certain key points from previous conversations, even get the prospect involved in circulating our message to other important people in the organization, thus involving other players to help us expand our influence and access within the sale.

Once we have established the relationship, we can accelerate the sale, and e-mail is a good tool for doing that. The people we are talking to can help us move the sale forward more quickly because we can stay in contact with them not only through face-to-face and voice communications, but in a very direct way by means of tactful, nonharassing e-mail messages. I'm talking about e-mail messages that say, basically, "I'm still here, and we're still working together to make X happen for you."

This is basically e-mail selling by *staying on the radar screen.*

E-mail, in my experience, is not always a great tool for *getting* salespeople on the radar screen. (There are some ways you can use e-mail to get on the radar screen, but you can't build your whole prospecting strategy around e-mail.)

E-mail can be a superb tool for *staying* on the radar screen.

And, just as a reality check, we salespeople should acknowledge that a period of one-sided or noncommittal e-mail correspondence with someone may be a sign that we aren't quite as big a dot on the radar screen as we may imagine ourselves to be.

Fake Buying Signals

One thing I want you to watch out for is the possibility that information may come to you via e-mail that is in fact a fake buying signal masquerading as a real buying signal.

Why, you may ask, do we have to bear this in mind about e-mail messages in particular?

Because e-mail is, by definition, an inherently impersonal medium. If you're a salesperson, you will find that it is used by people who would rather communicate with you in a way that does not require any investment of time, effort, emotion, or energy whatsoever. The message from someone who doesn't really want to talk to you might look like this:

Subject: Fascinating

Bill, thanks for coming by today. You've given me a lot to think about. No problem if I bounce your idea off some of the people around here, I hope?

Thanks for taking all those notes. Please e-mail your proposal ASAP to my assistant Sandi *(Sandi@acme-org)* and I will call you back as soon as we get some consensus. Also, I forgot to mention to you that I'm off to England next Friday for a couple of months. Hope to be in touch when I get back.

Best to you and the kids,

Milt W. Stopcallingme

VP of Everything

I hope you have gathered, from my definition of "buying signal," that this kind of e-mail is a clear violation of the Next Step standard. You should call Milt before he gets on the plane to England and try to *set a date* for the two of you to review the proposal he's planning to circulate on your behalf.

All too often, e-mail messages are camouflaged so as to *look like* buying signals. Here's another example.

Subject: Link?

Thanks for your e-mail message. Can you e-mail me a link to your product list so I can take a look at what you have to offer?

Milt W. Stopcallingme

VP of Everything

That might sound like somebody who is actively engaged in figuring out whether or not it makes sense to work with you. But in fact, as with the previous message, there is actually no commitment whatsoever.

So what do you do? Of course you cannot refuse to let the person look at your Web site.

As a practical matter all you can do is comply with his request and briefly suggest something at the end of your message that *you* are going to do at some point in the next two weeks. For instance:

Subject: Re: Link

Thanks so much for your recent message; below is the link you requested.

www.ourcompany.com/productlist

I am going to be in your area on Tuesday morning at 10:00 meeting with the ABC Company. Why don't I stop by at 11:00 and meet some of your tech people?

Brenda Nextstep

This kind of request for a Next Step should become second nature to you in your e-mail messages. Some people will say yes. Most people will say no. And that's okay! You want to know who's really saying no to you.

Do it!

There is absolutely no excuse for not asking for some kind of future time commitment from the person with whom you are trying to build a relationship.

Asking is what salespeople do for a living!

In fact, you can rest assured that this person you are corresponding with knows that asking for such commitment is in fact something that salespeople do on a regular basis. So there is not going to be any hostility as a result of you making this suggestion, either via e-mail or in person. To the contrary, there is probably going to be a more direct and more authentic exchange of information than you might otherwise get. You are going to get one of these two messages:

"Thanks for the suggestion, Tim, but we are really not ready to sit down yet. Do me a favor and give me a call around the first of February so we can try and set something up then."

Or:

"That sounds fine, Tim, but I have only fifteen minutes or so to spare. If you're willing to work with that, I can introduce you to some of our key people around here during that period."

Obviously, that is a buying signal. It is distinguishable from a "not buying signal" because—you guessed it—the person is actually taking a piece of his or her calendar and giving you access to it.

Suppose you get that first message instead? That is no problem. We call this kind of lead an opportunity. It is not a prospect. It is simply an opportunity for future business. Mark it in your tickler file or whatever other mechanism you have to remind yourself that this person asked you to get back in touch on such and such a date—and set up a meeting. Then call or e-mail without apology around that date, and suggest that you get together on June 1 at 10:00 A.M.

See what happens!

The Message Template

I want to share with you now a template for a basic format of an effective person-to-person e-mail message. This is a good model—but not the only possible model. It's a sound approach to a "basic" e-mail message that focuses on a Next Step.

Notice that its subject line connects to a date that coincides with the Next Step that we want, and that the first line references a competitor or other company with which the recipient is familiar.

"GOOD" TEMPLATE

Subject: Meeting on April 19

MAXWIDGET

We've done a lot of work for people in your industry, including Max-Widget. My boss suggested that you and I meet to discuss your widget retooling plans for the coming year.

Could we meet this coming April 19 at 2:00 P.M. at your office?

Sincerely,

Mike Conway

www.retooler.org

978-555-0555 (office)

978-555-5550 (cell)

978-555-5050 (home)

CONFIRMING APRIL 19TH MEETING AT 2:00 P.M.

The purpose of this message is simply to secure some type of involvement or Next Step or confirm an involvement or Next Step. There is absolutely no way anybody reading this message could misinterpret what it is about, get lost in a long paragraph, or mis-understand what kind of action is required or requested.

Notice, too, that the message can be read in full on a single computer screen display. As in, the person doesn't have to hit "page down."

The information at the beginning and end of the message is what is most important. If the reader is going to skip anything here she is going to skip the material that shows up after the word *Max-Widget*. The human mind is trained to ignore that which it does not process. By making an editorial decision to place the most important material at the beginning or end of the message, and by putting the least important information in the middle of the message, we are taking advantage of how the human mind works. All too often, people compose thoughtless e-mail messages where the most important information is buried in the middle of a long paragraph in a message like the following.

"Bad" template

Subject: Your skyrocketing profits

Your profits certainly will start to skyrocket once you realize that we've worked with some of the key people in your industry, including MaxWidget. That's why my boss suggested that you and I get together. What would be a good time for us to hook up? Maybe sometime next week? Let me know.

Mike Conway

Sales Associate

Retooler

See the difference?

The first message is the message I strongly suggest that you to use as your model.

The second message is the message I want you to avoid like the plague. Dumb subject line. No Next Step request. Key information (the name of a competitor) buried in the middle of the text. No phone contact information. Nothing to catch the eye at the bottom of the screen. And even though it's quite short, it somehow seems long-winded.

Especially if you are still at the beginning of the relationship and still trying to secure some kind of initial commitment, keep it short and make sure it follows the outline of the "good" template.

The Perfect E-Mail Message?

No, you don't have to send exactly the message I out-lined in the previous chapter. Just follow the basic outline, and edit intelligently. Let's talk for just a moment about principles for making (minor) variations on the template you just saw.

The title of this chapter really does require a question mark at the end. There is no single perfect e-mail mes-sage that is applicable to all situations where we have the opportunity to move the sale cycle forward.

There is, however, a set of standards we can apply to most of the e-mail messages that go out to prospects when we hit "send." I want to share those with you now.

There are basically three questions that we have to answer. They are:

- How *long* should the message be?
- How *detailed* should the message be?
- How *casual* should the message be?

I want to take you through these in order and share some thoughts on the types of answers that you should be giving as you create your messages.

Let us look at the first question: *How long should the message be?* The best answer is: pretty darned short.

As a general rule, the *only* people I will read long e-mail messages from are people who are either my customers or people I am related to by blood. When it comes to anyone else, I either skip the message entirely or read the beginning and the ending and decide from there what I should do.

Be honest. This is probably very similar to your own standard. My guess is that, in your world, the only people whose long messages do get read are those from your own customers, your boss, or relatives. (And let's be honest again: some of those messages from the people we are related to, we may not read every single solitary word of those, either.)

So. We're creating messages that we want people to read. It is incumbent on us to keep our messages short if we want to get anything accomplished by means of an e-mail message that moves the sales process forward. How short? Again, think in terms of a single computer screen.

Everybody who uses e-mail uses it in one of two ways these days: either by means of looking at a computer screen or by looking at a display that is considerably smaller, like a BlackBerry. That means that we who write messages actually have a very small amount of space in which to make our point. For my money, it is best to keep the messages so short as to be impossible *not* to read if you glance at them.

I advocate an effective length of two to three sentences tops for the main portion of the message. Note that I am talking about the message that shows up in the body of the e-mail and not the subject line or the signature, which are separate animals.

Here's the second question. *How detailed should the message be?* The answer here is that the message should go into relevant detail and feature few of those details. For instance, if the message can emphasize that we have worked with a company in this prospective customer's industry, that is the level of detail we want to encourage—but we do not want to spend more than a sentence or three exploring that. We just want to mention the name of the company if we can and suggest what the person ought to do about it (usually, meet with us or talk to us.)

In other words, we want to be just as detailed as it takes to provoke curiosity and get a response—but no more detailed than that.

Let's look at the third question: *How casual should we be?* This is a very difficult question because the e-mail message has become, for so many of us, a replacement for verbal interaction. That means that during the course of our working day, if we are sending around e-mail messages internally, we may be tempted to adopt the same level of discourse that we would use if we were hanging around the water cooler. But in fact, if we are reaching out to a brand-new person or someone we have only recently spoken to on the phone, we actually have to assume a somewhat higher standard.

You never know. You might run into a grammar cop, someone who will disengage from your message the moment he or she finds a minor writing error in it. (This is another reason to keep the message short, by the way—fewer possibilities for error.)

Consider the e-mail message to be a relatively formal document. (See also Chapter 71, on unforgivable e-mail mistakes.)

About the Subject Line

THE SUBJECT LINE is as important as anything you put into the body of the e-mail message.

In fact, what we looked at above—that terse, concise template that is easy for people to respond to or forward to someone else—is very likely the least important part of an e-mail message. The most important part of the e-mail message, and the part that I would urge you to pay attention to and strategize more closely than any other part, is the subject line, and that is the subject of our present chapter.

Many people imagine that the subject line of an e-mail is comparatively unimportant, and then wonder why their messages get no response or a confused response. In fact, the subject line of the e-mail is the single most important determinant of whether the person will ever open, read, or acknowledge the body of the message—which means that we need to find a way to strategize that subject line at least as carefully and probably with much more thought than the body of the message.

Here are some examples of subject lines sent by real, live salespeople that are well intentioned enough and are certainly not making any attempt to mislead the reader but that still fail miserably at the task of getting the person to open the message and consider its contents. (I've changed the content of these headings very slightly so as to avoid any confidentiality problems, but trust me, I really have received e-mails with headings like this.)

Subject: Article

Is this a request that I send the person an article? Is this a request that the person be allowed to interview me for an article? Is this a request for an article that I have written? Some people might argue that the ambiguity of the subject line here is a positive, but I have my doubts. Remember, this message is competing against scores or hundreds of other messages for my attention. In fact, the salesperson wanted to send me an article. But if the point was to get me to open the message, the headline, in my view, did a terrible job.

Subject: Your company's success

Again—there's nothing misleading about this. The salesperson really does want to talk to me about my company's success in the body of the e-mail. But what possible entry point to this subject does the single sentence here give me? My company's success depends on any one of a thousand different factors and all I get from a subject heading like this is that the person who's e-mailing me isn't willing to specify which one of those thousands of factors this message relates to.

This is another subject heading that is presumably so vague that it undercuts any actual content of the body of the message that might be of interest to me. In fact, the person was trying to meet with me to discuss ways for me to expand my network of sales training franchises by means of display advertising. I'm not saying he necessarily had to put the words *display advertising* in the heading, but might it have made sense to connect the heading somehow to the goal I already knew about—namely, expanding my franchise network?

Subject: Tomorrow

This is an example of a subject line that is self-contained and has no meaningful connection whatsoever to the message it precedes. Think about it for a second. I can understand two things when I look at the subject line and the heading. I can understand the content of the subject line, in this case "tomorrow," and I can understand whether or not I recognize who sent the message. If I recognized who the message is coming from, this could be a great heading because I would be interested in finding out what the person has to say about tomorrow. But in this case, I had no idea who this person was, and so I was left a message from a stranger about something unspecified that would happen tomorrow. Would you open that message? The only reason I did was that I was writing this book, and had a duty to identify what messages hooked up with stupid e-mail headlines. The person who was planning to call "tomorrow" wanted to discuss my investments. I missed the call.

Unless you're writing a book about e-mail techniques and looking for examples of lousy subject headings, as I was, you'll want to find a way to avoid this sort of heading.

So much for well-meaning headlines that fail to engage the recipient. What do the best subject lines look like?

Here is one of my favorites:

Subject: June 23 meeting

The beauty of this heading is that it immediately answers the first question that everybody has when they are considering opening up an e-mail message, namely, "Is this something I really have to look at?"

In this case, the message makes it clear that it is something that requires attention, because there is a meeting in the short term. In fact, when I send this message, what I am doing is asking the person whether or not he or she is willing to meet with me on a certain date and time. I particularly like placing an emphasis on times and dates and months in headings, because it causes the recipient to wonder whether or not the message affects his or her immediate schedule. And by immediate schedule, I mean something that takes place during the next two weeks.

Commitments that take place within this particular time frame tend to mean much more than commitments that are made for three months or six months or nine months or twelve months away. The closer we get to that two-week time frame, the more meaningful that commitment is and the more important the communication about it becomes. So it stands to reason that a heading that focuses on a specific date within the next two weeks will probably have more interest than something that does not.

Here is another heading that works:

Subject: Joe Clark

This subject line is a good one to use when Joe Clark is someone known to both the sender and the recipient of the message. If Joe Clark is a personal acquaintance of the person I am trying to reach out to, it's almost a guarantee that the recipient is going to open the message and see what I have to say about Joe. Obviously I have to follow through on this and mention that Joe gave me a referral or explain how Joe and I have worked together in the past.

Here is another example of an e-mail heading that works:

Subject: McClusky Industries

This is when McClusky Industries is either a competitor of the e-mail recipient or a company otherwise familiar to the person I am trying to contact. Ideally, it should be a company that I have worked with, so I can build my message around the success I had in working with McClusky in the past.

The Secret Weapon

HOW THE HECK DO YOU CARRY ON an ongoing conversation using that basic template for a good e-mail that you saw in Chapter 58? You can't simply send an endless series of two- or three-sentence e-mails.

For more complex communications as the relationship deepens, it is imperative that you find a way to send a little bit more substantial message and carry on with the business of moving your sales cycle forward. You just have to do this in a way that takes into account two facts about the way people really read e-mail.

Fact Number One: Text is inherently boring, and it's more boring as it accumulates. A huge column of text that has an unbroken series of words and sentences will be almost impenetrable to your reader.

Fact Number Two: Human beings are visually driven organisms. They are driven to graphics. And, in the kind of e-mail messages we're talking about, graphics mean bullet points. Bullet points are your secret weapon.

Human beings respond well to pictures. In other words, we respond more easily and with greater facility to messages that are visual in nature.

I am not going to suggest that you should go out of your way to incorporate lots of snazzy graphics into your e-mail messages. There are some people who would argue that you should do that, but I personally don't think this is a great investment of a salesperson's time, for the simple reason that large graphics files (a) tend to take up a lot of space and (b) are likely to be blocked by spam filters.

No, what I am suggesting is that you keep your messages personal and keep them simple, but that you find ways to incorporate a secret weapon:

Bullet points.

Bullet points serve basically the same purpose as photos or cartoons would in a PowerPoint or other visual demonstration. But they are much easier to incorporate into e-mail messages.

Here is an example involving an e-mail message I might send to a prospect who is considering letting my team make a presentation to a critical group within his organization. Here's the first version.

To: Jim Prospect

From: Mike Salesperson

Subject: Upcoming presentation

Jim:

As you requested, here are some thoughts on why it makes sense for me to deliver the proposal in person in front of your regional vice president on May 3. For one thing, he will get a sense of me as a trainer and see how my personal style connects with the material. For another thing, I will bring twenty-five-plus years of experience to the task of explaining the principals that make up the substance of the program. Finally, I will be able to answer questions on the spot, rather than putting you in the awkward position of having to check with me and follow up afterward about any queries that the vice president may have about the program content. Jim, I really think this is the way to go. What would you think of putting me on the agenda on May 3?

Mike

Now take a look at the same message, reformatted this time using the "bullet principle":

To: **Jim Prospect**

From: Mike Salesperson

Subject: Upcoming presentation

Jim:

As you requested, here are some thoughts on why it makes sense for me to deliver the proposal in person in front of your regional vice president on May 3. I hope you'll share them with the board.

- For one thing, the RVPs get a sense of me as a trainer and see how my personal style connects with the material.

- For another thing, I will be able to demonstrate the Phone Coach equipment that is a critical part of the training program.

- Finally, I will be able to answer questions on the spot, rather than putting you in the awkward position of having to check with me and follow up afterward about any queries that they may have about the program content.

Jim, I really think this is the way to go. What would you think of putting me on the agenda on May 3?

Mike

Do you see the difference? The same exact information is getting across but the fact that the information is conveyed by means of bullet points makes the second message much easier to get into. The easier your message is to get into, the more eyeballs will actually read it, and the more eyeballs that actually read it, the more fingers will type a response to you and hit "send."

61 Signatures

A MAJOR OPPORTUNITY for spreading the word about your company and its products and services can and should be found at the bottom of every e-mail message you send. This is the portion of the message known as the "signature," and it should be written, revised, and updated as carefully as anything else that appears in your message.

Anyone who must make his or her way through a hundred or so e-mail messages sometimes notices the signature more readily than the body of the message. Why? Because human beings have a tendency to scan to the bottom of a message to see what the point of it is. We want to "cut to the chase"—so we hit that page down button or use our mouse to scroll to the very bottom of the message. What this means is that someone who receives a number of messages from us will, over time, receive more exposure to the signature we set up at the bottom of the message than to anything else we write!

It behooves us, then, to create a powerful and compelling signature, and to revise it from time to time so it retains the same basic theme but does not become so familiar that its message fades into oblivion.

Just as you would not send out a message to prospects or clients in written form that did not incorporate your company's logo and contact information on a sharp-looking piece of stationery, so you will also want to avoid sending out an e-mail message that contains no reference whatsoever to your company, its Web site, or your own role within the company.

Of course, there are some important differences between a carefully crafted e-mail signature and a good piece of stationery. For one thing, the stationery is a physical object, and it is an accepted convention to incorporate a logo at some point near its upper left-hand corner. There is no such convention these days regarding e-mail signatures, primarily because the act of sending an image as part of a logo can set off spam filter alerts.

Here is a model signature to consider adapting:

Stephan Schiffman, President

D.E.I. Franchise Systems

www.dei-sales.com

"We Understand Sales"

123 Metropolitan Way

Metropolis, NY 10107

212-555-5555 (office)

212-555-5557 (cell)

212-555-5556 (home)

You read right—that's a home phone number. When I leave a positive impression with a prospect or customer, I want it to be reinforced with accurate information on how to reach me by phone at just about any hour of the night or day.

My signature sends the clear and unequivocal commitment that these people can and should feel free to reach out to me at any one of the three numbers I offer.

I do get a lot of resistance to this from salespeople, and I have told salespeople in training programs that it is a perfectly acceptable alternative to list one's cell phone number and main office number if these are the only two lines that you want to use for business purposes. But supplying the home number sends a message of accountability that is hard to forget.

Remember this, if you remember anything at all about your e-mail message signatures: It should send the unspoken message that you wish to be accessible to the other person, and it should offer at least two valid phone options that the person can use to get in contact with you.

The P.S.

When you receive an appeal from the Red Cross or from somebody trying to sell you a new magazine subscription by mail, you virtually always see a P.S. message down at the bottom below the author's signature, whether the document is a single page or longer.

I think the reason that the P.S. message is so powerful in direct mail is that it allows the copywriter to restate all the critical facts of the message and even to issue a call to action. For instance, a P.S. might look like this:

P.S. Call 1-800-999-9999 today to lock in your special low rate of only $12.95 per unit!

The theory is that the person reading the message may drift down to the P.S. or even zip forward to it and read nothing else but that message.

On the whole I think this is an accurate way to look at direct-mail selling, but notice that in our e-mail message we're not trying to close the deal by means of our message. So if we do use a P.S. to restate key points, we want to make sure that we're not doing so in such a way that's going to make the letter likely to be confused with spam.

Feel free to use a P.S. statement at the end of your message to restate a key point and perhaps emphasize the Next Step you plan to ask for. But make sure that that P.S. is appended to a message that is suitably concise, and be sure you personalize it in such a way that the recipient knows it could only have been addressed to him or her.

My Pet Peeve

Now here is increasingly common e-mail correspondence habit—one that really annoys me. That isn't really such a big deal, but the fact this habit may be annoying your prospects *is* a big deal.

What annoys me is messages like this:

Subject: Re: Discussion

Okay, fine. Let's do that.

Did you understand that? Me neither. Nevertheless, I get messages like that from salespeople all the time. They assume I remember what the heck they were talking about. I don't, and neither do your prospects. They open the "conversation" (which I have little or no memory of participating in) with inscrutable phrases like "Why not?" or "Should I ask them first?"

People sometimes lose sight of the fact that the decision makers with whom they are discussing matters by e-mail have other things going on in their lives. There are multiple priorities, multiple objectives, and multiple contacts to juggle at any given moment. It is therefore incumbent upon you, as a salesperson, to give appropriate context within the body of your message—while keeping the message concise. Offer context that will allow the other person to make sense out of your message even after having had thirty other people interrupt his or her day.

This problem highlights a regrettable disadvantage of e-mail, which is that even though it often *feels* like a conversation to the salesperson, and perhaps even to the person with whom he or she is communicating, that "conversation" can be, and often is, interrupted by many other things during the course of the day. So what feels to you, the salesperson, like a small pause may end up feeling to the recipient like a totally different conversation.

Remember, a whole lot can happen between the time you hit "send" at 9:00 in the morning and the time I read your message at 4:00 that afternoon.

Three Critical E-Mail Selling Principles

THE PRINCIPLES I WANT TO SHARE with you now are so important that I want to cover each of them here, and offer examples as to what they might look like if they are expressed within the body of an e-mail message. But I also want to make it clear to you that the same principles apply in *any* setting where you are communicating with a prospect. These principles are relevant to any salesperson, in any industry, anywhere on earth. So whether you're sending e-mail messages, closing sales over the telephone, or casting a large blanket over a campfire in order to send smoke signals from the parking lot, you'll have the opportunity to use these principles to improve your relationship with the prospect (and, simultaneously, the size of the number on your commission check).

We train a lot of different salespeople in a lot of different industries. Sometimes they put up a fuss and insist that what we're trying to share with them doesn't actually apply to their sale. *That has never, ever happened when we shared the principles you are about to read.*

These three principles, in other words, actually work, *and* they are relevant to any and every selling situation. If you memorize them and use them on a regular basis, you will make more money. That's a promise.

The Three Selling Principles That Are Always Relevant to Every Situation are as follows.

Principle #1. Learn about what they do.

Principle #2. Be more concerned than they are about their problems.

Principle #3. If all else fails, ask where you went wrong or what mistake you made.

Got it? Great. We're done.

Seriously, before you try to implement any of these (deceptively easy-sounding) rules, let me share some insights on *how* to do so, and what kinds of mistakes are likely to present themselves when you incorporate these ideas into your e-mail communications with prospects and customers.

The first of our Selling Principles That Are Always Relevant to Every Situation is:

Learn about what they do.

In selling, we are not so much interested in identifying what the prospective buyer "needs." Instead, we are interested in identifying what he or she is actually doing right now.

Think about it for a second. If I send you an e-mail message asking you to identify your most critical "needs" in XYZ area over the next ten days, what are you going to tell me? You are either going to tell me something superficial and vague about what you are looking for, or you are going to tell me that you do not need anything. That second outcome is considerably more likely. (By the way, if you don't even answer the e-mail message, that's an eloquent way of telling me that you don't think you need anything at all right now.)

Need means "must have." *Need* means "die without." We need water. We need air. We don't need—or at least don't think we need—salespeople to tell us what has to happen next in our business lives.

You will run into a lot of people these days who tell you that sales is all about "finding the need." You will encounter a fair number of experts who insist that effective selling is all about asking "need" or "pain" questions like this:

- "What is it that keeps you up at night?"
- "What is your biggest problem with your current vendor?"
- "What is the one thing you would fix if you could change anything in your relationship with ABC Company?"

Many, many salespeople tell me that messages like this are the focus of their e-mail correspondence campaign with customers and prospects. What's the need? What's the pain?

Here is my question—how much meaningful information are you going to get out of a question like that?

How much meaningful information have you actually received from a question like that?

Instead of focusing on the superficial, need-based, problem-based, pain-based portion of the information picture, I am going to get a better picture of what is actually going on in the relationship if I say something like this:

- "What are you doing right now to . . . ?"
- "How many times before have you . . . ?"
- "Who else have you spoken to about . . . ?"
- "Why did you choose to . . . ?"

Let me give you an example of how this works. Sometimes, if I am in a face-to-face selling situation, I will have the job of determining whether or not somebody I am talking to is actually the true decision maker for selecting a sales trainer. No doubt, you have had a similar challenge in face-to-face interviews that you have conducted when *you* are trying to determine whether or not the person in question really is the decision maker for what you sell.

So we have a question to ask. What should that question sound like?

Here is what most people ask:

"Are you the final decision maker for this product?"

Here is what I ask:

"Just out of curiosity, how did you do this the last time?"

Or:

"Just out of curiosity, why did you choose XYZ?"

Or:

"Just out of curiosity, what made you decide to do it X way instead of Y way?"

The responses I get to this will instantly tell me whether or not the person I am dealing with really is involved in the decision-making process.

Can you see how focusing on the "do" of the situation gives me more information about what is actually happening in that person's world than any other approach?

And you know what? I can ask about the "do" of the situation as it affects this person both *as an employee* and *as an individual*. Two levels! Each informs the other. If I don't know what the other person is trying to "do" professionally—what deadlines are coming up, what new customers have to be kept happy, how old customers are going to be retained—how much progress am I really going to make with this person? And if I don't know what the other person is trying to "do" as an individual in this job—what promotion he or she is after, how he or she got the job, how happy he or she is with the current position—how much progress am I really going to make on the professional front?

If we show genuine, open, and enthusiastic curiosity about what the person is doing on both the personal and organizational level, then we are going to find out that we have a lot higher quality of information and a much more robust picture of what is actually happening in the relationship and in the organization. Certainly we're going to know more if we ask these kinds of questions than we would if we simply fired off a lot of e-mail messages asking the person to tell us what keeps him or her up at night.

If there is nothing that keeps the person up at night, we are in trouble. And even if there is something that keeps the person up at night, we are going to get a better picture of it by asking what they are doing right now to deal with the situation.

We should be curious about the person. We should be curious about the organization.

We should be curious about the past. We should be curious about the present. We should be curious about the future.

We should be curious about how. We should be curious about why.

Wherever possible, build your e-mail messages around a genuine curiosity about what the other person is actually *doing* in an area where you know for sure that you can add value to the person's day.

■ ■ ■

The second of our three Selling Principles That Are Always Relevant to Every Situation is:

Be more concerned than they are.

Once you have done an effective job of finding out what the other person is trying to do or accomplish or has done or accomplished in the past, it is incumbent upon you to project yourself into his or her position and express deep, genuine concern about *how* the initiative he or she has committed to—whatever it is—will actually get off the launching pad.

In other words, you want to be *more* upset by the possibility that the contact will not accomplish his or her goal than he or she is.

All too often, people within the target companies we try to sell to have a hard time finding allies to worry or be as concerned as they are about achieving critical goals. In my business, the sales-training business, people are typically trying to increase sales production by a specific percentage marker within a particular period of time. As a sales trainer, it is incumbent upon me to buy heavily into that goal once I identify it and understand all its parameters. That means I express deep (and quite sincere!) concern about everything connected to that goal—everything that might help my contact attain it, as well as everything that might stand in the way of attaining the goal.

And you know what? When I express a concern about one of those obstacles that might stand in the way of attaining the goal, I will often share a *strategy* for overcoming those obstacles!

So once I have identified what the sales target for the next quarter is—let's say it is exceeding quota by 15 percent in all sales territories—I am going to open up every communication with the people involved and express my concerns about what is standing in the way of our attaining exactly that.

To: Mark Bigshot

From: Stephan Schiffman

Subject: Beating quota by 15 percent in all seventeen of your territories

Mark:

BEATING QUOTA BY 15 PERCENT IN ALL SEVENTEEN OF YOUR TERRITORIES

Great talking to you by phone today. I have some ideas that I think will help you to accomplish this, but I'm concerned about some of the obstacles you're facing. Can we meet in your office this coming Tuesday at 9:00 A.M.?

Stephan Schiffman, President

D.E.I. Franchise Systems

"We Understand Sales"

123 Metropolitan Way

Metropolis, NY 10107

212-555-5555 (office)

212-555-5556 (home)

212-555-5557 (cell)

—REQUESTING MEETING AT 9:00 A.M. ON TUESDAY, APRIL 10, 2007—

When I get this meeting (which I will), I am going to mention that I have been very preoccupied with all the possible obstacles standing in the way of Mark's attaining that goal of his. In fact, I am going to enumerate those obstacles in as much detail and with as much emotion as I possibly can. And then I am going to express exactly how much information I have been able to track down that seems relevant to the neutralization of those obstacles, and I am going to talk about the resources that I personally can bring to bear to overcoming them so Mark can attain his goal.

All of this is by way saying that in your e-mail messages, if you have to pick a single theme that is going to appeal to your prospect, probably one of your best bets will be to select the "message of concern" e-mail. It should look something like the example I've shared with you in this chapter.

■ ■ ■

The third of our three Selling Principles That Are Always Relevant to Every Situation is:

If all else fails, ask where you went wrong or what mistake you made.

Assume full responsibility.

What I mean by this is not that you send nonverbal signals of responsibility, or even a formal proclamation to the prospect that you personally are responsible for delivering a positive outcome. Those things are good, of course. But it is just as important to use this principle of taking responsibility to figure out whether you have any daylight, any option to move forward, when things go wrong.

For instance: Suppose you have been working for seven or eight weeks on a major deal, and one morning you receive the voice mail message that salespeople have nightmares about. You hear your primary contact at a huge prospect—one that you thought was at 90 percent likelihood of closing—saying:

"Hi Jim, this is Bart Overwhelm at Massive Company. I just wanted to let you know we have had a bit of a change of thinking here. I had a chance to chat with the CEO about exactly where we stood on the proposal you put together for us and while I personally think it has all kinds of potential, the CEO feels differently and so we are going to be going a different route. I am sorry this did not work out, but I hope we can keep in touch and possibly get together on another project. Best to you and the kids. Talk to you soon. Bye."

Now suppose that your attempts to reach out to this decision maker (or purported decision maker) go nowhere. So you do everything you're supposed to do. You call at 7:00 in the morning. You call at 6:00 at night. You try to get help from Bart's assistant. Nothing works. You cannot get through. You've been shut out.

You have a feeling there *might* be something that could save the deal. If you act fast. But you have no idea what that "something" is.

What to do?

You might be tempted to think that there's nothing you could do wrong at this stage if your goal is to get Bart's attention and re-establish a dialogue. Actually, there is plenty you could do wrong. You could show up in the Massive Company parking lot and howl a lament to the skies. You could hire a small aircraft to write the words "Surrender, Bart" in the sky above the company's headquarters. But assuming that you are not up for theatrics like those, you will want to focus instead on the one *right* thing to do in this situation, which is what I call the "taking responsibility e-mail."

It could look like this:

Subject: My CEO

. . . wants to know what I did wrong here. I feel like I must have screwed something up. Did I miss something?

Jim Jarhead

WidgetCo

Want to hear about an even more effective message? This would be for your boss or CEO to send the message. (Hey, you're not proud. If it would help you land a huge deal, now or in the future, would it be worth asking your CEO to send an e-mail message? Sure it would.)

Here is how it might look coming from the CEO's e-mail address.

Subject: Jim Jarhead

Just between you and me—what did Jim do wrong on that proposal?

Ed Intensely

CEO

WidgetCo

212-555-5555

Messages like these have an extraordinary galvanizing effect. (Another strategy that is just as powerful is for your CEO to make a call, leaving a message "Concerning Jim Jarhead"—with no other information besides his title and contact number—on your contact's voice mail.)

In almost all situations, the person you are reaching out to will in fact respond, and fast, with an explanation of what happened. You might not get the deal, but you will get the straight story about what actually caused you to fall out of the running so suddenly. The response, whether it comes by e-mail, voice mail or somebody actually picking up the phone when you call, is probably going to sound like this:

"Actually, Jim did not do anything wrong at all. It's just us. We found out that our budgets are frozen for the next six months and we do not have any way to pay for this. I wish I had known that up front, because I certainly would have told Jim that was the situation so that we could have avoided putting all this effort and time into setting up the proposal. But that is where we stand."

At this point, it might be a good idea for your CEO—or whoever—to suggest billing the program or product delivery later, to take advantage of the budget allocation that will unfold.

When in doubt, use e-mail to take responsibility. When something goes wrong, ask where you went wrong or what mistake you made. Then try to get face to face, or at least voice to voice, so someone in your organization can offer a suggestion about how to get around the problem that's presented itself.

E-Mail "Branding"

WE HAVE ENTERED A FASCINATING PERIOD in human history, one in which a single piece of information can emerge as a defining identifier and even a determinant of your own identity.

Think about it. If you have an e-mail address that connects to your business—*Johnsmith@ABCcorp.com*—then, when you share that information with someone, you are not merely giving them a way of getting in touch with you, but also sharing an important piece of who you are.

By giving the person that e-mail address, you give him or her the right to begin a correspondence with you, to maintain that correspondence over time, to forward it to other people, and to reach out to you at any and every time the person feels it's appropriate to do so—2:00 in the morning, 1:00 in the afternoon, whatever. In a strange way, your business persona *melds* with that e-mail address, in a way that your business identity does not meld with a phone number or a physical address. In cyberspace, your e-mail address is not only a way to get in touch with you, but an expression of your business self.

The reason I bring this up is to remind you that when you share your e-mail address with a business contact, you are basically sharing with them the right to archive and retrieve an ongoing series of messages that you share with them. E-mail is different from written correspondence in that it tends to stick around for a while. Whereas we can throw away a written memo, it is quite common for electronic correspondence records to exist in three or four or more forms. This is not to suggest that you should become paranoid about giving out your e-mail address—quite the contrary; you should relish the opportunity to create and support a "business identity" that sends a consistent brand message about you and the organization you represent.

Just as your company goes out of its way to send specific brand messages about its products and services, you can and should use your e-mail address to evoke certain distinctive brand messages about you as a person: your trustworthiness, for instance, and your ability to respond quickly to questions, your diligence in following through on commitments, and so forth. Just make sure the messages you send are consistently positive ones, and you will have no problem.

And—to support your brand—do be sure to check your e-mail at least once a day. (Any other standard is tantamount to sales malpractice these days.)

E-Mail and Online Newsletters

JUST ABOUT EVERYONE ON EARTH who has an e-mail account hates spam. By the same token, just about everybody on earth likes to get something valuable for free. Someone may ask to receive something you or your business offers for free—an article or report, say. The act of your signing prospects up for an e-mail newsletter is not spam, assuming that you give them the option to remove themselves from the distribution list, and assuming that you honor their request if they make it.

We must learn to operate between two all too familiar extremes—flooding somebody with irrelevant, unsolicited information on the one hand, and giving away "too much" free content online. Ultimately, of course, it's a matter of trial and error, but this is a balancing act that you and your company can, with just a little practice, get right.

People who agree to have their e-mail addresses added to a distribution list usually receive what is known as an "opt-in" newsletter. There's a pretty obvious reason for this name: they have opted in to the distribution list, meaning they have agreed to receive your newsletter.

At my company, DEI Franchise Systems, we have a free booklet on starting your own franchise business that anyone who visits our Web site can request. The act of making the request for the free booklet—which we send along to anybody who requests it—enrolls you on our e-mail distribution list. We have also purchased opt-in e-mails from e-mail list brokers. Between the two sources, we have compiled a master list with the names of approximately 13,000 people who have requested our content. Every single one of those names belongs to somebody who once agreed to give their e-mail address in exchange for receiving something in return. And every single one of them can opt out as easily as they opted in.

Our challenge, in working with this list, is to make absolutely certain that we are having a good dialogue with these people and that they feel that the information they receive as a result of joining the list is worthwhile.

So what do I send them? Well, approximately once a week, I send out an article—and a request for information. I want to know what kinds of topics they would like to see covered in future newsletters. I may also use the list to broadcast information about upcoming public events that involve DEI or my own speaking appearances.

Obviously, I am hoping to encourage a dialogue by means of passing along specific helpful information to this group, which consists almost exclusively of salespeople, sales managers, and senior executives at companies. Some of those conversations turn into discussions about face-to-face training programs. And some of those discussions, thank goodness, actually turn into revenue for me and my company. The key to getting a good dialogue going, in my experience, is picking content that seems likely to be easy to implement for the people in my opt-in list.

I mentioned a little bit earlier that the e-mail newsletter to this opt-in list goes out "approximately" once a week. That is a conscious decision. One of the mistakes that people make about e-mail newsletters is that they make them too predictable.

If the newsletter always comes out on Monday or always comes out on the first of the month, people become attuned to it—and that can be a bad thing. It's possible, of course, that the person is eagerly awaiting the latest installment of the e-newsletter, just waiting for the moment he or she can read the articles and forward them to everybody else in the organization. To my way of thinking, though, the odds are fairly long against that possibility. Much more likely is the scenario where the person gets habituated to seeing the newsletter show up in the mailbox on a certain day, and learns to ignore it.

So by altering the production schedule—by making it come out on the tenth day and then on the fourth day and then on the ninth day and then on the eleventh day—we help the audience develop a sense that the content is on the way at some point in the future. But we do not set up a pattern that they become so used to that they instantly delete the newsletter every Monday morning.

Along the same lines, I try to alter the headings that I use in setting up the subject line for my e-mail newsletter. Here are some examples of actual headings that we have used with the newsletter. Notice that each and every one is different.

Subject: Stephan Schiffman on increasing the value of your key accounts

Subject: Ten "musts" for a successful speech

Subject: Sixty-second overview: Time management techniques for salespeople

Subject: DEI Update: The five stages of the sales career

Subject: Sales managers: Are you measuring these fifteen skills?

Here's what I *don't* do for the subject line:

Subject: Stephan Schiffman's E-Newsletter, Volume 2, Issue 4

It never ceases to amaze me. People really do repeat subject lines like that for their newsletters, week after week after week. No benefit, no highlight—just the name of the newsletter and the volume and issue number. How boring is that?

Vary your subject lines. Vary your content. And always highlight the benefit the person will receive by clicking on your message.

On Opt-In Lists

HERE ARE SOME THOUGHTS on creating and managing your opt-in lists.

Failing to give people an opportunity to give you their e-mail address is a big mistake. If you have a Web site, you should have a place there where people can get something free—if only your company's brochure in PDF format—in exchange for giving you their e-mail address. You will need to develop a form that makes it easy for people to give you this information. Free resources on how to build such a form can be found at *www.htmlgoodies.com/ tutorials/forms/index.php.*

Do not ignore requests from people who want to be taken off your list. We use a tool called EmailLabs, which I recommend highly—you can find out more about it at *www. emaillabs.com.*

One of the things I like about EmailLabs is that it makes it extremely easy to manage drop requests. There is a single spot where you can pop in a given e-mail address, and the software will instantly ensure that the e-mail address in question is utterly and completely deleted from any and all distribution lists that you may be managing. In other words, if you have fifteen or so distribution lists that you are keeping track of—and we do at my company—EmailLabs gives you a single step you can take to make absolutely sure that a drop request has been honored by each and every one of those fifteen lists.

Create messages that look cool. Another thing that I like about Email-Labs is that it gives you an extremely easy interface for HTML code development. To put this in the language of the layman (which I certainly am), their "HTML helper" feature allows people who only know how to use a program like Microsoft Word to create an extremely attractive newsletter—without having to master HTML programming skills.

Don't waste time sending messages to bad e-mail addresses. Yet another thing I like about EmailLabs is its ability to handle and eliminate "bounce backs"—those pesky messages that come your way when an address is invalid for some reason or out of date. Get them out of your list quickly.

Learn how to manage exclusion lists. Did you realize that your competitors have access to your Web site? Well, they do, and it is a pretty good bet that they are using your stuff if you are circulating a free e-mail newsletter. If you do not want somebody who is directly or indirectly competing with you to have access to all of the material you are putting together, you can enter the appropriate domain names into a suppression list. Again, EmailLabs is excellent in this regard, as it has a suppression feature that is extremely easy to use.

Back up everything. What you want to avoid is having any situation where a catastrophic accident or unforeseen computer glitch instantly vaporizes twenty or thirty thousand contact names at a time. If you are handling this information on your own, you will want to make sure you back up everything (as in weekly and monthly) by transferring your database into a format comprehensible to a database program or spreadsheet. Keep a separate file accessible at all times.

You may be tempted to assume from the previous that I have been lavishly compensated by the good people at EmailLabs in exchange for the complimentary things that I have said about them in this part of the book. That is not true. What you have read here is based solely on my own experience with the software, and with the good results that it has delivered for us. It is, I can say without reservation, an excellent product: easy to use, reliable, and regularly updated. There are other resources you can use to manage and create your opt-in e-newsletter campaign, but I think I have given you a pretty clear indication here about which one I think you should be using.

E-Mail and Article Distribution

I LOVE USING E-MAIL to alert prospects and customers to the fact that an article about my company has shown up in a media source unconnected with my company. At the end of these messages, I usually suggest that the prospect and I get together to discuss new ideas. (But notice that the e-mail is technically "about" the link I'm passing along.)

Sometimes, when I suggest that salespeople use e-mail for just this purpose, they balk at the idea, and say, more or less, the following:

"That's all very well for you, Steve—you're an author with lots of experience in getting articles placed. How the heck am I supposed to point people toward articles about my company when none exist?"

Well, I have two responses. First of all, how sure are you that articles about you, your company, or your products really don't exist? Have you entered your own name or your company's name or the name of your most popular products and services into Google, the omnipresent search engine of our time? Once you do this simple experiment—and we're talking about an experiment that takes only five to ten minutes to perform—my prediction is that you will find more than one article that's easy for you to pass along to prospects and customers by means of a message like the following.

Subject: Warranty coverage article you might find interesting

Hi Todd:

Below is a link for an article I came across in the Yahoo! News section the other day. It had some interesting points about our recent product launch, and I thought you might find particularly interesting the piece at the end about choosing the right warranty coverage.

http://linkarticle.com/87890708970

I have some ideas for Q4 I'd like to share with you over lunch next week. I'll call tomorrow to see when you're free.

Take care,

Susan

Now, on to the second point. Even if you do have some coverage of your company, your products, or even yourself that you feel like sharing with the world of prospects and customers, it's likely that you could use more. Believe it or not, it's not at all difficult to put together a strong article that delivers value to your prospective customers; and it's only a very small investment of time, effort, cash, and energy to place those same articles in venues where they'll get more visibility than they're getting right now. Check out the following sites for more information on how to get more exposure for the articles you've developed:

www.prnewswire.com
www.marketwire.com

You can also make this sending-a-link message a "staying in touch" e-mail—one that doesn't (directly) reference a Next Step, but simply gives you a reason to call the person a day or so after you hit "send." Here's how it works. First, you pick someone you want to reconnect with—say, that prospect who's been "pending" for the last three weeks and hasn't gotten back in touch with you about your proposal. Next, you select an article with diligent care, making sure that it really does match something that is happening in this person's world. Then, you place the easiest call in the world: "Hey, I sent you an article on yada yada yada; I don't know if you had the chance to see it, but I wanted to let you know that it's on your e-mail system. How are things?"

I wasn't calling about trying to get business.

I wasn't even calling to check whether the person remembered the last e-mail message I sent. (That's a no-no.)

I was calling to *make sure he didn't miss* the article about yada yada yada—it's on his e-mail system. "And listen, as long as I've got you on the line . . . what's up in your world?"

I much prefer making this type of call to somebody I would like to work with than any other kind of call. I *hate* (and will not make) the call where I say, "Hey you told me you were going to have a decision about working with us this week, and it's already Friday. What the heck is the deal?"

Talk about a call that isn't going anywhere! Why bother? You remember what we learned about controlling the flow and people responding in kind? That's not the flow I want. That's not the response that I want to hear back in kind.

So I don't call to ask, "What the heck is holding us up?" Ever. If I have some other reason to initiate contact—the article on yada yada—then in nine instances out of ten the person will, on his or her own, bring up the issue that I really want to talk about— namely, the thing that's standing in the way of us doing business together. Then I can suggest a Next Step that makes sense for both of us.

67   "Hey, Would You Take a Look at My Web Site?"

IT SHOULD GO WITHOUT SAYING—but I will say it anyway. Suggesting that the person visit your Web site and then get back to you to let you know what he or she thinks of it is not a great strategy for moving the sales process forward.

I get this all the time, usually from people I don't know who phone me and e-mail me and who are trying to establish some kind of first contact. "Hey, let me give you my Web site address. I want to know what you think of it."

This is basically the same as requesting that the person read your brochure and then give you a call to let you know his or her thoughts about it. If you can beat quota by doing that, my hat is off to you, but I suspect that neither you nor any other salesperson on earth can pull off that trick.

We want the call to go well. We want the e-mail message to produce something. We want to be liked by the decision maker to whom we just reached out. So we make a huge mistake.

We want so desperately to think that we are satisfying the other person that we sometimes fall back into the habit of not challenging the prospect in any way.

That's the huge mistake. "Oh, I'm not asking you to actually do anything meaningful in this relationship—just, in your off hours, of which I know you must have plenty, to review my brochure—er, Web site—and tell me what you think of it."

This common sales mistake loses sight of the fact that there has to be some kind of creative tension in any selling relationship. If the prospect is already happy doing exactly what he or she is doing right now, that person would have no need to talk to a salesperson. We, as salespeople, have to challenge our prospects' conception of what they are doing right now; we have to learn what they're doing right now and shake things up a little bit. We think it is possible that there may be a match between what we do and what they do. We think that the match may have aspects of value that they have not previously considered.

If none of this were true, our job description would not read "salesperson." It would read "order taker."

No, you don't want to overwhelm the person. At the same time, you don't want to fall into the trap of avoiding any possible tension in the exchange.

Ask directly for a meaningful Next Step. Instead of saying or writing, "Why don't you take a look at our Web site and then e-mail me back," call and say this, either directly or by means of a voice mail message:

"I came across an article that I want to e-mail you; it is a link that shows up on our Web site and it is a little hard to find. I am going send you the link because I think it has some good ideas for your blah blah blah initiative, and then I will call you tomorrow. I have some thoughts on how it might affect your business. I am planning on calling around 8:00. Talk to you then!"

Then send the article—as a link, not as an attachment. And call when you said you were going to call. Try to set a Next Step.

It's a pretty simple principle, but it's so easy for people to lose sight of it. Let's say that I am calling you to set an appointment, and you tell me that you are not interested in meeting with me. Well, you'll recall that I have a very specific response for that, one that I have worked out over countless prospecting calls, and it tends to have a pretty good statistical likelihood of at least continuing the conversation, and perhaps even moving forward to a scheduled first appointment. I say, "You know what? That's exactly what Joe Smith over at XYZ products told me, and now he's one of our best customers. Just out of curiosity . . ." (and then I ask a question).

I've trained salespeople on this stuff for over a quarter of a century. So can you imagine how it makes me feel when I get a prospecting call and I hear a salesperson say, "Hey, that's okay. Do me a favor. Jot down the name of my Web site and take a look at it and then let me know what you want to do."

I hang up instantly. This is the sort of thing that might make it sound as though some kind of meaningful discussion has taken place. But in fact, there is no discussion taking place. This is just a salesperson volunteering a "nonbuying signal" of his very own!

This suggestion provides absolutely no tension whatsoever in the relationship, and as I pointed out, a certain healthy tension is essential to forward progress in the sales discussion. How do I know whether or not you could conceivably add value to my organization if you are not willing to make the case that you could?

How likely would you be to invest a chunk of your day reviewing the contents of a Web site based on a thirty-second discussion with a total stranger? Not very likely at all. So, if you are going to close the call with something, close it with an attempt to meet again or talk again or a suggestion about a way that you might be able to get face to face with the person at some public event. Do not issue meaningless and irrelevant suggestions that the person monitor your Web site. It is just not going to happen.

Why E-Mail Is Not Enough

I'VE SEEN A LOT of "brilliant new e-mail approaches to sales" over the past few years. They usually have to do with prospecting. The prospecting plans take lots of different paths, but they tend to have these two things in common.

- They never involve actual discussions with strangers.
- They do involve sending out lots of e-mail.

Every single time one of these schemes is submitted for my approval, I try to talk the person out of building his or her whole quarter, month, or week around the plan. To explain why, I have to give you some background.

According to the breakthrough work of Howard Gardner in his book *Frames of Mind*, human beings have seven distinct levels of intelligence. We all function on all seven of these levels, not one, and we function at different degrees in each of those seven intelligences. Given this, the idea that a single IQ test can accurately evaluate human intelligence is simply absurd.

Based on this concept, it turns out that e-mail correspondence neglects vast chunks of the human intellectual system. In fact, it only appeals directly to a couple of the intelligences Dr. Gardner identifies. Let me outline them for you now so you can see exactly what I'm talking about.

Gardner identifies the following specific intelligences. As you read what follows, remember that we all have these intelligences; we're just not all equally brilliant in all seven.

1. Verbal/Linguistic Intelligence

This has to do with how one uses language. People who are born writers are gifted in this area of intelligence. Clearly, verbal and linguistic intelligence is part of what happens when you compose a positive and compelling e-mail message. For people who are very "good with words," the act of composing, reading, and responding to e-mail messages takes advantage of this type of intelligence. People who have extraordinary verbal or linguistic intelligence can also communicate effectively by listening, by speaking, by reading, by writing, and by making connections between concepts and ideas they identify in different sources. Important: It is possible (and quite common) for someone who has great verbal skills not to be a particularly good reader or writer; such a person might be incapable of responding effectively to an e-mail, but would be better attuned to a telephone conversation.

2. Musical and Rhythmic Intelligence

Gardner identifies a rhythmic sense in which some people excel and others do not. He identifies people with high intelligence in this second area as extremely sensitive to the musical elements of pitch, timbre (by which he means the characteristic markers of a given tone), and rhythm. To get your head around this level of intelligence, consider that even people who cannot hold a tune can still be moved by a powerful piece of music, or can find a commercial jingle compelling enough to recall it at various points throughout the day. When we do these things, we are using our musical and rhythmic intelligence, even though we ourselves may be poor musicians. Notice here that musical and rhythmic intelligence has nothing whatsoever to do with reading or responding to e-mail messages—unless of course (1) there is a sound file attached to the message, (2) the organization's spam blocker has not blocked the message because of the attachment, (3) the recipient decides to open the attachment—which is not at all a certainty, given the prevalence of concerns about viruses—and (4) the person has the software necessary to listen to the attachment. That's a lot of "ifs," so let's just say that the second variety of intelligence is not closely linked to receiving e-mail messages.

3. Logical and Mathematical Intelligence

People with high intelligence in this area have a passion for abstraction and a deep-seated need to explore and discover. They enjoy analyzing, breaking down, and resolving problems. They may or may not be great at math, but they almost certainly have a lot in common with Sherlock Holmes. Those blessed with very high intelligence levels in this third area may take great pleasure in identifying inconsistencies or errors in reasoning that others have missed. Now, it is possible that somebody who employs this kind of intelligence may do so by means of an e-mail message. But notice that e-mail messages from this person are likely to be long, that they may require a great deal of technical understanding, and that they may identify more problems than opportunities. So even though this third level of intelligence does technically connect with a type of functioning relevant to the medium of e-mail, the resulting communication may not always move your sales process forward. To the contrary, the person with high-level logical and mathematical intelligence may delight in sending e-mail mes-sages that identify new (and, often, insurmountable) obstacles for salespeople!

4. Visual and Spatial Intelligence

Here Gardner identifies the intelligence that allows people to understand visual reality. People who score high in this realm of intelligence know how to create, interpret, and transform visual images. They may think in terms of pictures. Inasmuch as salespeople must usually avoid incorporating visual imagery in the body of their e-mail messages, primarily for practical reasons (spam filters may pick up the image and keep the message from ever reaching its intended recipient), it's safe to say that the types of e-mail messages that we are primarily discussing in this book do not appeal to people who score high in this fourth realm of intelligence.

5. Bodily/Kinesthetic Intelligence

This variety of intelligence, according to Gardner, has to do with things one can do with one's body, and the fluency and grace necessary to execute physical movement. Bodily and kinesthetic intelligence takes the form of both highly sophisticated movement of the body, like that of a ballet dancer, and intricate manipulation of physical objects, like the work of a sculptor. Notice that in the example of a sculptor, the bodily and kinesthetic intelligence compliments the visual and spatial intelligence. If it is your job to create a business relationship with someone whose most developed intelligence is bodily and kinesthetic, e-mail should not be your medium of choice. Think about it. Reading and responding to e-mail is essentially a sedentary activity. It might well be the polar opposite of bodily and kinesthetic intelligence—the kind of activity someone gifted in this area would be likely to go out of his or her way to avoid.

6. Intrapersonal Intelligence

This kind of intelligence, familiar to anyone who has ever written a love letter or received one, has to do with expressing one's own feelings and perceptions. Consider the achievement of a great poet, raconteur, novelist, or playwright, and the potential of this unique intelligence area will become clear to you. Such people understand their own reactions and emotional patterns, interpret them effectively, and can even reproduce them or simulate them in a way that allows others to participate in them. Since research indicates that much human decision making is driven by emotion rather than cold logical assessments, appealing to people's emotions—how they feel and why they feel that way—would seem to be a powerful and important sales strategy. Unfortunately, people with high levels of intrapersonal intelligence are sometimes strongly internally oriented, which means that they may need a strong personal bond with you before they even begin to evaluate your written message.

7. Interpersonal Intelligence

This is not to be confused with intrapersonal intelligence, which, as we have seen, points toward the individual's own feelings and perceptions. Interpersonal intelligence, on the other hand, is pointed toward other people. People with high levels of interpersonal intelligence are often considered charismatic and powerful leaders. Here's the extraordinary thing about people who score high in Intelligence Level Seven: They often intuitively understand, and adapt their communication styles to, people with high intelligence in any of the other six categories. Salespeople often score very high in the area of interpersonal intelligence (so consider yourself lucky if this all sounds strangely familiar). Great politicians and great speakers may score high in this seventh level of intelligence; this is the "leadership intelligence." In general, this level of intelligence is the one that allows someone to "bond" powerfully with individuals or groups; somebody who has a "knack for dealing with people" is likely to have high levels of interpersonal intelligence. But here's the catch. If you are aiming to sell to somebody whose primary intelligence connects powerfully to human interaction, it is unlikely that you will want to base most (or any) of your initial contact with that person on an activity that requires him or her to stare at a computer screen.

■ ■ ■

You can see, I hope, that Gardner's system gives salespeople important new insights about the intelligences that are operating simultaneously within all of us—and on the importance of using different methods to connect with people based on that.

Now here's the part I want you to remember. If your strategy for uncovering new prospective customers relies solely (or even primarily) on pointing them toward words you have written, words that can only be displayed on a computer screen, it seems likely to me that you will be missing huge chunks of the audience—and that missing that many people will be a mistake.

For some people—perhaps a majority of people—eye-to-eye, face-to-face, and/or voice-to-voice interaction will be an intrinsic part of their intelligence set. Interpreting (or even noticing) e-mail from strangers will feel, to them, like translating a foreign language.

Use e-mail as one of the tools in your outreach campaign, but be ready for in-person activity, too. You should be ready to engage in one-on-one linguistic and verbal exchanges; you should be ready to play a great piece of music or a powerfully cut video that uses music; you should be ready to prove your case with logical precision if necessary; you should be ready to use imagery during face-to-face presentations and in your organization's marketing materials; you should be ready to "walk around the plant" and allow a prospect to show you a physical location or demonstrate a product; you should be ready to ask a prospect how he or she feels about something, and be ready to listen to the answer; and you should be ready to allow somebody with a very high level of interpersonal intelligence to turn you into one of his or her audience members.

Mastering all seven of these intelligence skills, and then using e-mail intelligently to support the relationship, will move you forward in ways that relying on e-mail alone as a prospecting tool simply cannot.

E-Mail and Blogging

CHAPTER

69

FOR THOSE OF YOU WHO HAVE BEEN UNDER A ROCK for the past few years, a "blog" is simply a diary or journal that somebody shares with the rest of the world via the World Wide Web. The term comes from the phrase "Weblog," and the fact that that six-letter word—shortening the phrase World Wide Web Log—has been further condensed to the monosyllabic "blog" is as telling a signal as I can think of that our world's attention span is collapsing.

Now we don't even have time to say "Web log." We only have time to say "blog."

Most people who write blogs write them for very small audiences—and by very small audiences I specifically include audiences that do not exceed one. That's the bad news about blogging. What is the good news about blogging? The good news is it is, technically, free. In other words, assuming you have access to the Internet and a fairly reliable connection that gives you access to a Web resource for your blog, actually composing the entries on the journal will be as free as the air you and I breathe. Or at least part of the monthly package you are paying for anyway to connect to the Internet.

The six-million-dollar question is this: Why should anyone be interested in reading your blog? Well, there are two possible reasons for people to be interested. Either what you write will entertain them, or what you write will be useful to them.

Let's tackle entertainment first. Many, many people spend large amounts of time, effort, and energy trying to be controversial, funny, or otherwise engaging by means of a blog these days, and very few of them succeed. Of those who do succeed, only a tiny minority attract any audience of any size. The question here is not whether you are capable of writing something that makes you feel good for having written it, but whether you can write something that will enhance the visibility—and perhaps even the profitability—of your products and services. So I am going to suggest that you focus, not on tickling people's funny bones—or, God forbid, infuriating people by being purposely controversial or abusive—but rather on being useful. The job of your blog should be to keep people abreast of new developments that they are likely to be interested in, given their status as your customers or prospects. Leave the entertainment to the pros.

Yes. I am asking you to think of the journal you keep online (if you decide to keep one) as something that people familiar with your stuff, or searching for something like it on the Internet, will be happy to stumble across. I am also suggesting that you merge your e-mail newsletter content with your blog content, and find ways through both channels to issue and share roughly the same information about what it is your company is actually doing these days.

Use your blog to:

- Tell people about changes in your product or service lines.
- Tell people about changes to your Web site.
- Share free advice that people can use instantly on how to do what they do better.
- Share links to articles of interest to people who fall into your market niche.
- Collect responses and feedback from blog readers.
- Update your readers about a business or news event that connects to their business objectives.

Of course, each and every one of these ideas is something you could also adapt to your e-mail newsletter copy.

So how do you do it? How do you set up a blog? There are really two options. The first is to purchase software, and the second is to use an online source to power your blog. Two of the most popular are blogger.com and livejournal.com. Check them both out: I think you will decide that working with one of these two sites makes the most sense.

A side note—don't bother trying to promote your business by means of participation in newsgroups. If you want to join a newsgroup, do so because you enjoy communicating about the subject in question. Don't assume that joining the newsgroup will produce prospects in any predictable way.

If you want, and if the editors of the group agree, you can include your name and contact information in the signature of your posting software and share an occasional article or resource or comment. As I say, though, you shouldn't expect this to turn into a revenue source.

E-Mail as a C-Level Selling Tool

SUPPOSE YOU FOLLOW THE ADVICE of the various "take it to the top" C-level selling experts, muster your courage, and actually make that dreaded call to Jane Intimidator, the CEO of Amalgamated Data.

Please understand: At this stage I am not talking about sending a "blind" e-mail message to Jane. I am talking about calling her up on the phone and asking her for a meeting.

And suppose that Jane is actually willing to meet with you. Suppose that she actually remembers and is present for your meeting when you show up at her doorstep.

How long do you think that discussion with Jane is actually going to last?

If Jane is like most of the CEOs that I deal with, it's going to be a pretty brief conversation. Why is it going to be brief? Because Jane got to be CEO of Amalgamated Data by delegating work to other people. So whatever it is I am trying to sell Jane—sales training, computers, sewing machines, rubber mats for the floors of her factory in Thailand, or the little paper umbrellas you put in tropical drinks at the company's annual retreat in Maui—you can bet that Jane is not going to sweat out the details of the decision to implement it. Even if Jane likes my suggestion (and eventually signs on), somebody else is going to do the heavy lifting.

No, the best outcome I can hope for in that situation, and in any similar situation with a similarly high-powered executive, is to receive an endorsement from Jane that allows me not just to talk with Joe Achiever, the high-flying VP of Operations for Amalgamated Data, but to do so under the auspices of the CEO, Jane Intimidator.

Do you see where I am going with this yet?

Before I leave my meeting with Jane, I want to ensure that I can keep her in the loop—and broadcast the message to others at Amalgamated Data that Jane is engaged with me and supports my efforts. I want Jane to be kept up to date on exactly what happens between me and Joe, and I want that to happen in a way Joe has to respect.

It might be nice if Jane would agree to meet with me again so I can update her on exactly what is happening between me and Joe. But in the real world, this is not very likely.

No, what is actually likely to happen is that Jane will agree, if I ask her directly, to let me update her on all the important conclusions that Joe and I reach after Jane refers me to him. How do I want to make those updates to Jane? Well, if I know how Jane likes to communicate, I am going to pick the medium she is most likely to engage with, review regularly, and trust. But in a lot of these situations, I really will not have any idea what Jane's preferred method of communication is going to be, so I am going to suggest, by default, that I keep Jane—and everybody else I connect with at Amalgamated Data—up to date by means of e-mail messages. That's why I'm going to ask Jane to give me her e-mail address so I can personally give her a summary, from time to time (not every day), of exactly what I am doing with Joe. And so I can copy Joe on the very same message.

It is very important to understand that when I ask Jane for her e-mail address so I can give her occasional updates, what I am really doing is setting up a barometer of sorts that will tell me about the quality of my communication with Jane. I want to gauge Jane's willingness to get an occasional summary of how my initiative is going, and the prospects that it really will add value to her organization.

If Jane tells me, "No, I don't want to give you my e-mail address. I get enough messages already . . . work with purchasing" that is really not a good sign that I should invest a lot of time and effort and energy in my discussions at Amalgamated. It is possible, of course, that Jane would rather hear about how my discussions with Joe are going by some other medium, but if the simple request for an e-mail address—which is, after all, a pretty common means of keeping in touch with the business world these days—falls flat, then I know that there is likely to be a problem somewhere down the line.

In that situation, to identify where I really stand, I might even consider asking Jane a question like this: "Wow. I'm a little surprised by that. I didn't expect that you'd say that. Usually at this stage of a conversation, when I talked to some of your colleagues at other companies in your industry, they're more than happy to have me set up these updates by e-mail. I'm just curious why wouldn't you want to get an update from me about how well or poorly things are going?"

By asking this question, I am actually very likely to get a direct answer from the CEO, one that might sound like this: "No, it's nothing like that, Steve. It's just that we're really not planning on doing any spending in this area over the next twelve months. You're probably better off trying to talk to somebody else."

My experience is that CEOs tend to be very direct about things like this. If they are asked a direct question, they will give you, more often than not, a direct answer. That really is the key: You have to be willing to ask them a direct question. You have to learn not to beat around the bush.

Another big issue in this situation is trust. We have to make it absolutely clear to Jane that we will not be bombarding her with fifty e-mails a day. Who could blame her for wanting to avoid that? So we have to make it abundantly clear, from the very beginning of the conversation, that what we are talking about is an e-mail that will take place at some point between

Time Frame A and Time Frame B, say fourteen to twenty-one days from now.

You remember that earlier on I told you that sales was all about getting commitment to a Next Step. In this case, when you are dealing with a very high-level person, you may not be able to secure a Next Step that takes the form of a face-to-face meeting with the very topmost person in the organization. (No matter what anybody says, it is unlikely that you will be able to work directly with the CEO of a large organization, and it is unlikely that he or she will agree to meet again with you one on one.)

The whole point of the meeting, from the CEO's point of view, will simply be to plug you in with the right people in the organization. That's if you're lucky. That's the best possible outcome to that meeting. In that case, you will want to "take the temperature" of the relationship and just make sure that the CEO really does want results of the kind you think you can deliver. If so, he or she should have no problem agreeing to a brief e-mail message from you that summarizes how the initiative is going.

Once you establish that, the e-mail message you prepare for the CEO will have the most remarkable effect on others in the organization. It will remind Joe Achiever that you are in fact working with Jane Intimidator's blessing. During your next discussion with Joe, you can make it clear that you set up this arrangement with Jane, that she has given you her e-mail address, and that she wants to have a concise summary of exactly what you found out between now and the middle of March.

Let me be honest about something. You cannot expect to play this card alone to victory, because obviously Joe has a relationship with Jane Intimidator, too, and in all likelihood, it is significantly stronger than yours is. But you can make it clear that you are each working along the same lines, in the same direction and toward the same goals. You can make it clear that implementing Jane's vision is the whole reason you are showing up to meet with Joe. If you use e-mail to send and reinforce that message, you'll be on the right track.

22 Unforgivable E-Mail Mistakes

THERE ARE ANY NUMBER OF MISTAKES salespeople make in composing e-mail messages. In this part of the book, I'm going to warn you about twenty-one of the most dangerous—and offer some advice on what to do instead.

Mistake #1: Not Asking for, or Confirming, or Setting a Next Step

Not building a reference to some kind of Next Step into your e-mail, or preparing for one you plan to ask for, means breaking a basic commandment of selling.

You are a salesperson. Your income is built on asking for, and receiving, Next Steps. You are communicating by e-mail with someone to whom you wish to sell. It follows that your every communication should either propose, or directly or indirectly reference, what's happening next, or could happen next in the relationship.

Use a personalized e-mail message to:

- Request a face-to-face meeting at a specific date and time.
- Confirm a face-to-face meeting at a specific date and time.

- Send along a link to an article of interest, then phone the person afterward to make sure the person saw the link. (As I've mentioned elsewhere in this book, I like to do this with people who are "still thinking" about a proposal, and it has been pending for a while. Inevitably, they *volunteer* information about where they are in the selling process, at which point I can recommend, over the phone, an appropriate Next Step.)
- Say that you have a new idea to discuss and suggest a specific date and time for doing so. (This is often helpful after a presentation has gone poorly.)
- Set expectations for an upcoming meeting at a specific date and time.
- Establish timelines with current customer.
- Float an idea for a proposal before you actually deliver the formal proposal at a specific date and time.
- Pave the way for a phone call at a specific date and time that will set up a face-to-face meeting.
- Confirm the date and time of a post-meeting "debriefing" appointment *before* you deliver a presentation to a committee or meet with a group.

(As a footnote: Personally, I don't like "confirming" an initial face-to-face meeting I've recently set up, since that gives the recipient an opportunity to cancel the meeting. If you've already established a good initial dialogue with the person, however, you may wish to confirm the meeting by e-mail or phone contact ahead of time.)

Mistake #2: Stupid Subject Lines

The following messages are very likely to be instantly discarded or ignored. Don't use them.

- Messages whose subject line pretends that the person has already won something
- Subject lines that reference nonexistent acquaintances

- Subject lines that try to use off-color jokes (or outright obscenity) to win the other person's attention
- Subject lines featuring any variation on "What on earth do I have to do to get in touch with you?"
- Subject lines featuring any variation on "You asked me to get in touch with you" when that is not the case
- Lies (for instance, "We found your wallet")
- Half-truths (for instance, "We might have found your wallet")

Would *you* open any of those messages? I didn't think so.

Mistake #3: Tone Mismatch

I'm assuming you were careful enough to send an *initial* message that struck a professional tone and piqued the other person's interest. What I'm talking about here is the message you send *in response to an incoming message from the other person*. Often, the messages salespeople send out in such situations are hastily composed, and they miss out on important conversational cues from the other side.

Put bluntly: We're sometimes so excited about getting a response that we write text that looks as though it were composed by baboons.

Suppose you get the following message:

To: **Jerry Salesperson**

From: Mark Bigshot

Subject: Re: Beating quota by 15 percent in All seventeen of your territories

Hello there, Jerry:

This does sound intriguing. Alas, I'm not available to meet with you on April 12.

Is there any time the following week that we could get together? I am free from 2:00 P.M. to 3:00 P.M., Monday through Thursday. What's the best day for you?

Best,

Mark

What can we conclude about the person's communication style, just from those few sentences? Well, for one thing, we can conclude that this is someone who takes a good deal of time to compose text with care. All the capitalization is correct. All the punctuation is correct. All the sentences are complete. Mark even used the word *Alas*, which is at least circumstantial evidence of an English major somewhere in his family tree.

Since we know that we're dealing with a careful writer who adopts a studious, careful, almost academic tone, we should do our best to mirror that tone in the message we send back. All too often, however, we don't do that. Instead, we tell ourselves that the most important thing is to get back to Mark *instantly*. Nothing else matters! We may even fool ourselves into believing that Mark is probably sitting at his monitor, waiting impatiently for our response, at this very moment. So what do we do? We send something like this:

To: Mark Bigshot

From: Jerry Salesperson

Subject: Re: Beating quota by 15 percent in all seventeen of your territories

hey Mark:

what abt next Mon at 1:30?

I"ll be mtg w/another client that AM near you pls advise

J

Even though we will have to take a few extra minutes to compose a sentence or two that matches Mark's studious tone, we are better advised to do that than to hit "Send" upon composing the barely comprehensible message here. Following's a better model:

To: Mark Bigshot

From: Jerry Salesperson

Subject: Re: Beating quota by 15 percent in all seventeen of tour territories

And hello to you, Mark:

Thanks so much for getting back to me so quickly.

Could we possibly meet in your offices on Monday, the 19th of April, at 1:30? I have a meeting that morning at Centennial Bank.

Looking forward to hearing from you,

Jerry

A side note: Unless you are absolutely certain you have achieved what might be called a "verbal" level of e-mail interaction with your correspondent—the kind of relationship in which an occasional misspelled word or forgotten punctuation mark will do you no discredit—you really should go to the trouble of composing your message carefully, checking it for grammar and spelling errors, and perhaps even asking somebody else to review it before you send it out. Hitting send before you are really ready to is one of the most common causes of "e-mail stress" among salespeople. By the way, most good e-mail platforms now feature a spell check function, but be forewarned that this function will not correct misspellings of proper names or errors like "lead" for "led." I once lost a prospect after thoroughly confusing him by making a reference to "gold" when I was actually asking about "golf." That is the kind of thing that slips through spell checks, and it's something you should be vigilant about, especially when suggesting a round of golf to a high-ranking C-Level decision maker.

Mistake #4: Getting the Person's Name, Company, or Title Wrong

Unforgivable. Check the person's name, company affiliation, and title against an unimpeachable outside source. Again, it is quite possible for you to get the person's name, company, or title wrong . . . and for such a message to sneak past a computerized spell check program. If the person disengages from your message for a heartbeat, that heartbeat is long enough for him or her to hit "delete."

Mistake #5: Sending Attachments Too Early in the Relationship

Sometimes, spam filters will refuse a message that carries an attachment, or will regard an image within the message as an attachment. Even if the message with an attachment or image makes it through, people will generally shy away from a message from an unfamiliar correspondent that has an attachment. Can we blame them? This is how computer viruses are spread. Leave off the attachment until the other person tells you that it is okay to send one.

It is worth noting here that there has been a constant battle between those who are engaged in sending out voluminous amounts of e-mail to people who have not requested the message and the forces of technology committed to keeping people from having to deal with vast amounts of spam. This battle is an ongoing one, in which one side perpetually attempts to top the most recent technological work-arounds and insights of the other. I am going to strongly suggest that you keep your messages *very simple*, lest you be perceived as one of the bad guys. I am also going to suggest that you avoid wasting your time and energy trying to figure out ways to get around spam filters and firewalls. If you are having difficulty connecting with an individual by means of e-mail, pick up the phone and try calling the person directly. That will be a much better investment of your time and effort than convening a summit conference of engineers and asking them to close the gap between you and the perspective customer's IT department.

Mistake #6: Sending the Wrong Attachment

This can be particularly embarrassing if you send an attachment that is non-work-related or contains sensitive information.

Mistake #7: Sending No Attachment When the Body of Your Message References an Attachment

I have a theory that salespeople are the members of the work force most likely to commit this blunder. It is a great way to extend your selling cycle and confuse your prospect. Check twice before you hit "send."

Mistake #8: Using All Caps

This is the online equivalent of shouting at someone across a desk.

They say President Clinton had a habit of sending e-mail messages with the "caps lock" key on. That's just one of the examples by which his presidency is destined to live in infamy. (Capital letters in subject lines are okay in certain situations where your aim is to signal emphasis.)

Mistake #9: Cursing or Using Off-Color Humor

No bad words. No innuendo. No Monica jokes (see above).

Mistake #10: Using Humor That Is Not Off-Color, But Is Nevertheless Inappropriate

Ethnic jokes, for instance, are off-limits.

Humor in general is an iffy proposition in e-mail correspondence. Much of the interpersonal connection that makes a joke funny in the first place is missing online, thanks to the absence of body language and vocal inflection. (No, little smiley faces are not appropriate in sales communications.) And let's face it—people have gotten tired of having the same joke forwarded to them by fifty different people.

Even well-intentioned humor can backfire in an e-mail message to a prospect or customer. My basic rule is: Save the jokes for the New Year's Eve party, choose them carefully, and tell them in person.

Mistake #11: One-Word Messages

Even in response to a one-word message from the other person. Even if the person does understand you (which is far from a certain thing), you will run the risk of being perceived as arrogant. Do something a little more creative than writing the words "yes" or "no" in the body of the message.

Mistake #12: Ranting

Don't ever send an e-mail message to a prospect or customer when angry. Don't ever send an e-mail message to a prospect or customer in order to "get something off your chest."

Mistake #13: Making Any Reference to Religion

There is only one possible exception to this: the prospect brings the topic of religion up first, and you and the prospect or customer are of the same faith. In this case, you have a possible opportunity for establishing commonality—but this type of discussion is still fraught with risk. Tread carefully. Remember, you are selling, not preaching.

Mistake #14: Making Sexist or Racist Remarks, Even in Jest

Any discriminatory language may come back to haunt you. Always assume the person with whom you're speaking has no sense of humor. Always assume that your message will be archived and/or sent to your boss.

Mistake #15: Communicating in Long Blocks of Text

Break it up and use bullet points, as discussed in Chapter 60.

Mistake #16: Using Cheesy Tricks in Your Subject Line to Try to Get Past the Person's Spam Filter

By using the number 3 instead of an *e*, for example, as in: LOW INT3R3ST RAT3S. Why on earth would you resort to this trick if you weren't sending massive amounts of blind e-mail?

There is probably no better way to convince your correspondent that you are in fact a spam artist.

Mistake #17: Sending the Message to People Who Should Not Receive It

Responding to a query or comment that has come your way from someone else? If you do not mean to reply to everybody who has up to this point received the message, *do not use the "reply all" feature.*

Copying people unnecessarily, in this situation or any other, is a common breach of e-mail etiquette. One of the reasons that our e-mail boxes are overflowing—not the only reason of course, but one of the reasons—is that we are sometimes far too eager to copy everyone who might conceivably have even a tangential connection with the message in question. If your query really is meant for the VP of Operations at BigCo, you should probably think twice before copying the CEO, every member of the Board of Directors, and every person on the sales staff. If nothing else, you will tick people off because they will assume you are always sending them messages they do not have to read—and they will be less likely to read the messages that really do relate to them. Use the "cc" field sparingly. (But do use it to keep key contacts, like the CEO, in the loop about your progress toward key goals.)

Mistake #18: Encouraging a Multiparty Shouting Match

When you are raising a controversial topic, and you have absolutely no option but to send a message to more than one person at a time, think hard about whether you really want everyone who reads your message to be able to respond to everyone else about what you've said.

Let me give you an example. If you have to pass along bad news about a delayed shipment, and you do not want to enable an online debate about the wisdom of deciding to work with your company in the first place, your best approach will be to avoid the "cc" field entirely. Instead, send the message to yourself and place all the relevant recipient e-mails in the "bcc," or "blind copy," field. This means that no one will be able to respond to the entire group by simply hitting "reply all." Anybody hitting reply will be addressing only you.

Mistake #19: Being (Perceived as) a Jerk

Here's the interesting thing about e-mail: it is extremely easy to misinterpret.

We, as readers of e-mail, lack any meaningful visual information from the sender. (We can't read body language or facial expressions, the way we would in a real-life, one-on-one conversation.) Similarly, we as readers lack any information about the pitch or tone of the sender's intended "voice." (We can't hear whether the other person intends a remark to sound facetious, for instance.)

But, to the writer, e-mail correspondence often feels very much like verbal communication—so much so that many people who "let it all hang out" while writing messages type out things that look strange, offensive, or even menacing in an e-mail message . . . but wouldn't draw a moment's notice if the same words were spoken casually. (Example: "You don't want to go there." Say it with a smile, and you're humorously changing the subject. Type it in an e-mail message, and it sounds like you're planning to send over a guy with brass knuckles.)

Bottom line: We as readers may come to the conclusion that somebody is being a jerk—while he or she does not realize the words chosen seem at all jerk-like.

So what do I really mean here? What I mean is, read your stuff over twice before you hit "send." Don't let the other person conclude that you are a jerk. In the world of e-mail, all it really takes to "be" a jerk is for you to inadvertently give someone the ammunition necessary to conclude that you are one. Stay away from sarcasm and irony; make sure nothing you've written could possibly be misconstrued.

Mistake #20: Mixing Business with Pleasure

This one is so obvious that many people miss it. Send business messages from your business e-mail—that is, from the one with your company's domain name at the end of it. Send personal messages from your personal e-mail address. Do not mix the two up. I know of people who maintain as many as five or six different e-mail addresses for different functions. That's fine, of course . . . as long as they keep everything in the right bucket.

Never, ever use your company's e-mail system to distribute personal communications.

Mistake #21: Rambling On and On

Yes, even if your correspondent rambles on and on. The other person's long message to you is *not* permission to send a long message in return. If you think that *your* long message will be scanned and circulated reverently, as though it were a religious text, you have a fundamental misunderstanding of the job description behind the word *salesperson*.

If you really, truly cannot get the message across within the confines of a single screen of information, and you don't want to send an attachment, my suggestion is that you pick up the phone.

Mistake #22: Sending an E-Mail Message in Anger

Never send an angry e-mail message to any business contact. At any time. Ever.

For professional salespeople, this is, quite simply, *never* a good idea. Take a break and come back to the message in an hour or two, after you've had the chance to calm down.

Part Six

50 Sales Questions
to Close the Deal

Questions That Initiate Contact and Build Rapport

THIS SECTION OF THE BOOK is designed to help you ask questions that move you closer to closing the deal. The fifty questions here are designed to help you travel relentlessly toward that goal. The questions are arranged into these categories:

1. Questions that help you initiate contact and build a rapport with the prospect—*Chapter 72*.
2. Questions that help you figure out what the other person does (you can't sell effectively if you don't know this)—*Chapter 73*.
3. Questions that help you secure a Next Step with the prospect—*Chapter 74*.
4. Questions that help you identify the right presentation—*Chapter 75*.
5. Questions that help you deal with setbacks, formalize the decision, and negotiate the best deal—*Chapter 76*.

Question 1: What I'd like to do is get together with you this coming Tuesday at 10:00—does that make sense?

Obviously, you cannot spring that question on somebody within the first five seconds of a call, so there is a little bit of preparation that must precede it.

For the record, the following is an abbreviated version of a calling approach that leads up to that question (much the same as the approach discussed earlier in this book):

> "Hello, Mr. Prospect, this is Steve Schiffman calling from DEI Management Group. I'm not sure if you've heard of us, but we're one of the largest sales training companies in the United States and we work with firms such as This Company, That Company, and The Other Company. The reason I'm calling you today specifically is that we just completed a program with Big Company that helped them to dramatically increase their first appointment totals, and I'd really like to meet with you to show you the success that we had with them. I'd like to get together with you next Tuesday at 10:00; does that make sense?"

Notice that this is a standardized approach, which means that it is a script that I memorize and can deliver over and over in exactly the same way. It always leads directly to that closing question.

Question 2: Can I get your advice?

There are any number of reasons for scheduling a face-to-face meeting with a prospect. Among the most creative is a request for information about whether what you sell is applicable within that person's industry.

Let's say you are trying to sell for the first time to a group you have never sold to before—accountants, for example. And suppose that you have successfully sold to another group that the group you are trying to reach would have heard of—banks, let's say. Here is what your initial call could sound like:

"Hi, Mr. Jones, this is Steve Schiffman calling from D.E.I. Management Group. I'm not sure whether or not you've heard of us, but we're a sales training company here in New York City and we work with companies like The Blah Blah Banking Group. The reason I'm calling you today specifically is that I'm trying to figure out whether or not a program we did for Fleet Bank has any application whatsoever within the accounting industry. I'd like to get together with you to show you what we did for Fleet Bank and get your feedback on it, to see if we should be marketing to people in your industry. Can we get together this coming Tuesday at 10:00?"

Notice that this is a very low-pressure way to sell. It is an intriguing variation on the standard call, one that you may find helpful when you are branching out into new markets in which you can appeal to your contact as "one professional to another."

Question 3: Why don't we just get together?

This is an extremely effective question you can use to overcome objections, stalls and longwinded responses from people to whom you are prospecting on the phone. The advantage of the question lies in its straightforward nature. I cannot tell you the number of times that I have used this question to "cut to the chase" and deliver a friendly reminder to a new contact that the point of my call is to schedule a face-to-face meeting.

This question basically says, "Shouldn't we advance this relationship to the Next Step?" If the answer is a definitive no, you are going to find out then and there. If the answer is maybe, you are going to find out the reasons why there is some hesitation to getting together or to moving forward toward the Next Step. If the answer is yes, you are going to find out instantly; at that point you will pull out your appointment book, set the time and date, and politely get off the phone.

Question 4: So I've got us down for (date) and (time), right?

Ask this question and then get off the phone. Politely, of course! It is important to *conclude* the phone conversation with the prospect once you have set the appointment, however you ask to do so. If you set the appointment and then keep talking, only one thing can happen—the person can decide it does not really make sense to meet with you!

Question 5: The Knockout Question

In almost all the questions you will read about in this section of the book, you will find a specific structure and a clear indication of precisely what words you should say. When it comes to this question, however, there is really no way for me to give you that. This is the question you should ask very early in the relationship—perhaps during the initial prospecting call, but definitely before you get too far into the first meeting. It is a question that allows you to determine exactly how close this person comes to matching the profile of your "perfect" customer.

Please understand that I am not advocating that you subject the person on the other end of the line to an extended interview that will allow you to conduct a regression analysis about how well they match up with your 100 top clients. I am talking about a *single* question that will help you to understand whether or not this person matches your criteria and is worth meeting face-to-face.

There always is an inherent danger in telling people to build this question into their prospecting call, because the temptation is so strong to embark on an in-depth conversation with the prospect. As we have seen, if that is not your selling model, you want to keep the call clearly focused on one topic and one topic only: whether or not the person will meet with you at a specific date and time. However, I have found that with just a little bit of practice, people can learn to keep their calls focused and also deliver this very simple kind of question. In my industry, the sales training industry, the appropriate knockout question is quite direct and sounds like this:

"How many salespeople do you have?"

By asking a question like this, I can instantly determine whether this opportunity is worth scheduling my day around. If the person I am talking to has two salespeople, that is a good distance away from the ideal answer I want to get, which is usually a minimum of ten salespeople. I wouldn't take that person out to lunch.

If, on the other hand, the person tells me he or she is in charge of 250 salespeople, I know that this is potentially going to be a major deal, and I am going to need to bring references about some of the larger accounts with whom we have worked. In either event, I will get valuable information that will make it very clear to me whether or not I want to move forward with this prospect.

Questions for Building Rapport

Question 6: How's business?

This is an all-purpose conversation starter that will give you insight, not only on the person's present situation—not only the company's current level of success, but also how your individual contact measures that success. I have more than once met with a CEO who had a hot product or service in an expanding market that his company dominated, but who was nevertheless quite worried about the company's business prospects. My simple question, "How's business?" allows people to share the fact that their business is well positioned for success today, but vulnerable to competitive forces in the future, forces that may be deeply troubling to your contact.

So the simple-sounding question, "How's business?" is a great way to get the other person talking, and also an important tool for measuring both what is happening in this person's world and how he or she interprets and evaluates what is happening.

The following is also an effective question with which to begin the meeting:

Question 7: How did you become a . . . ?

Or . . .

What do you have to study to become a . . . ?

Asking about the person's early career or educational choices is among the safest and most reliable rapport-building strategies. It is very, very difficult to go wrong in the early parts of the meeting with a new person by asking the person what led him or her to the current job. In most cases, you will want to step back and let the person go on a bit about this, because the act of sharing one's history is an important part of the process of bonding with somebody professionally.

Question 8: So how did you come to work here?

Most contacts will be more than happy to fill you in on all the relevant details of how they got the job. Again, the simple act of their sharing this information is just as important as the content of what they pass along. The key in the rapport-building phase is to get the person to open up, to take part in the discussion, and to conclude that it is safe to share information with you.

This question will not work well, of course, if you happen to be meeting with the person who built the company up from nothing over a period of time. For entrepreneurs and other such movers and shakers, you should probably consider a question like . . .

Questions for Managing the Transition to the "Business Portion" of the Meeting

Question 9: Before we get started, would it help if I told you a little bit about how our company got started?

This is the point in the meeting at which you will pose this question or something like it. Interesting variations include:

Would it help if I went first?

If there's a problem, and the other person wants to go first, that's fine. But at least you've initiated the discussion.

Would it help if I told you a little bit about the work we did for XYZ Company?

Share a few relevant details about the company you mentioned during your prospecting call, and then ask a question.

Question 10: Would it help if I gave a brief overview of what we usually do during this meeting?

All of these questions and their countless variations are important tools for you to use to establish control of the meeting. Can you see why? The mere fact that you have posed the question determines the subject that you and the other person will be talking about. This is what we mean when we talk about "controlling the flow."

Note that we are not asking the prospect, "What don't you like about the widgets that you are currently using?" We are instead choosing to put the focus on whether or not it would help if we "went first."

This is a very tactful way of establishing our position as the coordinator of the meeting, and of soliciting an initial response from the other person. There is a cliché that prosecuting attorneys will not ask a question to which they do not know the answer. The same is not exactly true for salespeople—we have to ask lots of questions that we do not know the answer to—but we are nevertheless responsible for posing questions and then anticipating where they are going to go. And at this crucial junction in the meeting, we do not want to launch questions that can lead us into a direction with which we are completely unfamiliar.

Question 11: What made you want to consider purchasing [widgets]?

Not long ago I had the pleasure of taking a call from someone who had decided that he wanted to contact our company to deliver sales training to his organization. This is one of these "dream calls"—the kind of call where the person says, "I have 150 salespeople and I would like you to come in and train them. I read your book, I love what you guys do, and I am ready to set up training. What do you charge?"

Now, twenty years ago, I would have taken that call and started in asking about timing, pricing, and what kind of schedule for the day the prospect was trying to set up. But nowadays, I handle this kind of call a bit differently. Here is what I said:

"That's great. Thanks for calling. Just out of curiosity, what made you decide that you wanted to invest in sales training for people?"

For a lot of people, a question like this is a little scary. They assume that the sale is closed, and that asking questions about motive or decision will only increase the likelihood of losing the deal. But actually, just the opposite is true.

Question 12: What is the main thing that you are trying to accomplish this month/quarter/year?

This is an opening you can use in a situation where you really do not have a lot of information to work with. It is the kind of question that will, with any luck, give you insights into precisely what your contact envisions, what he or she is responsible for making happen, and perhaps even an early glimpse about how you might fit into the overall picture.

Question 13: How do you think you stack up against the competition?

Do not be afraid to ask a decision maker within the organization how he or she feels the organization stacks up against the competition. A fair number of senior executives seem to make a lifetime commitment to the job of identifying areas where the competition is outperforming them, analyzing ways to combat this and all the possible strategies for overcoming the performance gap identified. Someone who takes this approach to the question is very likely to be a person of authority or a person "on the way up." By the same token, a person who is complacent about the competition and who believes that it represents no real threat to his or her employer's operations, is unlikely to hold a position of great practical authority and influence within the company.

Note that I am not suggesting that every key decision maker will have a cynical or pessimistic answer to this question; only that these people will be more likely to take a realistic look at the challenges they face from the outside. These decision makers are also quite willing to share what they feel to be their company's competitive advantages with you, but they must, by definition, develop some sense of what is working and what is not for their competitors in the marketplace.

Even significant market share is not any guarantee of dominance of a given market, and most successful executives know this. That is why this question, and intelligent follow-ups to it, can be such an eye-opening experience for a salesperson eager to identify the priorities of the "movers and shakers" within the organization.

Question 14: My guess is, your people face challenge X— what do you think?

This is an extremely important question, but one that must be used with great skill and followed up appropriately (see the next question).

This question is only to be used in those situations where you really feel that your product or service can add value to the person's operation. The fact that you've reached this conclusion is interesting, but it's really not as relevant as what your prospect has concluded. Instead of doing what most salespeople do, namely proclaim that we have the solution and start reciting a memorized speech about it, we're going to ask a question that very subtly introduces our interpretation of the situation, and then asks for the prospect input and endorsement before we proceed any further.

Question 15: Why do you think that's happening?

This is the all-important follow-through question to Question 14. Notice that before I supply any explanations of the facts that the prospect and I agree are before us, I am going to give him or her a chance to interpret and explain the situation. Nine times out of ten, however, the person *won't* have meaningful input. There may be a stock response, but in fact they know full well that I work with a lot of sales teams, and so they'll turn to me and say, "Well, I think it might be a number of things, but I'm most interested on your take on this. Why do *you* think it's happening?"

It's at that point that I'll go into a much more detailed overview of what my company offers. I'll say something like this, "My guess is that they're not prospecting enough, and that the basic daily activities really haven't been built into their routine. My feeling is that

333

they're probably just coasting on referrals from existing accounts, and that they could go to the next level if they just did a little bit more prospecting and made that a regular habit."

Note what I've done here. What you just read is exactly what I wanted to say, probably from within about five minutes of shaking hands with the prospect. It's entirely possible that I would have had an initial fix on what the situation in that person's sales staff is right off the bat, after just a few questions. But even though I have the feeling that I "know what's going on," I can't simply lead the meeting with my recommendation. I must both establish rapport with the individual, open lines of communication, *and get his or her take on what's going on*. Then, and only then, can I start to give an initial sense of where I think the problem may be.

To offer an example of how this very important question sequence works, I've used my own industry. But the same strategy can apply to virtually any field of endeavor, and I think you'll find it very easy to insert the specifics of your own sales environment. Follow the same sequence, and make sure you get the other person's input before you launch in on a brief overview of what you think might be the matter. This is a question sequence that should be saved for some point in the second half of your face-to-face meeting.

Follow-Through Questions to Figure Out What the Person and the Company Do

Question 16: "So—are you currently . . . ?" (The Framed Question)

A framed question is one that builds on an assumption contrary to what you assume the prospect believes. It is an extremely important interview tool, because it gets you corrected, and getting you corrected not only gives you the right information but also encourages the dialogue with your prospect.

We have already noticed that when we ask people directly whether or not they are responsible for making decisions in a given area, they are likely to inflate their importance—at least during the first face-to-face meeting. People may not always be willing to give us the precise information we want, but we may rest assured that they will usually be willing to correct us and thus demonstrate their expertise.

During the sales interview, you should be ready to use a question that uses this principle to uncover information that would otherwise not be forthcoming. This kind of question is *designed* to get you contradicted.

I realize the idea of posing a question that's meant to encourage the other person to contradict you sounds a little strange at first. But it does work, because human beings love to be right! So when you ask this kind of question, you're going to let the other person "right" you—and when he or she does so, mark my words, you'll get a whole long story about what's really going on in the organization.

Here's how it works. At a certain point, you're going to incorporate a specific assumption within the question or question sequence—an assumption that points in the opposite direction from the answer you "expect."

Framing can be adapted to virtually any type of information gap you need to fill. You can use this approach, for example, when you want to learn which, if any, of your competitors, your prospect is talking to. Here's what it might sound like.

You: So, are you working with Plattsburgh Services to get a proposal together for this project?

Prospect: Plattsburgh? No, no, they're way too small for a job like this. We're only talking to the bigger firms: yourself, Megacorp, ABC Development, and Business to Business. We had had some problems with the initial pricing Business to Business was talking about for this project, but our CEO used them exclusively at his last company, and he thinks very highly of their technical support team. So we had to get them in there.

Did you notice that the prospect, after correcting us, offered a little story that gave us some essential background information? My experience is that you'll be *much* more likely to get this kind of information if you ask a framed question than if you ask a question like, "Who else are you talking to?"

Framed questions are designed to "harness" the other person's natural inclination to inflate his own importance, to be right, and to correct us. I recommend these questions for situations where you are having a little difficulty getting the other person to open up at the beginning of the meeting.

Again, how do you construct a framed question? Simply build in the assumption that you think the person is likely to correct, and then ask the question with the opposite assumption.

Question 17: You don't mind if I take notes, do you?

Asking this question at an early point in the meeting, of course, is a perfectly acceptable way to set the tone. You may also choose to simply remove your yellow legal pad, pull out a pen, and begin writing down every word or key concept the other person shares with you.

I include the question here because many salespeople I train are skittish about taking notes without "permission." I'm not big on asking for "permission," but I suppose that if you are dealing with someone who is sensitive about revealing competitive information, or routinely handles materials that have legal or regulatory implications, it would probably be a good idea to confirm that the person has no problem with you taking notes.

In any event, you should make a point of recording, by hand, all the key points from the discussion. Doing so sends an impossible-to-ignore message: *I am listening to you.* Writing key points down during a meeting encourages your contact to open up, makes the conversation flow more smoothly, and establishes your credentials as someone who is willing to make a significant effort to get the right information down in black and white.

Question 18: Just to get a ballpark figure, what kind of budget are you working with?

When I suggest to salespeople that they pose this question during the first meeting, and preferably during the early portion of that meeting, they stare at me in horror. Among their responses are:

- "I haven't even developed a rapport with the prospect yet."
- "The prospect doesn't know anything about us yet!"
- "I haven't had a chance to probe yet!"
- "I haven't determined what the person's needs are yet!"
- "I haven't determined what the person's 'pain' is yet!"

The prevailing thinking among so many salespeople today is that you cannot possibly discuss price in the most general or vague terms, without having engaged in some elaborate ritual. This ritual supposedly includes the determining of all the benchmarks and the criteria for success, as well as the "pain" or "need" that is keeping a person up at night, so you can craft a "value statement" that reflects the "cost" of doing business with your competition.

Nonsense.

The plain fact of the matter is that you have every right to ask, at least in general terms, whether or not this person has a budget that could result in the two of you working together. If this person does not know where or how big that budget is, or has a budget that is too small, you are in trouble. And you should know about that trouble early on, sooner rather than later.

Question 19: What is your average sales cycle?

A fair number of the people you ask this question will not be familiar with the term "sales cycle" so you may have to explain to them that what you are talking about is the amount of time it takes them to move from initial contact or first discussion, to a decision to purchase. You can expect to get an answer that begins with the words "It depends . . ." when you as this question, but you should also be prepared to press, ever so tactfully, for some kind of meaningful explanation of where the upper and lower boundaries lie.

I have worked with companies whose sales cycle was twenty minutes (their upper-end duration of a telesales appeal). I have also worked with companies whose sales cycle was upwards of two years. The answer you receive will tell you a great deal about the culture of the organization, and the processes it must implement to attract customers, keep them happy, and begin the process all over again.

If you do not have a good sense of how long it takes a given company to turn a prospect into a customer, you should not expect to be treated as a business ally in any meaningful sense of the word. Make a point of getting some kind of response to this question, whether or not the answer directly relates to your product or service. It is important strategic information.

Question 20: Can I tell you what some of your counterparts of the organizations that we have been working with are concerned about in this area?

This is a transitional question designed to help you introduce a relevant success story. Obviously, you will want to avoid sharing anything that is even close to being confidential business information, but there is a great deal more you can do to share information and insights, especially by passing along stories from companies that do not directly compete with one another.

You really are an expert. You really do have a right to pass along such information, and to analyze it for your prospect. This is one of the exciting things about working in sales. After you have been with it for only a very limited amount of time—say six or eight weeks—you realize you and your organization really do have a wealth of direct, practical experience that some of your prospects will definitely benefit from hearing. Do not be afraid to volunteer relevant advice and success stories that have come about as a result of working with other companies. Too often, salespeople seem to be apologizing for even stepping into the prospect's office when they should, by rights, be charging consulting fees!

You are an expert in what you do. If you were not, you would not be making a living this way. You know your industry, and you know your product or service, and the odds are that you know enough relevant situations to this one to be able to add value to the person's operation. Think of yourself as less of a convincer and as more of a specialist, someone with valuable experience that can be brought to bear in any number of different professional settings. Intelligent variations on this question include:

Can I tell you how some of my clients in the (X) industry dealt with this problem?

Or . . .

Can I share with you how we handled this when we faced a similar situation with (ABC Company)?

Or . . .

Can I tell you about something that happened to me that may be helpful?

Or . . .

Can I tell you what my boss did about this when he faced the same situation?

Or . . .

Can I give you the highlights of a case study we did that was very similar to this?

All of these are excellent transitional questions. Tailor them to match the story you are hoping to share.

Questions That Move You Toward a Next Step

**Question 21: Can we meet next Tuesday at 2:00—so
I can show you an outline of how we might be able
to work together?**

This is a request for an Outline Meeting. There's a very
good chance this kind of meeting should be your primary
Next Step option.

The outline is, first and foremost, a reason to come
back to meet with the prospect. As a general rule, this is
the single most effective strategy for regaining a meeting
with a prospect after a face-to-face meeting. If the meeting has gone well and you have identified a potential area
of benefit to the prospect, you should have no difficulties
winning this particular kind of Next Step. If the meeting
has not gone well, you will know, because the person will
be hesitant or completely resistant to the notion of meeting with you again to discuss this outline.

Sometimes salespeople ask me, "How do I put it
together? What is an outline?"

Basically, an outline is a document that says, "I am not
a proposal." This is an opportunity for you to offer a condensed overview of your ideas about:

- Timing
- Pricing
- The specific products and services that could help the prospect gain the goals that you discussed together

You should practice your request for the Outline Meeting carefully. As a matter of fact, I am going to strongly suggest that you will act out the end of the first meeting with a sales manager or colleague before you attempt to incorporate this question. The way you ask this question will depend on the specifics of what has gone before in your relationship with the prospect, and it will probably be different every time you pose it.

In practice, this may end up being a *longer* question than any other question you ask—because it is, in essence, the conclusion of the meeting. Here's a variation that will show you what I mean. This is how I might ask for an Outline Meeting:

Question 22: Okay, Mr. Prospect, I think we are thinking along the same lines—at least I hope we are. Here is what I want to do next. I would like to go back to my office and share what you have told me about your recruitment goals with some of the senior people at my company, and then what I want to do is brainstorm with them and give them the opportunity to share their insights on how we might be able to put together a plan for you. I don't think we are ready to look at a *proposal* yet, but what I do think we are in the position to do is show you an outline. I would like to come back here next Tuesday at 10:00 just to show you some of our initial thinking about what might go into the proposal, and then I would like to meet with some of the other people on your team who might be able to help us develop the program more fully. Does that make sense?

Whew!

It takes practice, but believe me when I tell you that you can learn to deliver this kind of question smoothly.

Did you notice how the "request" for the meeting to go over the outline appeared in the middle of all that? That is a fairly sophisticated technique, but it is one I would recommend that you practice and master. Simply asking, "Can we get together next week on Tuesday at 2:00?" will not deliver quite the same results as outlining your battle plan and incorporating the Next Step as an assumption within it.

In the best situation, what you want to do is give a verbal summary of your battle plan, with fairly detailed, comprehensive steps—and then simply ask your prospect whether or not "that makes sense." (Notice that before we can ask the ultimate question, "whether it makes sense" to buy our product or service, we have to ask ourselves whether it "makes sense" to take these preliminary steps.)

Even if you do not get the prospect to agree to meet with you again to go over your outline—you must ask the prospect to do something!

Question 23: Why wouldn't you want to meet next week?

This is the all-purpose follow-through question when your request for a Next Step is shot down. If you don't know why the person doesn't want to meet with you again, you should.

Have this question ready in case you encounter resistance, tactful or otherwise, to your request for another meeting. It is best delivered not as an indictment or an accusation, but out of an emotion of genuine surprise.

I like to deliver this question at length, and with a tone of very mild alarm that I may have committed some lapse in etiquette. Take a look:

Question 24: Wow—I am kind of surprised to hear you say that. Usually by this point in the meeting, people are very eager to meet with us again. Just out of curiosity, why wouldn't you want get together again to look at our outline?

The key, at this point, is to shut up and wait for the other person to talk. This can take some discipline, because there may be an awkward silence that follows. It is absolutely imperative that you allow that awkward silence to remain, and that you not make any attempt to fill it.

Eventually, the person will begin to give you a clearer picture about exactly where you stand. This answer will typically begin with the words, "The thing is . . ." It is not uncommon for prospects who have held back on providing critical information—about budget, about timelines, about decision-making processes, about any number of other important aspects related to your sale—to offer them in detail at this point in the meeting.

Notice that you are asking directly for the Next Step, and then following up with a serious, nonconfrontational question, from one professional to another, about why there would be a problem in granting such a Next Step. This situation is sometimes what yields the real picture about what is going on in the organization. The point is to make the most of the capital—the time and energy you have invested—that was required to make this first meeting happen at all. You might as well use that investment to get a straight answer as to why the person does not want to meet with you again.

Questions to Use for Backup Plans

Question 25: Can I meet with your team and report back to you on (May 31)?

This is one of my favorite "backup" Next Steps. When I find myself face to face with a top decision maker who, for whatever reason, does not wish to meet with me again in the short term, I will often say something like this:

"Why don't we do this, then: Let me meet with your team, let me listen to them in action, and let me take some notes. Then, when your schedule frees up, you and I can meet—let's say at the end of this month on the 31st at 2:00 P.M.—and I can debrief you on what I have learned and how we might be able to help. Does that make sense?"

If the person is not willing to work with you along these lines, it is a very good bet that you simply do not have a prospect. After all, you're basically offering to do free consulting work. *Do not make the mistake of investing vast amounts of time, energy, or attention with such a person.*

Question 26: Why don't we get my boss to meet your boss?

This is a classic "up the ante" maneuver, a great way to justify expanding the relationship and moving out of a situation where you are "stuck" with someone who has little or no decision-making authority.

You will have to pick your shot carefully, but this is a perfect example of a question you can use to escalate the sale and expand your network within the organization.

Question 27: Why don't you come to one of our company events?

This can be a training seminar, a tradeshow, an investor meeting, a company celebration, a holiday party, or even an event you design specifically for the benefit of this one contact. The closer the theme of the event is to your contact's business goals or key concerns, obviously, the more likely you will be to get him or her to agree to attend.

Here, as with every Next Step request, your goal is to make it easy for the person to say "yes." Do not make the mistake of encouraging the person to come, and then charging him or her an arm and a leg to do so. Ideally, the event should be free.

Question 28: Why don't you come take a look at our facility?

This can be an office, a manufacturing plant, a display room, or any other location that seems relevant to your business and will show your company in the best light. Sometimes, you can win a Next Step that involves your boss more easily by scheduling a time for the prospect to come "drop by the office" and "happen" to meet your superior. Whatever works.

Question 29: Why don't I come back and show you . . . ?

How you finish the sentence is up to you, but it should have something to do with seeing your product or service in action.

If you sell software, offer to come back and show the prospect a demo version of the particular program you think might match his or her situation. If you sell promotional items, offer to bring back a variety of samples so that your prospect can take a look at some of the most likely matches with his or her organization. If you sell consulting, offer to come back with a demonstration of what has worked well for other clients in the past.

Again, make sure that the date you are asking for occurs at some point within the next two weeks. *If the Next Step is scheduled for further than two weeks out, it is significantly less likely to take place.* (Think about it—isn't it easier for you to make a halfhearted "commitment" for a slot that's a month away than for next Friday?)

And If You Can't Get a Next Step . . .

Question 30: Is there someone else in your industry that you think I should be talking to?

When in doubt, ask for referrals. (Actually, you should ask for referrals anyway, whether or not you get a Next Step!)

CHAPTER 75

Questions That Help You Identify and Deliver the Right Presentation

Question 31: Before we get started, can I share with you what I got from our last meeting?

This is one of many possible variations on a "verifying" question. I like to begin the "business portion" of the second meeting with a question like this, because it allows me to restate the key points that I gathered from the initial meeting, and to move into a side by side review of an important sales document: the outline.

An outline is a one-page or two-page summary of how you might be able to work with this person, based on what you got from the prospect during your last meeting. Its goal is not to sell, but to encourage the prospect to take part in direct revision.

What I usually do is pull the outline from my briefcase when I ask the question above. I proceed then to revisit all the key points that I "got from our last conversation," and will elicit direct input from the prospect by stopping after each point and saying something like "Here are my assumptions," followed by questions that sound like the following ones in this chapter.

The phrase, "Before we begin" is a very nearly perfect transition phrase—in this case, for the beginning of a second or subsequent meeting. The phrase helps you move from the small talk portion of the meeting into the "business" portion of the meeting without any difficulty—and actually marks the "beginning" of the reason for your visit, even though it pretends not to.

Question 32: Has anything changed since our last meeting?

An extremely important question and one that should be part of any second meeting. I cannot tell you the number of times I have spoken to salespeople who swore that absolutely nothing of consequence had changed between the first and second meeting—only to tell me later that the competition had somehow wormed its way into the account.

Look the person straight in the eye—not threateningly, but with genuine interest—and pose this question. Stop talking. See what happens.

Question 33: Did you have a chance to talk to anyone else in the organization about what we discussed last time?

This question brings up an underexamined issue within the sales process—and a vitally important subject for the second meeting.

Maybe your prospect has been circulating your ideas around the target organization; maybe not. Either situation is worth examining; either will affect the way that your second meeting proceeds.

If the person has been discussing your initiatives with others in the organization, you will certainly want to know what the feedback was and who is "in the loop."

Pose the question earnestly and with curiosity, and find out what is happening by using the most effective rhetorical "weapon" of them all—silence.

Question 34: Are we thinking along the same lines in terms of price?

Verify the dollars: Offer a specific price or, alternatively, a price range for a variety of possible offerings. *Get a reaction before moving on.*

Question 35: Is this product/service what you are looking for?

Verify that the product/service offering really does make sense to the other person. *Get a reaction before moving on.*

Question 36: Have I got the timing about right?

Verify the timing: Be specific about the delivery or rollout schedule. *Get a reaction before moving on.*

By specifying timing ("I think we could start next month"), you will usually get some kind of reaction from the prospect!

If you don't—if you sense hesitation, but the person does not offer specific changes or feedback, say . . .

Question 37: I'm sensing that there is a problem somewhere—where did I go off track?

Stop talking! Wait until you get a response.

You cannot verify your information without feedback from the prospect.

As we have seen, this "verification" step is an extremely important concept, and is one of the more important and frequently ignored areas of sales questioning. We must be willing to elicit new facts from a prospect, and to confirm that the information we got last time really is correct. Even if posing a question like this feels awkward, *that awkwardness is better than investing more time in the relationship without specific guidance from the prospect.* These are essential preliminaries to the presentation; if we simply rush forward to deliver our presentation, we may miss the mark.

Use this question, and your outline, to bring out objections and issues in a "safe environment"—while you are still in the interviewing phase.

Question 38: I feel like I'm missing something—what do you think I'm missing here?

This is another question that can be very helpful when you're dealing with a decision maker who is interested in moving the relationship forward with you, but has not provided much in the way of meaningful feedback about the outline you are using to develop your proposal.

When in doubt, say that you feel like you have made a mistake or oversight, and ask for a correction.

Some salespeople do not verify their information because they are afraid of making a mistake in front of the prospect. They should be afraid of investing a week or more of their time in developing a proposal for someone that does not match that person's world! The key to improving your closing ratios lies in being willing to be corrected by the other person. If you are never corrected by your prospects, guess what? You are not asking the right questions!

Make sure that you conduct the verification phase of your sales process with the right demeanor. Your goal is to come across as an ally who has a couple of questions and needs some guidance, not as a private detective or, worse, a prosecuting attorney. If you never get any clarifying or corrective feedback from your prospects, you may want to step back and look at why this is so. You may be intimidating people or you may be trying to move forward in the sales cycle too quickly. Do the responses you get tend to become shorter and shorter, and contain less meaningful information, as the relationship progresses? If so, you need to work on your willingness to be corrected!

Always remember, the opposite of wrong is right—you want the prospect to "right" your "wrong." When your prospect corrects you—you win!

Question 39: Just between you and me, what do you really think is really going to happen here?

This is among the most important sales questions of them all—but you have to know *when* and *how* to ask it.

If you ask it during the body of the second meeting, you may or may not get the straight scoop. And you may get a long monologue that serves as more of a distraction than anything else.

If, on the other hand, you were to wait until the "business" portion of the meeting is over, make all the small talk, shake hands, and let your prospect walk you to the door . . . and *then* pose this question, you will get a direct, honest assessment of exactly where you are in the sales cycle. You might even get the "inside information" you need to complete the deal.

Try it!

Question 40: Can you and I set up a time to debrief right now?

The point here is to secure the Next Step with your prospect *before* you actually make your presentation.

Question 40 is extremely important—be sure you ask it before you start investing the time necessary to develop your presentation! If the prospect is unwilling to schedule a time to meet with you after the meeting, there is a very good chance that there is some deal-killing obstacle or difficulty that you have not yet uncovered.

Let's say it's March 1. The committee is meeting on March 15, and you will be making your presentation to them at that point. It is incumbent upon you, *right now*, to set up a Next Step with your prospect—and schedule a meeting with him, or with someone else in the organization, to debrief on how the committee meeting went. That meeting might be scheduled for, say, March 17.

What you do *not* want to do is allow the meeting to conclude without some kind of Next Step in your prospect's calendar.

Remember, this is a series of exchanges. You are trading your knowledge, insights, and expertise for ongoing commitments of time and attention. Do not invest heavily without receiving a parallel investment from the other side.

Question 41: Just out of curiosity . . . what makes you think that's the right figure/date/deal?

Or:

What makes you say that?

Or:

What were you expecting?

Remember, as sales reps, we often overreact when we hear an initial "objection." What we should be doing is giving the other person the chance to identify the problem (if there is one) and help us get to the bottom of it . . . *before* we commit to solving it. For example, if the prospect says, "The pricing isn't what I expected," don't just say, "Stop! Let me tell you why this is a great price!" or "I can ONLY cut it by 50 percent!"

(By the way, I've heard *both* of these "turnarounds" offered by seemingly rational salespeople when they heard about a tenth of a second's worth of price resistance from a prospect.)

It might make more sense to explore the issue further by asking, "What were you expecting?" Your prospect might respond by saying, "Well, so-and-so told me he paid X." By the same token, the prospect might say, "Well, I really didn't have any expectation, because I've never worked with a company like yours before."

These are two totally different frames of reference! STEP BACK and ask more clarifying questions. Find out what's really going on.

Question 42: Can I tell you how we handled this issue when I worked with Company X?

A classic get-back-on-track question. Use it!

The prospect says, "It's just too expensive."

Instead of offering to discount, you say, "What makes you think it's too expensive?"

The prospect says, "I have only X dollars in the budget for this—I can't touch another penny until next quarter."

You say, "Can I tell you how we handled this issue when I worked with XYZ bank? They agreed to pay X up front, and we billed them 120 days later for the balance. It was no problem."

If the solution makes sense to the other person—you're in business. If there's another problem, keep cool, try to find out what it is, and offer another relevant success story.

Question 43: Did I do something wrong here?

This is the biggie. Use it when you have put a lot of work into the proposal—and you feel as though the prospect has, too—but you're suddenly running into a brick wall that has no name or description, and didn't seem to exist yesterday.

Your goal is to find out what's really happening, of course. Ultimately, you will recall our closing strategy is based on recommending what "makes sense" to the other person, and then asking directly whether or not it makes sense. Our classic formulation for this is, "It makes sense to me . . . what do you think?"

In this situation, you honestly *thought* you had something that made sense from the other person's point of view, but you find out now that you don't. What's missing? What has really changed that the other person hasn't told you about? This question is your best bet for filling these mysterious information gaps.

In practice, it can be brief, as above. My suggestion, though, is that you practice it and deliver a slightly more elaborate version, as I have outlined below, and tailor the longer version to the specific situations you face.

> **Question 44: Mr. Prospect, I have to be honest with you. Something is wrong here. Usually, when I have gotten this far through the process of meeting with someone, people are very excited about what I have recommended, and they do, in fact, decide to work with us. Actually, I pride myself on not making a recommendation until I am really sure that the other person is more excited about it than I am. I know for a fact that we have got the best program for you, and that it will deliver the results that you and I spoke about. So, I have to assume that I have done something wrong in outlining this plan for you. So help me out. *Did* I do something wrong? If I did—what was it?**

Obviously, this takes a little longer to practice than #43, but I think you will find it is worth the effort. If you ask this question honestly and without sarcasm, you will usually get the "straight dope" on what's gone wrong, typically preceded by the words, "No, you didn't do anything wrong. You see the thing is . . . "

It is entirely possible that your sudden reversal of fortune within the sales process is the result of some higher individual within the target organization taking control of the process. If that is the case, you have a right to lay all your cards on the table and ask directly for an opportunity to make your case to that senior decision maker.

Variants on the "Did I do something wrong?" approach can be employed at different points throughout the sales cycle. Just be sure not to overuse it, and not to employ the "full apology" I have outlined here more than once.

Questions for Specific Sales Obstacles

Question 45: We haven't heard from you in a while—did we do something wrong?

A variation on Question 44, designed for use with an existing customer. Use this question to reinvigorate a relationship with a client you have not heard from in a while. It is considerably cheaper, of course, to hold on to a current client than it is to find a brand-new one. With that in mind, you should probably ask some variation on this question to any customer whose sudden absence is troubling to you. It is a great way to find what is going on in the other person's world, and the same dynamic applies. Nine times out of ten, your customer will correct you by saying, "No, you didn't do anything wrong, it's just that we have been dealing with this crisis here and we've been distracted." (Or some such reaction that gives you some insight into what is going on in the other person's world.)

Regardless, you will get a clearer picture of the forces and pressures that your prospect is facing, and you'll have a great opportunity to request a meeting.

It is possible, of course, that you *did* do something wrong, but just don't know what it is. In that case, asking this question has a very good likelihood of pointing you toward exactly what happened, and will also leave you well positioned to schedule a face-to-face meeting so you can evaluate exactly what took place and how your organization can work to help keep it from happening again. (Note: In such a situation I do strongly recommend trying to find a way to schedule a *face-to-face* meeting with the customer who got less than your best.)

Question 46: I was just thinking of you, and I'd like to see what you're up to these days. Can we get together?

A less intense—and perhaps slightly easier to ask—variation on Question 45. This question, like that one, is designed for current customers who haven't been ordering from you lately.

You really don't need a "reason" to call a key customer and ask for a meeting to catch up on what's going on, of course. This question will help you reinforce the important message that you don't just talk to customers when you want their money or when there's a crisis you have to deal with. Not a bad impression to leave if you intend to secure more deals with this person!

Questions That Will Help You Negotiate the Best Deal

Question 47: Just out of curiosity, how did you handle pricing questions/issues last time?

Use this if the prospect is intent on sticking to an arbitrary pricing figure, and your attempt to identify meaningful benchmarks and standards goes nowhere.

This is one of four critical information-gathering questions you must be prepared to ask at this stage. The others are . . .

How did you handle invoicing/terms last time?

And . . .

How did you pick the (specific product/service, or element of the product/service) last time?

And . . .

What was your timetable for implementation the last time you did this (or: did something like this)?

These four questions are also vitally important to the success of your discussions. At any given moment, your negotiating discussion is likely to center on one of four critical questions from the prospect:

- How much will it cost?
- When do I have to pay?

- What product or service am I offering?
- What is the implementation timetable?

If you don't know what the benchmarks were for the last similar purchasing decision the company made in each of these areas, *you are negotiating at a disadvantage.*

To be sure, the prospect may choose not to share some of this information with you. But you have gotten this far by asking intelligent questions. Why stop now?

When you are pressured on any of these points during the later phases of a sales discussion—price, invoicing, product/service offering or availability, or delivery dates/implementation, it *always* makes sense to disengage and get the relevant facts about the person's past experience in the area in which you are working.

If there is no precise equivalent, disengage a little more, then ask your prospect what he or she thinks is the most likely situation he or she has faced.

The point is to encourage your contact to step back from a "hard-line" position, and also to identify, if possible, the relevant benchmarks you can both use to discuss what the final package would look like.

Question 48: Can we come back to this?

An *extremely* important negotiating question. If you don't ask it at least once, you are not doing your job well.

If you have an impasse on one of those three things you can always step back and ask to look at one of the other three elements.

If an issue is only producing disagreement and frustration, there is no sin in asking that it be postponed in order to allow you and the prospect to discuss something that you do agree on. Emphasize commonalities, and you will eventually be able to build up enough trust to move forward to the most difficult issues.

It is also true that by postponing the most difficult issues, at least with someone whom you know to be committed to finding a way to work out a deal, you may improve your negotiation position. But this depends, to a large degree, on who really has the most control of the negotiating session. If you have reason to suspect the prospect will in fact walk away if you put off discussing X for too long, and you don't want the person to walk away, you're probably going to have to discuss X sooner rather than later.

Question 49: Let's assume that I come up with a great program/ product/offering for you, and it costs ($X). Would you buy it?

It should go without saying that you will not want to volunteer prices along the lines suggested here until you are well along into the discussions with your prospect.

With that warning out of the way, I do want to emphasize that your goal in the negotiation phase should be finding *something* that will work for this organization, at this time, through this series of discussions. This question can be an effective tool for identifying what that something is.

Question 50: It makes sense to me—what do you think?

This is the question that we have been working our way up to throughout the entire sales process, and indeed throughout the course of this book. It is, ultimately, the only question that matters.

I have included it here as the question you can use to "clinch the deal," and it is certainly the most effective strategy I have ever come across for doing that. It is also, however, the underlying question behind just about everything else you have read here.

Sales is a matter of throwing out the ball. If I toss a ball to you, you have to react somehow. You can let the ball drop to the floor, you can catch it and throw it back to me, you can catch it and take it away. But you do have to do something. This question, for all its simplicity, *is* that act of throwing out the sales "ball," condensed to a few simple words. It is the question you should ask when you want to execute the plan you believe, in your heart, to be in the best interests of both parties.

On its own, however, it is useless. If you simply deliver a memorized "spiel" for half an hour, and turn to the person and say, "It makes sense to me, what do you think?" you will not be selling at the optimum level. You will, of course, close some sales—the sales to the people who are already in the marketplace, and who are already predisposed to buying, and who have more or less made up their mind to buy from someone. Those sales will come your way no matter what. But in order to get to the highest level of sales, you must be willing to ask some variation on this question *throughout* the process, not merely at the end.

Does it make sense for the person to meet with you in the first place? Does it make sense for him or her to allow you to interview key people within the organization? Does it make sense for him or her to share personal insights and experiences—the "stories" that have made this person a unique asset to his or her organization? Does it make sense for this person to share sensitive reports and data with you? Does it make sense for him or her to go out on a limb and introduce you to the president of the company? Does it make sense to him or her to meet with you a second or third or fourth time? Does it make sense to him or her to allow you to develop the presentations that will be delivered before the all-important committee meeting?

All these questions and their hundreds of potential variations are the necessary precursors to the question above.

Don't just ask the final question . . . ask all the questions that lead up to it and make it possible. That way, if the recommendation you are making really does make sense, you will be in a great position, not only to close a sale, but to build a future.

Two Lumberjacks

TWO LUMBERJACKS WERE GIVEN AXES and told to go into the forest to cut down trees. The first lumberjack went up to his first tree and started to chop away. He chopped all day long without stopping.

The second lumberjack also did his share of chopping and cutting, but at various points during the day, he would stop, walk away, and come back a few minutes later. Meanwhile, the first lumberjack kept working away.

At the end of the day, the lumberjack who worked nonstop, who never stopped working, had cut *less* wood than the lumberjack who took breaks.

Do you understand what happened?

The lumberjack who took breaks went to sharpen his ax.

The point is that both men were given the same tool, but only one of them learned how to use the tool properly.

We're all given the same tools. We all play on the same field. We all play by the same rules, yet certain people really learn how to use those tools properly. In the end, it's not the playbook that's important, it's the execution. Every basketball team, every football team, plays on the same field. What makes one better than the next? It isn't their playbook. It's their execution. What will make you better than the next person? What will give you the success you need? Your execution. Your ability to carry out the plan.

■ ■ ■

In my office, we have regular sales meetings, but they're a little different in one respect from the meetings in many offices.

Certainly you've heard the expression, "Have a nice day." Where I work, we don't say that; we say, "Make it a productive day." It reminds us that we're in control of our destiny, that our success or our failure is in our own hands. It's just the same with you.

Make it a productive day!

Sample Cold Calling Scripts

ALMOST EVERY PRODUCT THAT YOU BUY TODAY has a set of instructions; many even state something along the lines of "use only as directed." I take a slightly different approach on the matter of tinkering with the simple prospecting scripts that follow. Certainly you should feel free to adapt them to your own personal style. But do so in keeping with the spirit of the program outlined in this book. Don't overembellish.

As you look these scripts over, you may find them a little ambitious. They're meant to be. They're simple, and they're direct. That's why they work.

At one of my seminars, a group of salespeople expressed some reservations about these scripts. Why were they so aggressive? Where were the probing questions? How were they to "draw the prospects in"?

Their problem, of course, was that they were wasting their time talking to people they should have classified as simple rejections in the first minute of the conversation. And anyway, selling over the phone is not what cold calling is about.

To address the concerns these people raised, I decided to try a little experiment. I sat down one Tuesday and made seven cold calls in a two-hour period. I got through to two people and got one appointment by using one of the scripts reproduced here—word for word. That's 50 percent. I asked the sales manager if he could match that figure using his current methods. He couldn't.

When the salespeople finally saw the results of the program, they decided to give it a try.

The salespeople I'm talking about were lucky. They kept an open mind. If you do the same thing, you'll see a marked improvement in your performance.

The scripts outlined here are the basis for the work you're about to undertake. Obviously, as you get more proficient at your phone prospecting work, you'll change a word here and there to fit your own style and requirements. But the same approach applies—and that's the point. You'll stop wasting time by having extended conversations on the phone. You'll be direct in asking for the appointment. You'll know what you're going to say in advance.

When I start my seminars. I usually begin with the sentence, "When God wanted to punish salespeople, he invented the cold call." That actually sums up my feelings, and possibly yours as well, about the cold call. You, and only you, can turn that "curse" into an opportunity—by beginning to use the techniques I've shown you, and the scripts provided here.

Initial Contact Script
Good morning _____ , this is _____ from _____ . The reason I'm calling you today specifically is so I can stop by and tell you about our new _____ program that increases _____ . I'm sure that you, like _____ , are interested in _____ .
(Positive response).
That's great _____ ; let's get together. How's _____ ?

Third-Party Endorsement Script
Good morning _____ , this is _____ from _____ .
(Insert your brief commercial on your company.) The reason I'm calling you today specifically is that we've just completed working on a major project for _____ , which was extremely successful in increasing _____ . What I'd like

to do is stop by next _____ to tell you about the success I had at _____ . How's _____?

Referral Script

Good morning _____ , this is _____ . *(Insert your brief commercial on your company.)* The reason I'm calling you today specifically is that _____ just suggested I give you a call to set up an appointment. I wanted to know if _____ at _____ would be okay.

Follow-Up Script

Good morning _____ , this is _____ from _____ . A number of weeks ago I contacted you, and you asked me to call you back today to set up an appointment. Would _____ be good for you?

Nine Key Principles of Sales Success

My only real concern when it comes to sales training is whether the training I offer helps people make more sales. If it doesn't, then the training really doesn't make any difference. The purpose of sales training is to help people do what they do—that is, sell—better—that is, make more sales.

With that aim in mind, let's look now at some of the basic principles for sales success. If you only memorize one portion of this book, make it this one!

1. All Steps Lead to the Next Step

The only reason you're making a cold call is to get an appointment. The only reason you went on the appointment is to get to the next step in your sale. Your next step could be the second appointment or it could be a close. It doesn't really matter to me what it is, as long as you know what it is. Too many salespeople go on appointments without having any idea what their objective for the visit is.

The objective of every step of the sales process is to get to the next step. If what you're doing doesn't get you to the next step, do something else that does!

2. The Difference Between Success and Failure Is Seventy-Two Hours

I think each and every one of us has had a great idea that went unattended. We said, "Boy, I ought to write a book about that," or, "That's a great idea for a movie," or, "I should design something that does that better." Then, six months or a year later we see that our idea has actually been implemented by someone else. Well, what happened? The difference was that the other person took action on the idea.

You can read this book, but if you don't begin to implement the concepts that we've talked about here within seventy-two hours, and then maintain the activity for twenty-one days, you're not going to be successful.

People tend to fall back on what they know. And if you don't get started with these concepts within seventy-two hours, you'll fall back on what you already know, and you'll have missed an opportunity to be far more successful than you are now. Respond immediately! Find something to implement! Take action now!

Changing your selling techniques within seventy-two hours really is the key to success.

3. All Objections and Responses Can and Should Be Anticipated

Everything that I've ever created in selling has been based on the premise that I can know in advance what a prospect's response will be—that I can learn to predict how people will respond to me during a cold call or in person.

I know, for example, that on a sales call I'm going to be asked certain questions about my training techniques and about how my seminars work. I'm prepared for these questions. I have my answers ready. If I didn't prepare an answer, that would be like going on a sales call without a business card. I would never do that. Would you?

4. Follow-Through Is an Integral Part of Sales

I prefer "follow-through" to "follow-up." Don't you? In fact, I very rarely say to anybody, "I'm going to follow up with a telephone call." What I like to say is "I'm going to follow through by calling you next week." In other words, I'm going to follow through on what I've started. I'm going to complete it. I may not make every sale, but I'm going to follow each relationship through as far as I can.

5. You Must Find Out What the Prospect Does

Find out what people do! Ask them what they do, how they do it, when they do it, where they do it, who they do it with, and why they do it that way. Your job is to help them do it better.

6. Prospects Respond in Kind

I've said it throughout this book, and I'll say it again here. People respond to what you're asking, and they respond in kind to how you ask. As I've pointed out repeatedly, if you ask, "Do you need my service?" the odds are you're going to hear a "no." If you talk instead about how you can help them do what they do better, you're going to be successful.

This concept of asking the right questions comes from a discussion Socrates and Plato had about pleasing the gods. They concluded that the pious person was the person who pleased the gods; that is, who made the gods happy. I believe that, in order to make the gods happy, we have to ask the question, "What, exactly, will make them happy?" Therefore, to my way of thinking, a pious person is one who asks the key questions.

If you don't ask questions like "What is it that you do?" or "What are you trying to get accomplished?" you will not get the success you deserve.

7. It's Necessary to Ask for the Appointment

One of the biggest mistakes salespeople make is failing to ask for the appointment. I've heard salespeople ask for just about everything except an appointment during a cold call. Guess what? They don't get the appointment!

8. It's Necessary to Understand the Four P's

In order to become a more successful salesperson, you should concern yourself with four basic areas of knowledge:

- Professional development
- Product malleability
- Presentation skills
- Prospecting

Let's look at each of them in turn:

Professional Development

Ninety percent of all salespeople in the United States fail to read one book about improving their sales techniques in a given year. Furthermore, most salespeople will not pay for their own sales training; 90 percent of all sales training is paid for by the employer. Salespeople will pay for their own swimming lessons, quilting lessons, riding lessons, tennis lessons, horseback riding lessons, driving lessons, and (of course) golf lessons, but they won't pay for their own sales training. You may want to give some thought to whether or not you need to sign up for a program that will help you improve your sales skills. (You've already beaten the odds, however, by reading a sales-related book!)

Product Malleability

"Product malleability" means repositioning your product or service to fit your prospect's specific needs.

Remember, the purpose of your product is to help people do what they do better. Strictly speaking, your product doesn't matter as much as your ability to take it and apply it—and that means, of course, that you have to understand your prospect's business. So product malleability comes from your understanding of what your prospect does, and how you can apply what you offer to the prospect's unique situation.

Presentation Skills

Presentation skills account for an important part of your overall success, but they probably aren't as important as you might think at first. Many people practice their presentations constantly, using role-playing, memorization, and even video-taping to hone their "moment" with the prospect. Do they realize that the ratio of calls to appointments is usually three-to-one—and sometimes even higher?

I would be foolish if I told you that making a good presentation to your prospect is not important. But in the overall scheme of things, it is still not as important as getting in the door—prospecting. And, of course, no amount of practice can perfect a presentation that is not based on solid information about the prospect.

Prospecting

Prospecting is really what sales success is all about. It's what makes the difference. We did a study of successful salespeople making between $75,000 and $125,000 a year consistently for ten consecutive years. We learned that 45 percent of the success of an individual salesperson comes directly from his or her ability to prospect. Twenty percent comes from presentation skills. Twenty percent comes from product knowledge or product malleability, and the remaining 15 percent comes from sales training. In other words, 65 percent of what successful salespeople do is finding people and talking about potential applications; that's prospecting and presenting combined.

9. It's Necessary to Understand the Three Most Important Words in Sales

The three most important words in sales today are *obsession, utilization,* and *implementation.* Let's consider those:

Obsession

You need to be obsessed by what you're doing. You have to be willing to think about your job seven days a week, twenty-four hours a day.

Utilization

Obsession without discipline results in chaos. If you're not disciplined enough to stay focused, to make the calls, to do what you have to do to reach your goals, you're not going to be successful. Successful people understand how to utilize everything. So take all the material, all the things that you've read in this book, and use as much as you possibly can to become more successful.

Implementation

And finally, we come to implementation. You just have to do it. You have to implement the plan. You have to do the work. If you don't do it, you're not going to be successful.

Ten Traits of Successful Salespeople

IN ALL THE YEARS THAT I'VE TRAVELED and during all the programs I've done, I've given more than 8,000 speeches and trained more than a half million salespeople. I've found that there are certain key characteristics that make people successful in sales. Here are the top ten.

1. They're Not Normal

You've decided to go into sales and, therefore, by the very definition, you're not normal. Sales success is not a normal state. Sales success is not normal—because success means being willing to act differently. When you're successful, you're not normal, and because you're going to maintain that success, you're comfortable with the idea of never being normal again!

2. They're Committed

Successful salespeople are committed to their goals, and they have goals. Not only do you have to be committed to your own goals, but you have to be committed to the goals of your company. Do you understand those goals? Do you understand fully what your company is trying to accomplish?

You're also looking to work with the goals of your customers. As soon as salespeople say to me that they're concerned about their commission checks, then I start worrying whether or not they're concerned about their customers. If you help customers accomplish their goals, if you help them do what they do better, you will never, ever lose.

3. They're Motivated

Successful salespeople are self-motivated. They know what they have to do and they know how they're going to get there. Interestingly enough, the role of the sales manager in the successful salesperson's career is really minimal. You and I both know what we have to do. We know we have to make calls. We know we have to follow through and do the things you've been reading about in this book each and every day. We know we have to take action. We have to make things happen.

One of my favorite stories is about a great Hollywood literary agent named Swifty Lazar. His actual name was Irving, but everybody in the business called him Swifty. Swifty Lazar died a number of years ago, but in reading about him, one of the things that struck me was that every single morning, he said he would get up and he would look at his calendar and see what was going to happen that day. And if there was nothing that was going to happen, he made something happen every day . . . before lunch! And that's exactly my philosophy—you make something happen every day . . . before lunch. You get an appointment. You make a call. You start some activity. Because the activity you create today is going to give you business down the road.

4. They're Self-Declared

Being self-declared means that successful salespeople feel good about themselves. Successful salespeople carry themselves well, they talk themselves up, and they understand what it is they have to accomplish and how they're going to get there.

5. They Sacrifice

If you've ever watched the Olympics, or any committed athlete, you realize that an athlete makes tremendous sacrifices. They make choices each and every day in order to be successful. They understand that the gain is worth the choice that they're going to make.

6. They Delegate

Successful salespeople also understand how to prioritize and how to get the things they need to do done. They know how to take best advantage of the resources and the people available to them.

7. They're Optimistic

Successful salespeople are part of the solution and not part of the problem. It's easy to find problems. Anyone can do that. And yet I'll bet the person you remember most in life, the person you consider your mentor (whether it's your parent, grandparent, coach, or a college professor), is the person who helped you find the solutions.

Successful people are believers. They believe the great mission can be accomplished. They not only believe it; they live it.

8. They're Enthusiastic

I absolutely, positively love doing what I do. The reason I tell you that is that I want you to be enthusiastic each and every day. Every single day, get up as if it were the first day you've ever sold. Do you remember the very first sales call you went on? Remember that anxiety, that nervousness, the adrenaline pumping through your body? It was exciting! Live that excitement every day!

9. They Live Off-Peak

Successful salespeople don't drive onto the highway at 8:30 A.M. and sit in traffic. They're going earlier, or they're going later. They're not going with everybody else.

They constantly rethink their options. They're not standing in line at noon for a restaurant. They go earlier or later. They're not like the woman in New York City I heard of recently who stood in line for an hour and a half . . . to complain about the lines.

10. They're Consistent and Persistent

Successful salespeople have the focus and the discipline to follow through on their projects and not get bored. Successful salespeople aren't fickle. They have a plan and stick with it.

Seven Questions You Should Be Able to Answer Before You Try to Close the Deal

WHY DO SALESPEOPLE FALL INTO THE TRAP of attempting to close the sale with silly "closing tricks"—like saying "I'll lose my job if you don't buy from me?" The short answer is that they're afraid. Specifically, they're afraid the prospect will turn them down if they ask for the business straight-forwardly. So to overcome this fear, they practice delivering some manipulative, supposedly foolproof "technique" that somehow will magically make the person say "Yes."

The truth is, their fear about asking for the business is usually well justified. Most salespeople who try to close the deal don't yet know enough about the other person to ask for the business.

Here are seven questions you should be sure to ask your prospect before you attempt to close any sale. If you don't know the answers . . . you're not yet ready to make a formal recommendation. You should get face-to-face with your prospect, pull out your pen and your yellow legal pad, and find out the answers.

And by the way—asking these questions also serves an important purpose during the course of your discussion with the prospect. By posing a question that addresses one of the following issues and then taking notes on the response you receive, you regain control of the conversation and put yourself in a better position to make a recommendation about the next step in the relationship.

1. How did this person get this job?

Was your contact one of the founders of the company? Was he or she recruited by a pricey executive search firm? Did he or she answer a classified ad a month and a half ago? Your aim here is to determine your contact's level of influence.

2. What's the person's role in the organization?

Is your contact a leader or a follower? What part did he or she play in the past when it came to deciding whether and how to use companies like yours? What major projects is he or she working on right now? If the person you're talking to does not have any projects that are relevant to your selling area, you are not talking to the right person. Your aim here is to find out what this person can or cannot do within the organization.

3. Are you dealing with someone who is either (a) a decision maker or (b) a person who can get the decision made for you?

If your contact has no knowledge, access, or influence relating to your product or service, you need to find a way to get this person to help you connect with someone else in the organization. Your aim here is to identify who, in the organization, is likely to be able to help you get this deal done—and to determine with some certainty whether your contact falls into that category.

4. What's the organization's current plan for dealing with the area where you hope to make a contribution?

To find out, ask, "What were you planning to do this quarter in order to . . . ?" Your aim here is to identify any competitors who may already be involved, and to get a sense of how the target organization has defined the problem up to this point.

5. Why aren't they using you already?

Your aim here is twofold: to learn what the company already knows or thinks about your organization, and to find out what plans are already in place. (To this extent, there is a certain amount of overlap between this question and #4.) I suggest that, early on in the relationship, you ask some variation on this question: "I checked my records and I noticed you're not using us right now. I'm just curious—why not?" While you're at it, you could also find out if the company ever considered working with you or getting in touch with you in the past. You may have been on the short-list for a project and not even known about it.

6. Does this deal truly make sense to the other person?

The goal here is to find out whether you're on your own or whether you've got an ally. Sometimes salespeople ask, "How am I supposed to know whether or not what I'm proposing makes sense to the other person?" The answer is actually very simple. When the prospect begins to act as though closing the sale is as important to him or her as it is to you . . . you'll know it makes sense! I like to find out whether what I'm discussing with a prospect really makes sense by asking a question like this as I'm on the way out the door after a second meeting: "Listen—just between you and me, how do you think this is going to turn out?"

7. What does your contact think is going to happen next?

The idea here is to get clear on what the mutually agreed-upon next step in the relationship is. If your contact has no idea you're about to close the deal, there's a problem. Here's a good selling rule: Never make a presentation you don't think will close! Try saying something like: "You know, based on what we've gone over today, I have to say that this really makes sense to me. I'm thinking that the next time we get together, on Tuesday at 2:00, we'll go over all the changes and I'll show you our full proposal, and at that point, I think it's going to make sense for us to reserve the training dates. What do you think?"

The Five Stages of the Sales Career

THERE ARE FIVE DISTINCT STAGES to the sales career, five periods of professional change growth that apply specifically to the sales professional. If you manage people who sell for a living, you should know what these five stages are!

The Novice

The Novice relies heavily on other team members; he or she is still in the "learning the ropes" phase. The Novice may place too much importance on a single prospect and neglect the importance of effective prospect management.

The Contributor

The Contributor works more autonomously than the Novice, and can anticipate prospect expectations and manage the sales cycle more effectively. Contributors tend to be strongly goal oriented and to show a great deal of commitment to their work. They need less help than Novices when it comes to managing their own time, gathering the unique prospect information necessary develop the right "proposal," and closing the sale. A common challenge is an unwillingness to reach out to other team members for help in securing larger and more complex deals.

The Performer

The Performer serves as a role model for others in the sales organization and assists in the completion of large and complex sales. Performers tend to have a deep experience base and superior people skills. They support and motivate other team members in support of their key goals. These are usually the supreme "team players." Some (but by no means all) performers may become impatient with less experienced colleagues.

The Leader

The Leader chooses to assume a coordinating role in the sales team's activities; he or she is also comfortable developing and supporting new talent. Leaders can articulate the company vision and support key partnerships that arise within the sales team. Effective Leaders know how to win group support for new and challenging goals established by the higher-ups in the organization. Many Leaders find that balancing work and personal spheres can be a challenge.

The Builder

The Builder channels his or her entire personality into the mission of building the company, often at the expense of family ties. Builders are so committed to the long-term success of the group that they are often compared to people with religious callings or vocations. It really is a matter of faith to them that the company should overcome competitive and market challenges, grow, and prosper in the long term. Most chief executives and presidents are still very much salespeople regardless of their title. Whatever their job title, these salespeople tend to have superior executive, team building, and long-term strategic abilities. Their own high standards and extraordinary commitment are other important assets. A common challenge area for the Builder is that others may perceive him or her as eccentric, paradoxical or even autocratic.

■ ■ ■

Those are the five stages. You need not move all the way forward to the Builder stage to experience a satisfying career, but you should be able to identify where you are . . . and where you want to be . . . within this model. Trying to perform at one level before one has mastered the responsibilities of the previous level leads to what I call "stage uncertainty." This kind of uncertainty—on the part of the manager or the salesperson—is a major contributor to unhealthy stress and early burnout.

Finally, note this well: A salesperson's years of experience on the job may have nothing whatsoever to do with the stage he or she occupies. Seniority in sales is not the same as ability!

Five Steps to a Successful Coaching Meeting

IN ORDER TO BRING ABOUT INCREMENTAL IMPROVEMENT among team members, you must know how to conduct an effective coaching meeting.

The less often you have coaching meetings, the more difficult it is to get right to the point of what you want to discuss. Here are the five steps of the successful coaching session.

Step 1. *Know the team member.* Before evaluating performance, take time to understand the person. Why is he or she in this job? Does he or she want to grow? Is this person here for the short or long term?

Step 2. *Observe/evaluate work habits and skills.* Changes may be necessary in terms of general work habits (i.e., lateness, poor reports) or in specific performance skills that are unique to this job.

Step 3. *Plan your approach.* Develop an agenda for the coaching session. Limit yourself to one objective (for instance, to help a sales representative develop rapport with account contacts). Anticipate the team member's objections and prepare your own turnarounds/responses. Set up a strategy for the coaching session. How will you open the meeting? Where will it take place? How will you adjust for this person's personality or working style?

Step 4. *Coach.* Discuss why you are having this meeting, what you would like to accomplish, and what you have observed. Listen to the team member's side. Let him or her explain and discuss what has happened from his or her perspective. Explain your perspective on the situation; explain what changes can help the representative. Get agreement/verification on what the problem is, and what can be done to solve it. Develop a specific action plan with a timetable for completion and follow up.

Step 5. *Follow up.* Follow up with another observation/evaluation meeting and discussion to determine whether or not the problem has been solved. Then set another meeting/next step with this team member.

Sales Managers—Are You Measuring These Fifteen Skills?

SALES MANAGERS: WHAT ARE YOU MEASURING? Conduct this simple "value scale" analysis for each and every member of your team. It takes only minutes to establish your coaching priorities . . . and you'll have the information you need to begin a comprehensive coaching program with that salesperson. You'll get more accurate sales forecasts, too.

■ ■ ■

SCORING KEY

- **Zero to five total check marks:** LEVEL THREE PERFORMER (assume 25% of total value of "live" prospects will turn into revenue)
- **Six to ten total check marks:** LEVEL TWO PERFORMER (assume 33% of total value of "live" prospects will turn into revenue)
- **Eleven to fifteen total check marks:** LEVEL ONE PERFOMER: (assume 50% of total value of "live" prospects will turn into revenue)

ENERGY: SETTING FIRST APPOINTMENTS

O Understands own ratios. Is the salesperson monitoring activity ratios on a daily basis? What do the ratios look like? What specific ratio improvement would you like to see?

O Has time to complete call targets. Is prospecting a top priority on the average selling day? Does the salesperson make time to complete prospecting activities on a daily basis?

O Number of calls/day steady. Is the salesperson consistent, or are there (for instance) zero prospecting calls for five straight days, followed by thirty or forty calls the next selling day?

O Adequate appointments each week. Is the number of NEW meetings consistent from week to week? Is it the right number, given this person's ratios?

O Each first appointment (FA) takes no longer than thirty minutes to set. How long does it typically take this salesperson to set a first appointment?

SALES EFFICIENCY: THE SALES PROCESS

O Understands closing ratio. How many meetings or discussions does it take for this person to produce a single sale? Is that the right ratio? Can the salesperson discuss this ratio intelligently with you?

O Timeline and sales cycle understood. What is the average selling cycle on this salesperson's most profitable product/service? Is the salesperson capable of identifying this number without getting distracted by "exceptions" that turned into sales? Does the salesperson understand that what usually happens is what determines his or her selling cycle?

O Process-oriented (doesn't waste time with dead leads). Does this salesperson know when to move on?

O Masters product knowledge/product malleability. Can this salesperson make the product or service fit in a number of different situations or environments? Has this salesperson ever targeted an entirely new category of prospects?

○ Each follow-up appointment takes between sixty and ninety minutes to set and prepare for. Does this salesperson get parallel commitments and input from the prospect before committing large amounts of time and energy to proposal development?

VALUE EFFICIENCY: PRICE PROPOSITION

○ Understands pricing structure and margins. Can the salesperson explain to you the company's margin on what he or she sells? Does the salesperson understand why different products and services your company offers cost what they do?

○ Gap between proposed price and contract price is narrow. How close is the pricing in the first draft of the proposal to the final pricing?

○ Takes long-term view of account. Does this salesperson know when and how to use "strategic" pricing and bundling skills to close an initial "pilot" deal with an important prospect—and still make money for the company?

○ Negotiates from strength, not weakness. Does the salesperson avoid the trap of discounting without getting something in return? Does the salesperson live by the rule that you should never, ever, offer a discount before a customer asks for one?

○ Handles price issues honestly and forthrightly. Does the salesperson stand behind his or her company's pricing, and answer questions about pricing directly and with integrity?

Live Training Programs Offered by
D.E.I. Management Group

Appointment Making

D.E.I.'s Appointment Making workshop focuses on getting in front of more prospects by means of effective telephone prospecting.

Thousands of companies worldwide have successfully implemented Appointment Making skills, including Aetna, ExxonMobil. The Los Angeles Times, Nextel Communications, Sprint PCS, and Time Warner Cable.

As a direct result of this workshop, D.E.I. clients have reported increases in sales of as much as 30 percent, and increases in appointments generated from 33 percent to a high of 81 percent.

To learn more about this live training program, call us at (800) 224-2140, or visit *www.dei-sales.com*.

Getting to "Closed" (Prospect Management)

The D.E.I. Getting to "Closed" system is a patented, visually driven system for tracking prospects, strategizing forward movement in the sale, and forecasting income accurately.

Thousands of companies worldwide have successfully implemented the Getting to "Closed" system, including Airborne Express, ExxonMobil, Aetna, MCI WorldCom, LexisNexis, Trans Union, Motorola Canada, and Chase Bank.

Companies have reported a range of 20 percent to 40 percent increases in sales revenues as a result of Getting to "Closed" system implementation.

To learn more about this live training program, call us at (800) 224-2140, or visit *www.dei-sales.com*.

High Efficiency Selling Skills

The D.E.I. High Efficiency Selling Skills workshop introduces the sales process as a series of steps that will lead to a logical "makes sense" close when implemented properly. The premise behind the program is that we, as sellers, need to understand what our prospects do—in order to help them achieve their goals and do it better.

Over 8,000 companies worldwide have successfully implemented the principles in the High Efficiency Selling Skills workshop, including ExxonMobil, Aetna, Motorola, SEKO Worldwide, and Nextel Communications.

As a direct result of the High Efficiency Selling Skills workshop, D.E.I. clients have found they will actually present fewer proposals and close a far higher percentage of them—in some cases as high as 80 percent.

To learn more about this live training program, call us at (800) 224-2140, or visit *www.dei-sales.com*.

Online Training Programs Offered by D.E.I. Management Group

Visit us at *www.dei-sales.com/store* and learn how to log on to these and other popular online courses:

Sixteen Keys to Getting More Appointments
Sixteen proven techniques for getting more face-to-face meetings with prospects.

Using Questions to Accelerate Sales
Learn about the critical questions that will move relationships forward, speed up your sales cycle, and put money in your pocket.

Seven "Make It Happen" Questions You're Not Asking
This course includes the world's simplest—and most effective—closing technique.

The Monday Morning Meeting: A Manager's Guide to Increasing Sales
Learn to ask the questions that will boost your team's performance dramatically!

Telesales

The D.E.I. Telesales workshop shows both inbound and outbound telesales professionals how to open the conversation, build rapport, gather information more effectively, customize the recommendation, and close more sales.

Thousands of companies worldwide have successfully implemented the principles in the Telesales workshop, including Aetna, Intek/Sony, Nature America, Port, Inc., Reed Elsevier, Sprint, and Boise Office Solutions.

As a redirect result of the Telesales workshop, D.E.I. clients have found they better qualify their prospects and improve their closing ratios—in some cases by as much as 20 percent.

Index

Index

Index

high-placed ally making case for you, 192

inherent challenge of selling to, 187

knowing history of, 189

knowing who appointed members, 189–90

optimal situation with, 192

principles of dealing with, 189–91

Communication principles, 125–30

people communicate through stories, 129–30

people respond in kind, 125–26

responses can be anticipated, 127–29

Companies, large. *See* Large organizations, working in

Company name

identifying yourself and, 38–39, 73–75

leaving voice messages with, 84–85

Competitor(s)

acknowledging, in e-mails, 259, 261

asking how you measure up against, 332–33

biggest, 3

exclusion lists and, 291

identifying who prospect is talking to, 335–36

introspective questions about, 132

status quo as, 3, 54, 87

turning around responses about, 97

using e-mail more effectively than, 236–37, 244

Concern, having more than prospect/ customer, 280–82

Conferences, 29–30

Contributors, 377

Conversation(s). *See also* Communication principles; Interviews

asking do-based questions, 106–7, 109, 216

cable installer example, 149–50

confusing "products dumps" with, 183

in e-mail, 275. *See also* E-mail

giving full attention to other person, 109–10, 157–58

illustrating good and bad sales approaches, 102–3

real, with Ledge, 67–68

selling as, 106–7

verification step, 117–18

Curiosity

genuine, having, 279–80

using "Just out of curiosity...," 216–17, 218, 219, 220, 222–23, 279

Customers/accounts/clients

defined, 27

discerning long-term from "one-offs," 199–201

generating leads from, 31

giving them reason to call back, 109

knowing when to move on, 198–201

making them look good, 168–74

sending book to, 156

when you work for large companies, 154–56

Denial (false competence), 147

Difficult issues, raising, 140–42

Do-based questions, 106–7, 109, 216

Dollars per sale, increasing, 22

Doubling income, 20–23

E-mail

accelerating selling cycle with, 252–53

asking about where you went wrong/ mistakes, 282–84

Index

Index

Index

About the Author

Stephan Schiffman is president of D.E.I. Management Group, one of the largest sales training companies in the United States. He is the author of a number of bestselling books including *Cold Calling Techniques (That Really Work!); The 25 Most Common Sales Mistakes; The 25 Habits of Highly Successful Salespeople; Beat Sales Burnout; Ask Questions, Get Sales; Telesales; Closing Techniques (That Really Work!),* and *E-Mail Selling Techniques (That Really Work!).* Schiffman's articles have appeared in the *Wall Street Journal,* the *New York Times,* and *INC.* magazine. He has also appeared as a guest on CNBC's *Minding Your Business, How to Succeed in Business,* and *Smart Money.* For more information about Stephan Schiffman, and D.E.I. Management, call 1-800-224-2140 or visit *www.dei-sales.com.*